DEMOCRACY

IN ONE BOOK OR LESS

ALSO BY DAVID LITT

Thanks, Obama: My Hopey, Changey White House Years

DEMOCRACY

IN ONE BOOK OR LESS

★ ★ ★

How It Works, Why It Doesn't,
and Why Fixing It Is Easier Than You Think

★ ★ ★

DAVID LITT

ecco

An Imprint of HarperCollinsPublishers

HarperCollins books may be purchased for educational, business, or sales promotional use. For information, please email the Special Markets Department at SPsales@harpercollins.com.

Ecco® and HarperCollins® are trademarks of HarperCollins Publishers.

FIRST EDITION

Designed by Paula Russell Szafranski
Illustrations courtesy of Ben Orlin

Library of Congress Cataloging-in-Publication Data has been applied for.

ISBN 978-0-06-287936-3

20 21 22 23 24   LSC   10 9 8 7 6 5 4 3 2 1

To Jacqui, my daily reminder that good things happen

CONTENTS

PART I: WHO GETS TO VOTE?

PART II: WHOSE VOTES MATTER?

PART III: WHICH IDEAS BECOME A LAW?

A NOTE REGARDING FACTS
(ON THE THEORY THAT THEY STILL EXIST)

This book is about how quickly American democracy is changing. It's only fitting, then, that our democracy will have changed between me writing these words and you reading them. Maybe everything's better now. That would be nice.

Regardless, the numbers and statistics you'll encounter in these pages were the most accurate I could find as of late 2019 or early 2020, when I did the bulk of my revisions. I took notes when I traveled and recorded interviews when I could. Generally speaking, I used real names when referring to public figures, subjects of very long interviews, or cats. I used pseudonyms for everyone else. While this book has been professionally fact-checked, I am of course responsible for anything I missed.

Full notes on sources, which will take you down some very worthy internet rabbit holes, can be found at davidlittbooks.com.

DEMOCRACY
IN ONE BOOK OR LESS

INTRODUCTION
BROTHER MITCH

I am prowling outside Mitch McConnell's former frat house, which until fifteen minutes ago seemed like an excellent idea.

My plan is as follows: fly to Louisville, Kentucky; crash a party at Phi Tau, the old stomping ground of America's most powerful senator; win the trust of fraternity brothers; and uncover the secret of our democracy's deterioration, preferably by stumbling across an artifact or shrine. To that end, I've come up with a backstory (alumnus in his early thirties, in town on work travel) and put an ungodly amount of product in my hair. I arrived at the University of Louisville ready to party.

There was just one problem: no partying was taking place. On a Friday night less than twenty-four hours before commencement, campus was a ghost town. Passing by Delta Zeta's pristine flower bed and Beta Pi's unmolested dragon gargoyle, I found myself sincerely wondering what's happened to kids these days.

Phi Tau occupied Greek Row's prime real estate, a spacious corner lot, and at first appeared more promising. While the red brick building was clearly new, or at least expensively refurbished, the wraparound porch was decorated in classical Greek style: broken sofas, empty beer bottles, a well-loved propane grill. The remains of a mistreated armchair were arranged in prime lounging position on the roof.

Even so, the lights were off in the windows. No party. Nothing to crash.

And now I've spent a quarter of an hour peering through the front door of the two-story mansion. After a while I spot a pair of Phi Taus chatting in the hall, and I briefly consider knocking and telling the truth. But what could I say?

Hi there. I used to be a speechwriter for Barack Obama, and I've become quite certain that rescuing American democracy begins with me getting drunk at an organization once home to his political nemesis, which is why I'm here on a pilgrimage that is also technically, a business trip. Can I come in?

Such a plea, while honest, would likely be ineffective. I contemplate breaking and entering, but now that my twenties are behind me that's outside my comfort zone. Still, I'm determined to leave Louisville with something to show for my travels—some deeper understanding of what has happened to my country and what it means for our future. I take a deep breath, reassess my situation, and devise a new, far more sophisticated plan.

I start skulking around.

☆

"Remember *Schoolhouse Rock!*?" I say. This is back in D.C., and I'm not really asking, just changing the subject, the way I might say, "Remember Grandpa?" to a cousin. But Trent, the Capitol Hill intern who has asked to get coffee with me, doesn't understand my question's rhetorical nature. Where I expect a nod, I get a look:

I am confused right now, but my confusion is sad for you and not me, because I am young and you are old.

I know that look. I remember giving it. And finding myself on the receiving end, I begin to panic. "You know? The song? 'I'm Just a Bill'? Remember?"

Trent is the kind of eager nineteen-year-old who thrives in Washington. He carries a leather folder with a built-in legal pad upon which he has written questions in advance, and he wants more than anything to make a good impression. But I've given him no choice. Grimacing, he shakes his head, which is how I learn I might be the last of the *Schoolhouse Rock!* generation.

But if you're of a certain age (which I hasten to point out is still most of them), that show defined democracy. My grandparents owned a VHS of the children's cartoon, and whenever we visited, I'd pop the tape into the VCR, press play, hit rewind, and then watch it again.

For the handful of you too young to know what most of those words mean, here's a synopsis of "I'm Just a Bill," the show's most enduring segment: A homeless talking scroll befriends a male human child. Via song, the bill, whose name is Bill, explains our political process. Bill the bill started out as an idea held by the American people. A legislator wrote him into existence and brought him to the Capitol. If he's rejected, he will literally die. But if Bill's debated in committee, approved by the House and Senate, and signed by the president, he'll become a law.

"Gee, Bill, you sure have a lot of patience and courage!" exclaims the boy. The song ends with Congressman McCoy, a portly lawmaker in a 1970s-style brown suit with wide lapels, waddling down the Capitol steps and announcing that Bill's been signed.

"Oh *yay*-us!" squeals Bill. As a singer, Bill has a vaguely bluesy voice, but when speaking, he sounds like a cowboy who is also a drag queen. In retrospect, this was one of several strange elements of *Schoolhouse Rock!*

Yet sitting on my grandparents' shag carpet, I happily overlooked any oddities, vocal or otherwise. Like the millions of American children who have sung along to "I'm Just a Bill" since it first aired in 1976,

I was too busy rooting for the protagonist. It would be more than a decade before I cast a ballot, but Bill I could relate to. Here was this endearing little guy, full of charm and potential, determined to win over adults on his way to growing up.

And even if I couldn't yet articulate it, I could appreciate that the true hero of Bill's story was the very system of government he described. In other countries, citizens' lives were governed by a king's dictates or an aristocrat's whim. In America, we too had leaders, but we *ruled* ourselves. This was not a typical arrangement. Back when I sat in my grandparents' living room, eyes glued to the TV, fewer than half the world's people lived in a democracy. If you considered the full scope of history, all 105 billion human beings who had ever existed, that number fell to well below 5 percent.

But as an American, I was different. I was special. A working political process, one designed to turn the people's will into reality, was my birthright.

For the first few years of my own intersection with American history, our real-life system of government mirrored the one Bill sang about. In November 1986, six weeks after I was born, President Reagan signed sweeping, bipartisan immigration reform into law. When I was four years old we fought a war in Iraq for understandable reasons, won it decisively, and left on time. Under President Clinton we raised taxes on the rich, the economy boomed, and Americans of every income bracket saw their fortunes rise.

I don't mean to suggest that our republic made exclusively good decisions. Some ideas led to unintended consequences; others were just plain awful. But our democracy functioned. Most of us got the government we wanted most of the time, and when we were no longer happy with our leaders, we replaced them. That was the true promise of America—not perfection, but constant improvement. What made us great was that we could always make things better. As a child, I found it all immensely appealing: my country and me, brimming with patience and courage, growing stronger all the time.

Oh *yay*-us! Indeed.

Fast-forward a little more than a decade. In 2011, as I began my new job as a White House speechwriter, I brimmed with Bill-like enthusiasm. By the time I began working for President Obama, Republicans had won control of the House of Representatives, and I knew that the accomplishments of the president's first two years—the economic stimulus, a Wall Street reform bill, Obamacare—were unlikely to be replicated. Still, I assumed the process I learned about in my grandparents' living room remained intact.

Here's the way I thought our country worked: Our leaders, like Americans everywhere, might not always agree on the way forward. But they derived their power from the consent of the governed, feared the verdict of the voters, and sought to give the people what they want. When there was a problem, elected officials tried to solve it. When there was a crisis, they tried to confront it.

So you can imagine my surprise when, less than six months into my White House tenure, the greatest threat facing America was the behavior of our elected officials themselves. Plenty of people have written in detail about what came to be known as "the debt ceiling crisis," but the gist of it was as follows: Republicans in the House and Senate threatened to blow up the entire American economy if President Obama didn't cut social services for the poor. We, the People, were not happy to see our lawmakers take our nation hostage. A whopping 82 percent of us disapproved. But our representatives refused to listen. And when the next election arrived, most of them faced no consequences at all.

I suppose this was the moment I began wondering if our political process was not working properly. It was certainly the moment I first noticed who was really in charge. Then-Speaker of the House John Boehner seemed a step behind the extremists in his own party, a dog being wagged by his tail. But the Senate was a different story. There, the Republican leader appeared entirely in his element. It was as though he could see what was invisible to the rest of us, the political equivalent of ultraviolet light. In the corners of my mind, a fuzzy thought began to form: *Maybe Mitch McConnell knows something the rest of us don't.*

And then, for the next five years, I set these doubts aside. There were speeches to write and an Obamacare website to fret over and a tan suit that at the time qualified as a legitimate presidential scandal. True, our system of government had ceased turning good ideas into laws. But for me, my parents, and my grandparents, the story of America had always been the story of democracy becoming more real for more people over time. When I left the White House in January 2016, I was confident that progress was not just our history. Progress was our destiny.

What could possibly change that?

☆

On January 20, 2017, I could be found pacing the trails of Disney's Animal Kingdom, slurping frozen Cokes with double shots of rum and trying not to picture the words "President Donald Trump." As it happened, Inauguration Day fell on my wife's birthday. To celebrate the latter, Jacqui and I fled to one of the few places guaranteed not to show the former on TV.

I wasn't as frightened for my own safety as many of my fellow Americans. I'm a straight white male citizen—if I weren't Jewish, I'd hit surviving-the-Trump-era bingo. But each time I peeked at my phone to check on Trump's swearing-in, I didn't just feel worried about my country. I felt betrayed. America had held an election. One of the candidates was cruel, sexist, racist, frequently criminal, and a bit of a dummy. The American people, to their lasting credit, decisively chose someone else. We did our job. And the cruel, sexist, racist, frequently criminal dummy became president anyway.

Nor, on that Inauguration Day, was President Trump the only one preparing to govern without the people's consent. Over the previous six years, a clear majority of Americans had voted for one party's Senate candidates, yet a clear majority of senators belonged to the other.

In the House of Representatives, the new president's party had won a 1 percent victory among voters, yet somehow this earned them a landslide 11 percent majority of congressional seats.

I had been taught that America was a government of the people, by the people, and for the people. But as of January 20, 2017, that was no longer true. Instead, we had a government the people didn't vote for making changes the people didn't want.

Imagine trying to explain this political process to an extraterrestrial. Or a Belgian. Sitting on a bench at an outdoor restaurant called Pizzafari, still tipsy from the rum, I was struck by an uncomfortable realization: I *couldn't* explain it. I could list terms from AP Government. I'd worked in politics long enough to name a few villains. But the details of our republic, and the history that produced them, were a mystery to me. Why was it that our representative government no longer seemed interested in representing us?

It dawned on me that my relationship to my democracy was about the same as my relationship to my aging Subaru. When everything ran smoothly, driving was second nature. But when the machine broke down, I couldn't tell you what caused the problem or how the pieces fit together. I certainly didn't know how to fix it.

Until President Trump's election, I had never been much of a student. I majored in American history by skimming introductions and feigning confidence about conclusions. The shelves in my White House office were packed with weighty tomes I sincerely planned to read. But now, in a spirit of curiosity and occasionally of panic, I decided to look under the hood of my republic. I began downloading political science papers. I bought books packed with academic jargon and demographic tables.

I sought out their authors as well. I spoke with some of the professors and scholars who have been quietly sounding the alarm about our democracy for decades. Whenever possible, I escaped D.C., traveling our nation's fault lines to meet the Americans standing up for their country as the ground shook beneath their feet. My goal was not to transform myself into a leading authority, a bona fide political scientist, or a constitutional scholar. I simply wanted to become an informed American at a time when that seemed to matter.

Here's what I discovered: the democracy I live in today is different—not just a little different, but completely different—from the democracy I was born into.

If you're old enough to read these words, the democracy you were born into (or adopted, if you're an immigrant) has completely changed as well. Since 1980, the number of Americans legally barred from voting has more than doubled. Since the 1990s, your odds of living in a competitive congressional district have fallen by more than half. In the twenty-first century alone, the amount of money spent on Washington lobbying has risen by more than 100 percent, and in the last decade, the odds of a bill passing Congress have fallen to a fifty-year low. These are just a few examples. There are dozens, perhaps hundreds, more.

Most Americans don't know how radically their system of self-government has been altered. But Mitch McConnell does. In many ways, his thirty-six-year Senate career is remarkably undistinguished. He's no statesman. No major piece of legislation bears his name. But when it comes to understanding and shaping our political process, the man whom Phi Taus still call "Brother Mitch" is in a league of his own.

It's not the league he initially planned on joining. As a kid growing up in Augusta, Georgia, McConnell was a county all-star pitcher with dreams of stadium lights. Then his dad moved to Kentucky for a job and enrolled his son at Manual High School, and as a former future shortstop for the Yankees, I take no pleasure in telling you what happened next. Mitch discovered he wasn't very good. In his ninth-grade league, he failed to make the all-star team. In tenth grade he was left off the varsity squad.

In a parallel universe, one in which a young pitcher had slightly more zip on his fastball, America is a very different place. But here in our universe, this is what the stymied sophomore wrote about his experience, a half century after getting cut: "If I was going to excel at something, it wasn't sports. And the more baseball faded, the more something else was beginning to entice me, something that shared the same sense of competition, the team spirit, the need for endurance: politics."

With the sole, glaring exception of Trump, no politician in recent memory has been so blatantly transactional. And no politician, including Trump, has so openly treated accumulating power as a sport. McConnell even titled his memoir, appropriately and amorally, *The Long Game.*

Yet from the start of his new career, the rejected pitcher understood that in one crucial respect, politics was nothing like baseball. In politics, the players can make the rules.

This insight, coupled with his natural tenacity and single-minded determination, made Mitch McConnell the most important political figure of his lifetime. You were not consulted on the changes Team Mitch made to your republic. You didn't vote on them. If you're like most Americans, you probably didn't even realize they occurred. Yet more than any single issue, more than any political trend, certainly more than President Trump himself, our redesigned political process is responsible for the danger we find ourselves in today.

This book is about what happened to your system of government and why it matters. We'll go back to the beginning, and sometimes to before the beginning, to figure out how American democracy is supposed to function. We'll dissect our current political process to see where, how, and why we've strayed. Along the way, we'll meet forgotten Founders and scheming bureaucrats and a surprising number of stone-cold murderers. Just because the world's greatest experiment in self-government is teetering on the lip of chaos doesn't mean we can't have fun.

We'll also cover a lot of ground. Every chapter in this book could be a book unto itself, and most of them already are. At the same time, if you follow politics closely, you've likely encountered at least a few of the ideas and stories to come. My goal was not to write the first or last word on any of these topics. Instead, I set out to write the book I needed three years ago. If after reading it, you dive deep into political science, or history, or geography, or law, that's terrific. But if you're part of the vast majority of Americans who realize our democracy is in trouble, and you never venture past these pages, you'll nonetheless understand what went wrong.

More important, you'll understand how to set it right. This is not a book for students of politics. This is a book for practitioners. If you're a member of Congress, I wrote this for you. If you go to the occasional rally, or volunteer for a campaign, or donate to a candidate, or even just take voting seriously, I wrote this for you as well.

Because if there's one thing I hope to convince you of, it's that our broken system of government is far more fixable than you might think. We're in trouble. But American democracy has never *not* been in trouble. For all the dangers we face right now, a civil rights activist in the Jim Crow South or labor organizer in the Gilded Age would happily trade places with a U.S. citizen today. At every moment in our history, powerful Americans have sought to corrupt our political process for their benefit. Democracy survived because a far greater number of Americans came together to defend it.

We can do that now. While I didn't come up with any of the solutions you'll find in these pages, I picked them carefully. These ideas are doable. They don't require a constitutional amendment or Brett Kavanaugh's heart to grow three sizes one day. At the same time, the fixes I describe will make a difference. They won't mean the end of racism, or climate change, or Sean Hannity's career. They certainly won't guarantee that your political party always wins. But they're enough to restore our country's most basic promise: that we can solve big problems together. With these tools, we can once again have a democracy that reflects the will of the people and not the whims of a privileged caste.

But we're running out of time. Winston Churchill famously said that "democracy is the worst form of government, except for all those other forms that have been tried." Today, around the world and even here at home, a rising class of would-be tyrants is offering a new spin on Churchill's quote. "Democracy is the worst form of government you've ever tried," they ask, "so why not try something else?" These sales pitches don't always succeed. But they only need to succeed once. A defining feature of authoritarianism is the terrible return policy.

I'm not saying the United States will become Hitler's Germany or Stalin's Russia. It is, however, quite possible we will soon find ourselves in what Hungary's prime minister–slash–strongman, Viktor Orban, has coyly termed an "illiberal democracy." That's a system of government where the people are free to choose their leaders—so long as the ruling party remains in charge.

Even if our two-party system survives into the coming decades, there's no guarantee it will represent us in any meaningful sense. Consider Trent, the nineteen-year-old with the legal pad full of questions and zero knowledge of *Schoolhouse Rock!* He's about to cast his first vote for president, and his entire political life has been spent watching America ping-pong between disastrous government under Republicans and dysfunctional government under Democrats. No wonder that for so many of his cohort, what I still think of our country's founding promise looks more like a founding myth.

Nor is it just young people who are losing faith. The week I was born, the Pew Research Center found that 44 percent of Americans—including 55 percent of self-described conservatives—trusted Washington to do the right thing. The percentage of Americans who have trust in our government to do the right thing today? Just 17.

The news isn't all bad. Nearly 250 years after the start of the world's greatest experiment in self-government, its citizens are still more likely to believe in their elected leaders than in Bigfoot. Just not by much.

It turns out the maximum number of after-dark laps a grown man can take around a building occupied by college students without feeling like a serial killer from a horror movie is two. During my first circuit of the Phi Tau house, I spot a "Team Mitch" sticker on the rear door, which brings a brief surge of satisfaction. But the second time around feels less like an adventure than a misdemeanor, and I soon retreat to my hotel. I have one more night left in Louisville, and I vow to try again.

Yet when I return to campus the next evening, Greek Row is even sleepier than before. A stray cat pokes among the empty houses, but other than that, nobody stirs. I take up a position across from Phi Tau, and stakeout number two begins. On the top story of the red brick building, there's a window with a light on. It goes out.

Then, just when I'm on the verge of quitting, a car pulls into a parking space and a half-dozen college kids tumble from the seats. I never joined a frat in college—I had neither the fashion sense nor the inclination—and I immediately recognize this group of students as kindred spirits. Split evenly between guys and girls, the group begins moving someone's things into an apartment building, presumably for the start of summer classes. I'm still hoping to find some genuine Phi Taus, but at this point I'll take what I can get, so I approach the car.

I'm spotted first by a lanky guy of medium height in basketball shorts and a white T-shirt. He holds a beer in one hand and a sofa cushion in the other.

"I hear that's Mitch McConnell's old frat house?" I say.

"Yeah," he replies, diving right in. "He owns it!"

"He *owns* it?" To me, this is stunning. There's something farfetched, not to mention decidedly villain-in-a-Jimmy-Stewart-movie, about a politician snapping up valuable land next to the public university he represents. Yet if such a thought occurs to the young man in the baggy T-shirt, he doesn't show it. It's as though the world is a game of Monopoly, and his state's senior senator landed on a lucky square.

"The rest of Greek Row is owned by the university," he explains. "But that land is private."

"That's why Phi Taus do whatever the fuck they want!" exclaims another student, unloading a desk lamp from the trunk. But even this pronouncement is made less in a spirit of grievance than of campus truth: such-and-such a class is easy; professor so-and-so is a jerk; Brother Mitch's frat can get away with anything.

The lanky young man with the sofa cushion glances up, but instead of following his gaze to Phi Tau, I stay focused on his face. I thought, and hoped, I would see anger in his eyes. But I don't. Instead, his look doubles as a sigh, a subdued acknowledgment that in today's America, the meek and the powerful play by very different sets of rules. And while it isn't what I first came to Louisville to find, in this deflated expression, I've uncovered my terrible secret, not an artifact from the past, but a window into what our future will look like unless we do something, and soon. There's no fury in the young man's face. No outrage. Just weary resignation to the unfairness of the way things are.

"Come back here on a Friday in the semester," he tells me. "You'll see house after house of people, no one doing anything shady. And then you've got eighteen fuckin' Phi Taus drinking on the roof."

PART I

WHO GETS TO VOTE?

1

THE DRAWING OF LOTS

The Non-Voters

Three years ago in Virginia, a doofus cast a vote. Arriving at a polling place in Newport News, a small city on the mouth of the James River, this person was handed a paper ballot containing very simple instructions: To record your preference, fill in the oval beside a candidate's name. In the governor's race, our mystery voter carefully filled the bubble for Republican Ed Gillespie. Then he drew an "X" through it.

To our doofus's credit, he managed to get through the next few sections of his ballot without incident. But then he reached the race for State House of Delegates and the wheels came off the bus. Below the words "VOTE FOR ONLY ONE" were three names. Our illustrious Virginian chose two of them. Remarkably, he not only voted for the wrong number of candidates; he also voted for them incorrectly. While Republican David Yancey received a properly filled-in oval, Democrat Shelly Simonds, like Ed Gillespie before her, received both a filled-in oval and a slash.

Lord knows I have no right to lecture anyone about following directions. The last time I tried assembling a purchase from IKEA, I learned it's possible to flip a dresser inside out. Still, an adult human being, failing in three separate ways to fill in an oval with a pen? What a goober.

Six weeks later, that goober held the fate of 8.5 million Virginians in his hands.

Here's what happened. When the votes from the 2017 election were first counted and recounted, the ballot with the extra ovals and slashes was not among them. In election jargon, it had been "spoiled," like milk someone forgot to put back in the fridge. Meanwhile, the tally of unspoiled ballots revealed a seismic result. For the first time in twenty-two years, Democrats had won all three branches of Virginia government. In the first two of these, the races for governor and control of the state senate, their victories had been decisive.

But the race for the third branch, the Virginia House of Delegates, could not have been closer. Democrats had flipped the chamber by just one seat. One of those seats was in Newport News, home to our spoiled ballot. And there, Shelly Simonds had been elected by a winning margin of exactly one vote. Republicans grumbled at their bad luck. Democrats breathed a sigh of relief and prepared to make some major changes to Virginia's laws.

But back in Newport News, a middle school civics teacher named Kenneth Mallory, who had volunteered as an election observer for Shelly Simonds's opponent, was having second thoughts. Remembering a certain spoiled ballot, one pockmarked with unforced errors, guilt apparently crept in. After all, didn't every voter, even an outrageously careless one, deserve a chance to be heard?

That's how Virginia was treated to a Solomonic tussle over an answer sheet that would have been bounced from the SATs. Three judges were summoned from the state's Circuit Court. The Newport News doofus's ballot was placed before them. The room was locked. Deliberations began.

What happened over the next several hours remains a secret. We will never know what discussions took place, which theories were proffered, exactly how the three wise men attempted to read a voter's mind. But we do know that the judges reached a verdict. The person who cast the spoiled ballot, they ruled, had in fact intended to vote for Republican David Yancey. Shelly Simonds was no longer the winner by a single vote. The race was tied—which meant Democrats no longer controlled the House of Delegates. Their agenda was suddenly on ice.

Almost exactly one year later, in December 2018, I meet Shelly Simonds at a biker bar turned seafood restaurant called Harpoon Larry's. Unlike some politicians, she doesn't have a wax museum polish. Before she ran for office she was a mom and an elementary school Spanish teacher, and she still looks like both those things.

As we settle into a booth, the only difference between Shelly and the rest of Harpoon Larry's clientele is that her earrings and sweater were aggressively Christmas-themed. She's just come from taking a family photo that would double as a mailer for her next campaign, a rematch with David Yancey.

"I have a neighbor who's Republican who said, 'I'm going to vote for you next time,'" Shelly tells me proudly. I spear a bit of broiled crab cake onto a piece of lettuce and raise an eyebrow.

"Were you like, 'Where were you twelve months ago?'"

"No, no," Shelly assures me. But I am unconvinced.

"What about those two?" I ask, pointing to a white-haired gentleman and a much younger brunette casting bedroom glances across a shellfish platter. "Don't you look at them and wonder, 'Okay, which of you *didn't* vote?'"

Shelly shook her head. "You have to love everybody and accept everybody," she said. Then she shrugged. "Maybe it's maturity and yoga."

I am not especially mature, however, and I don't do yoga, so I frequently return to Shelly's 2017 campaign. Not the moment when a winner was finally decided—although we'll get there—but to the hours of deliberation that preceded it. The judges studying inky splotches. The spoiled ballot placed solemnly upon a table in a locked and windowless room.

It was a scene from a parable, the kind of story that demands a moral, and a moral soon emerged. "Every Vote Counts: 1 More Ballot Ties Up Virginia," read the headline on CNN. "It's proof that every vote counts," declared David Yancey, Shelly's opponent. "If you ever wonder whether every vote counts, talk to Shelly," said Tom Perez, the chair of the Democratic National Committee.

This idea—that all of us should vote because any of us might single-handedly decide an election—is inspiring and patriotic. It is also untrue. We might as well say "every plane crashes" or "every lotto ticket wins." Sure, Shelly's race was a reminder that, your ballot could theoretically prove decisive. But the probability of that actually happening is so small as to be virtually nonexistent. If you participate in every election for which you're eligible, odds are it will take centuries before one of them is decided by a single vote. And that's just for small local races like Shelly's. To personally tip a statewide contest, one for governor or senator, you'd likely have to wait eons.

Which is why when I think about the moral of Shelly Simonds's tied race, I don't imagine my vote deciding an election. Instead, I imagine what would have happened had the Newport News doofus not voted at all. If he had chosen zero candidates, rather than two, no wise men would have retreated to a locked room to determine his intentions. No reporters would have descended on his hometown. If he hadn't filled out his ballot, no one would have given him any thought at all.

But he did fill out a ballot. And whether you agree or disagree with the judges' final verdict, there's no denying this: Three of Virginia's most influential citizens spent their day pondering the inner life of a person you wouldn't trust to order a pizza on your behalf. All because he chose to vote.

The moral of Shelly's story, then, is not that every vote counts. The true moral, at once completely obvious and chronically overlooked, is this: in a democracy, people who vote are important in a way people who don't vote are not.

Benjamin Franklin understood the importance of voting—or, rather, the unimportance of not voting—before there was even an America to vote in. "They who have no voice nor vote in the electing of representatives," he wrote in 1774, "do not enjoy liberty; but are absolutely enslaved to those who have votes."

A lot has changed in the past 246 years, yet Franklin's warning still rings true. America today is made up of two separate and totally unequal countries. The first country, while far from perfect, is a republic. The people select their leaders. The people can reject those leaders when they fall short.

But here's the important thing: the people of the first country select the leaders of the second country as well. Citizens of that latter nation pay the same taxes, celebrate the same holidays, live in the same neighborhoods, send their children to fight and die in the same wars. Yet the decisions that shape their lives are made by representatives they never choose.

Because I am a creative professional who makes my living deploying clever turns of phrase, I will call the first country "Country Number One" and the second country "Country Number Two." As you've probably surmised, what determines which country you belong to is whether or not you vote.

Taken together, the inhabitants of Country Number One are more commonly known as "the electorate." The combined inhabitants of both countries make up "the population." But what do we call those living in Country Number Two? The only phrase we have to describe a group of non-voters is "a group of non-voters." In the last presidential election, 185 million Americans, including 44 percent of adults, didn't cast a ballot. And yet despite its enormous size, this gigantic slice of our country is chronically overlooked.

The goal of this chapter, and of the section of this book that follows, is to give what I'll call "the unelectorate" the attention it deserves. Who are America's non-voters? Why aren't they voting? And what does their lack of participation mean for the rest of us? If we want to understand our democracy, these are questions we must ask.

These questions are particularly urgent in America, because we have more non-voters, both in sheer numbers and as a percentage of the population, than nearly every developed democracy on earth.

We don't just trail countries like Australia and Belgium, where voting is mandatory. If our 2016 turnout rate had equaled France's, our electorate would have grown by 30 million people. New Zealand–level participation would have added a whopping 49 million to the rolls—a number larger than the voting-age populations of Florida, Pennsylvania, Wisconsin, Michigan, and Ohio, combined. When it comes to turnout, the United States also lags Sweden, South Korea, the Netherlands, Italy, Mexico, Austria, Denmark, Israel, Finland, Norway, Germany, Greece, the Czech Republic, the United Kingdom, Canada, Portugal, Spain, Slovakia, Ireland, and Estonia.

(We're slightly ahead of Latvia. So that's nice.)

And these rankings are based solely on America's performance in presidential elections years. In midterm elections, the biannual affairs where we choose one-third of our senators, more than two-thirds of our governors, and every single member of the House of Representatives, the electorate shrinks further. Consider what happened in 2018. Campaigns spent billions of dollars on ads, hundreds of thousands of volunteers knocked on doors, the president of the United States invented a terrorist-filled caravan to motivate his base. Thanks to all these efforts, midterm voter turnout soared to a new record high . . . of 53 percent. "The voters" and "the people" are not the same at all.

If the electorate were an exact replica of the population, only smaller, our low turnout might not matter. After all, the real purpose of elections—and the reason we'll spend so much time on them in the coming pages—is not just to win. Done right, elections make real the most basic promise of representative democracy: that the people have a say in what their leaders do. If the voters are demographically identical to the people, our representatives should pursue policies the public supports, regardless of turnout. We'll have leaders we trust. And if we stop trusting them, or they pursue some other agenda, they'll get fired.

As it happens, however, the electorate and unelectorate are not de-mographically identical at all. Voters, on average, have higher incomes than non-voters do. They are vastly more likely to possess a graduate degree or golf shoes. They are vastly less likely to have personal experi-ence with food stamps, community college, or payday loans. As with most things in America, when it comes to voting, there is also a racial gap: historically, white people have turned out at the highest rates, fol-lowed by Black people, followed by other nonwhite groups. Perhaps most stark is the age gap. Millennials are now the largest generation in America. But when the dust settles on the 2020 presidential election, Baby Boomers will almost certainly cast the most votes.

Here's an easy way to think about it: along nearly every dimen-sion, the average voter looks more like Donald Trump than the average American does.

Consider what happened in 2016. As Americans went to the polls, the United States was, thanks to changing demographics, more diverse than it had ever been. But that diversity wasn't reflected in the elector-ate. White voters cast 73 percent of the ballots, exactly the same per-centage as four years earlier. Meanwhile, in that same four-year span, the African-American population grew by 1.7 million. But the number of African-American *voters* actually declined by nearly 800,000. It was as though the entire Black population of Detroit vanished into thin air.

Perhaps unsurprisingly, Shelly Simonds puts it best. "The most im-portant thing isn't who people decide to vote for," she explains. "It's who decides to vote." We're walking along the banks of the James River, and she says that for months after her election ended in a tie, non-voters would approach her to beg forgiveness. I looked out over the water, the November sun glancing off the river and bathing the air in wintry glow, and tried to think, really think, about what she had just told me.

"Don't you want to slap them?" I asked.

☆

Perhaps my initial attitude toward the unelectorate was, as my highly diplomatic editor put it, "overly harsh." But in my defense, I wasn't alone. Just think about the language we typically use to describe the behavior of non-voters: "Staying home." "Sitting out the election." "Not showing up." These phrases drip with judgment.

Even on the Upper West Side of Manhattan, the Emerald City of well-meaning liberalism where I was born and raised, the idea that someone might have a good reason for failing to cast a ballot was never seriously considered. No adults I knew growing up would have suggested that those without jobs or homes were lazy. But non-voters were a different story. "People who don't vote have no right to complain" was a phrase so well worn it could have been embroidered on a throw pillow. Just a few years ago, I returned home for the Jewish high holidays weeks before an election. During the service, one of my rabbis lifted his hands and pointed his gaze skyward.

"How is it," he beseeched the heavens, "that anyone in America could not vote?"

I don't know if he ever received a divine answer, but let's run through some earthly possibilities. One explanation, volunteered by the late columnist Charles Krauthammer, is that Americans vote at lower rates than people from other countries because America is better than other countries. "Low voter turnout is a leading indicator of contentment," he wrote in a 1990 essay for *Time* magazine. Arguing that government was mercifully unimportant to Americans' day-to-day lives, he added that "it seems entirely proper that Americans should in large numbers register a preference against politics by staying home on Election Day."

One person who quite liked this argument was Mitch McConnell.

He quoted Krauthammer's piece in an op-ed about voting the follow-ing year. But just in case readers didn't agree that low voter turnout is a sign of contentment, he offered a second theory: non-voters are lazy. "Political couch potatoes," he called them, a phrase he later repeated to the *Washington Post*.

In retrospect, it's remarkable how readily the rest of the country adopted McConnell's framing. "Half the Electorate, Perhaps Satisfied or Bored, Sat Out Voting," read a *New York Times* headline in 1996. The *Times* is painstakingly careful to avoid taking sides, often to the point of ridiculousness. Yet when it came to the motivations of the unelectorate, Kentucky's leading Republican was in perfect harmony with Manhattan liberals, right-wing authors, and the paper of record. Some Americans, they all concluded, either don't care who governs them or are too lazy to cast a ballot. Either way, non-voters are non-voters by choice.

The problem with this assumption is that, while bipartisan, it's wrong. Let's begin with apathy. In Krauthammer's view, Country Number Two is made up of people with a "preference against politics." They believe their choices are all the same—equally good or equally bad. But on the rare occasion anyone bothers to ask non-voters what they think about politics, we discover that they aren't apathic at all. In the summer of 2012, for example, a team from Suffolk University and *USA Today* found that among the Americans least likely to participate in an election, those who weren't even registered, 80 percent nonethe-less had a favored candidate in the upcoming presidential race. These people had preferences. But for whatever reason, they didn't translate those preferences into votes.

If apathy doesn't explain non-voting, what about the couch potato theory? I should begin by pointing out that, given the demographics of voters and non-voters, arguing that the unelectorate is lazy quickly leads the arguer into dark places. Is an executive earning seven figures really more industrious than someone who punches in at a factory or picks fruit in the blazing sun? Are white people harder workers than

African-Americans, Asians, and Hispanics? For that matter, are active-duty members of the military, who vote at lower-than-average rates, lazier than the population as a whole?

Even if you put these nasty implications aside, the couch potato theory is a fundamentally conservative way of looking at non-voters. True, it's possible to find some examples of people who could easily vote and just don't feel like it. After years of campaign door-knocking, I've met some of them myself. But more often, blaming non-voters for "staying home" is like blaming a single mom working three jobs for not getting to the gym. Deciding to vote is like any other decision. You weigh the costs and benefits. And the benefits, quite frankly, are slim: a one-in-a-gazillion chance of swinging a close race and an "I Voted" sticker. From a purely rational perspective, the wonder isn't that so many of us don't vote. It's that so many of us do.

To say that non-voters "choose" not to vote is a vast oversimplification. Instead, non-voters reach the conclusion that, for whatever reason, voting is too difficult. That's a small but significant change in how we think about the unelectorate. The problem isn't that turnout is too low. It's that would-be voters believe the rewards of voting are too meager, and the barriers are too high.

Most Americans would like to see that cost-benefit equation become more forgiving. A whopping 90 percent of us agree that high turnout is beneficial for our democracy. Democrats, Independents, and Republicans view voting as a public good. Yet unlike with other public goods, we don't rely on the public sector to help increase the size of the electorate. In the United States, to an extent unknown in nearly every other democracy, getting people to the polls is the job of political parties and campaigns.

And in retrospect, putting the responsibility for high turnout in the hands of candidates may not have been the wisest decision. Because not every candidate *wants* high turnout. We don't like to advertise it, but in a republic like ours, you don't actually have to win over the people to represent them. If you can force your opponents' supporters out of the electorate, that works, too. All it takes to attempt this strategy is a lack of scruples—and unscrupulous politicians have never been in short supply.

Which brings us, at last, to the most plausible explanation for why Americans vote at such low rates. We aren't apathetic, or lazy, or indifferent. The reason so many of us don't vote is that so many of our leaders don't want us to.

☆

There's no good way to decide a tied election. In Nevada, true to form, candidates pick a card. In other states they draw straws. In Virginia, after Shelly Simonds's one-vote lead was erased by judges' decree, what followed was less an official ceremony than a poor man's Powerball.

The drawing of lots took place in Richmond. There, in a small auditorium, the chairman of the State Board of Elections, a youngish lawyer named James Alcorn, took his seat at the center of a long desk. A woman sitting to the chairman's left held up two slips of paper, one for David Yancey and one for Shelly Simonds. With great ceremony, she placed each slip into a film canister. She placed the film canisters into a ceramic bowl. Then an older lady to the chairman's right reached into the bowl, placed her hands upon the canisters, and solemnly jiggled them around.

Behind his glasses, James Alcorn's face was a mask of official neutrality. He stuck a hand in the bowl, selected a canister, and retrieved the paper slip within.

"The winner of House District Ninety-Four," he proclaimed, "is David Yancey."

And that was it. Shelly Simonds had been defeated. The people had spoken.

Except, of course, they hadn't. The *voters* had spoken. But in Newport News alone, there were approximately 24,000 non-voters—Americans eligible to cast a ballot who had not done so. They had voices, too. But those voices were never heard.

We're going to change that. In the coming chapters, we'll get to know the unelectorate: the Americans who aren't allowed to vote, or who are blocked from voting, or who decide it's simply too difficult. We'll dive deep into the gap between the voters and the people, with the ultimate goal of figuring out how to shrink it. And there's no better place to begin than just up the road from Shelly Simonds's house, where, more than four hundred years ago, one of history's great liars was booted from his democracy.

2

RICK VERSUS RICKY

The Officially Disenfranchised

On April 26, 1607, after four long months at sea, three boatloads of weary Englishmen disembarked on a buggy bump of land they dubbed Cape Henry. There was much work to do: homes to build, farms to establish, an unknown continent to explore. But first they had to stare at a box.

It is lost to history exactly what this precious container looked like. Big or small? Metal or lacquer? We'll never know. What we do know is that inside was a list of just seven names, handpicked by powerful men back in Britain approximately 3,700 miles away. The box had been sealed before the voyage began. No one, not even the chosen few, was told who had been selected.

Now it was time to find out. Still exhausted from the trip, New World mosquitoes buzzing around their ankles, the settlers gathered to watch. The seal on the box was broken. The lid was lifted. The seven names were read. For the first political campaign in the colonies that would become America, these seven—and only these seven—would make up the entire electorate. Elsewhere on the continent, most notably in the Iroquois nation, remarkably inclusive elections were being held. But there on Cape Henry, no one else could vote.

While most of the names from the box have faded from common memory, one remains famous today. John Smith. You almost certainly know his story. Kidnapped by the local Powhatan tribe, Smith was about to be executed when the chief's daughter, lovestruck Pocahontas, threw herself upon him, risking her life to save the man she loved. The chief's heart melted, and instead of killing the explorer he adopted him as a kind of surrogate son.

Almost none of this is true. Smith's biography is genuinely full of fascinating tangents—before crossing the Atlantic, he escaped slavery in Turkey; later in life he would coin the phrase "New England"—but his true talent was making up heroic tales starring himself. For one thing, when Smith was kidnapped, Pocahontas was either eleven or twelve years old, hardly an appropriate age for a romantic heroine. Also, it's nearly certain Smith's stay of execution was more of a ransoming. Rather than being "adopted," it appears he was swapped for some cannons and agricultural gear.

In real life, as opposed to in his own retelling, Smith's exploits call to mind not a Disney prince but a teenager auditioning for a prank show. During one expedition up the Chesapeake Bay, he failed to find a route to the Pacific but did manage to be grievously wounded by a stingray. (Smith ate the perpetrator and, to his credit, produced a highly accurate map of the area. It's still known as Stingray Point in his honor.) Back home in the colony, Smith was, in the careful words of the Jamestown Rediscovery Foundation, "Injured by a mysterious gunpowder explosion."

Lots of people had good reasons to blow up John Smith. In fact, the greatest threat to Smith's life came not from warlike Powhatans or ill-tempered stingrays, but from his own pissed-off fellow settlers.

On the journey from England, Smith attempted to mutiny and seize control of the expedition, a plot which immediately failed. After deciding (just barely) not to hang him, Smith's fellow travelers locked him belowdecks for the rest of the voyage. When the settlers made landfall, he was removed from the ship in chains.

So you can imagine the colonists' dismay upon learning that their least favorite person was about to become one-seventh of the electorate. A brief conference was held, and John Smith, rather improbably, became the first American to have his voting rights taken away.

The six remaining eligible voters were not a random sample. The names in the box had been chosen under the supervision of the London Virginia Company, a business venture set up to pilfer riches from the New World. Only the highly responsible—which is to say, only those whom investors *deemed* highly responsible—were on the list. Perhaps it's no surprise that the winner of their inaugural election was himself one of the London Virginia Company's largest shareholders, a middle-aged redhead with the delightful name of Edward Maria Wingfield.

Wingfield was a bad president. Under his administration, the colonists established Jamestown on a splotch of riverside marsh. On one hand, the site was conveniently uninhabited. On the other hand, this was because the native tribes knew better than to inhabit it. Diseases flourished there the way crops were supposed to. A freak drought made conditions even worse. Four months into Wingfield's first term, his constituents, understandably frustrated about starving to death, arrested him on fabricated charges and shipped him back to England. He spent the rest of his life as the principal of a posh boys' school, a leadership position to which he was apparently better suited.

But what of the political system that produced him—one where the electorate included six out of 100 adults, a mere 6 percent of the population? Is restricting the ballot to a small, select group of voters destined to result in tragedy? Or does the real danger lie in opening the ballot to everyone, thereby allowing an irresponsible public to muck things up?

These questions divided our country before it even was a country. And they divide us still.

☆

Four hundred years after Jamestown's first president was unceremoniously deposed, a bulldog mix named Mabel nearly bit my legs off.

This was in Canton, Ohio, where I was registering voters for Barack Obama's 2008 campaign. Like many of life's high-stakes experiences, my Mabel encounter is burned into my memory not as a film, but as a comic strip. In the first panel, I round a hedge into the kind of yard that doubles as a recycling bin. In the second, I am frozen mid-stride, just a few feet away from fifty pounds of drooling teeth.

The third panel is a close-up of Mabel herself. She's growling, but there's a delighted gleam in her eye. Millions of years of evolution have prepared her for exactly this moment. She was born to dispense carnivorous justice to strangers.

Suddenly, a fourth panel. I'm a hundred feet down the road. Mabel, straddling a border known only to her, is deciding whether to bask in the successful defense of her territory or disembowel me just for kicks.

It is here that the film version of my memory resumes. "Mabel!" A man lopes off his porch with a bemused expression on his face. He's in a T-shirt, and sports a curly brown mullet, bushy mustache, and significant paunch. He looks a bit like Dale Earnhardt, if Dale Earnhardt had spent less time racing in NASCAR and more time on the couch watching NASCAR.

"Mabel!" he repeats, although his tone is less "Cut it out!" than "Save some for me!" I glance at the beast, who pauses briefly at the sound of her master's voice. It's my chance to slip away.

But then I remember the clipboard in my hand, the responsibility I've shouldered, the stack of registration forms still blank. Retreat is not an option.

"Excuse me," I shout, while Mabel glares and growls. "Are you registered to vote?"

"Vote?" If Slowpoke Dale Earnhardt found the idea of my being torn to pieces amusing, he finds the idea of voting downright hilarious.

"Yes, sir." I quaver, keeping an eye on the growling dog. "Can we get you signed up?"

This time Dale doesn't bother containing his laughter. "Nah," he scoffs. "I don't vote."

To most people I know, even those who are pleased I was not eaten, this is an unsatisfying conclusion. We believe that all of us— even the poorly coifed and mean-spirited—should participate in our democracy. Every time an American scoffs at voting, an angel loses its wings.

But this is a modern view. The majority of our Founders would not have been disappointed that Mabel's owner declined to enter the electorate. If anything, they would have been appalled the option was open to him in the first place. The idea of extending the franchise to a guy who lives in a ramshackle home, fills his yard with trash, and keeps a low-class monster for a pet would have seemed ridiculous, no less bizarre than handing a ballot to Mabel herself.

"There will be no end to it," John Adams harrumphed in 1776, when the issue of expanding voting rights came before him. "New claims will arise; women will demand the vote; lads from 12 to 21 will think their rights not enough attended to; and every man who has not a farthing will demand an equal voice with any other."

Most early American leaders agreed with Adams when he argued that most Americans should be disenfranchised. (Even the word "franchise" reflects the view that voting is not for everybody. According to *Merriam-Webster*, it comes from a Middle English usage meaning "A right or privilege conferred by grant from a sovereign or a government." That's why we describe the government awarding you the ability to vote in the same way we describe Burger King awarding you the ability to sell Whoppers.)

But a few Founders took issue with Adams's grumpy view. Ben Franklin, whose liberal attitude toward the ballot we touched on in the previous chapter, was particularly miffed by the idea of property requirements for voting. "Today a man owns a jackass worth fifty dollars, and he is entitled to vote; but before the next election the jackass dies," he wrote. "Now gentlemen, pray inform me, in whom is the right of suffrage? In the man or in the jackass?"

From the start of American history, states were allowed to answer this question for themselves. Each could decide where to draw the line between the worthy Edward Maria Wingfields and the dangerous Slowpoke Dales.

In the debate between Franklin and Adams, most states initially came down on Adams's side. In 1790, the year the first census was completed, more than three-quarters had some form of property requirement for voting. Under this system, I would likely have had to wait until the age of thirty-two—when Jacqui and I bought our first house—to cast a ballot.

And I'm white and male. If you weren't those things, the situation was of course much worse. With one notable exception we'll return to, women were shut out of the political process entirely. Racial restrictions didn't just keep enslaved people from voting, but also disenfranchised free Black people in northern states like Connecticut.

Looking back on these harsh rules from a twenty-first-century vantage point, it's easy to conclude that our Founders didn't really believe in self-government. But that would be a mistake. By our modern standards (which are objectively less racist, classist, and sexist) voting in early America was indeed quite limited. But at our country's birth, the definition of "the people" was radically expansive, and not just compared to the British monarchy we left behind. In ancient Athens, strict citizenship requirements disenfranchised 80 to 90 percent of the population. In the Roman Republic, where voting rights never expanded beyond Italy, the unelectorate was larger still.

By contrast, Oxford historian Donald Ratcliffe estimates that in 1792, when George Washington ran for reelection, about 32 percent of the country's adult population could vote for him. On one hand, that still leaves out an awful lot of people. On the other hand, it's a long way from seven names in a box.

In the following decades, the electorate grew further. It happened just the way Ben Franklin had predicted: during economic downturns, previously enfranchised Americans suddenly found themselves without enough wealth to vote. When the economy rebounded and their voting rights were restored, these returning voters demanded a permanent end to property requirements. This change did not always come easily. In the 1840s, Rhode Islanders fought a mini-civil war between a "people's government" elected by the masses and the official government chosen by the landed elite. But by 1850, the idea that the ballot should be reserved for those who owned vast parcels of land or paid lots of taxes was history.

The end of property requirements for voting represented a change not just in law, but in worldview. We were now on the slippery slope John Adams had warned us about. And just as he predicted, we slipped.

If you went to high school in America, you likely know, or at least once knew, the rest. The Fifteenth Amendment guaranteed former slaves the right to vote. The Nineteenth Amendment extended voting rights to women. The Voting Rights Act of 1965 expanded the franchise to minority groups in practice and not just in theory. The voting age was lowered from twenty-one to eighteen during the Vietnam War. At the outset of American history, 7 in 10 adults were legally barred from voting. By the time I arrived, in 1986, that number had fallen to just 1 in 20. I was born into John Adams's nightmare.

But Americans didn't find it nightmarish at all. As the electorate changed, so did our view of elections. Today, just as we overwhelmingly agree that high voter turnout is good for democracy, 91 percent of us consider the right to vote essential to our personal freedom. In our modern understanding of the rights spelled out in the Declaration of Independence, casting a ballot is to liberty what oxygen is to life.

Yet our rules around voting haven't caught up to our attitudes. While we now live in a Ben Franklin world, we still vote in a John

Adams political process. The sealed-box origins of our democracy—the idea that ballots should be doled out as cautiously in America as guns are in other countries—remains evident throughout every part of our elections.

If you're hoping to win campaigns by increasing turnout, this is a problem. But if you're hoping to win campaigns by *lowering* turnout, it's excellent news. Because in a country where the ballot frequently remains a privilege and not a right, the most effective way to shrink the electorate is also the easiest. You can do to your opponents' supporters what fed-up colonists once did to John Smith. You can make it illegal for them to vote.

☆

In the spring of 2003, a lean, lanky executive named Richard L. Scott was in deep trouble. His company, Columbia/HCA, which ran hospitals across the southeastern United States, had recently been busted for ripping off taxpayers. During Scott's tenure as CEO, Columbia/HCA billed Medicare for false claims, paid kickbacks to doctors who ordered unnecessary medical testing, and used taxpayer dollars meant to fund community health education to pay for advertising instead. It was an all-you-can-eat buffet of fraud.

Richard L. Scott was never personally charged with a crime—executives in such cases rarely are. But Columbia/HCA's $1.7 billion settlement with the Justice Department was, at the time, the largest of its kind in history. As the guy atop the org chart, Scott resigned in disgrace.

Today, Richard L. Scott is better known as Rick. And Rick Scott is better known not for running a massive enterprise that committed crimes at taxpayer expense, but for being a senator from Florida. Before that, he served two terms as Florida's governor.

As you might expect, Scott's experience overseeing a Medicare fraud spree came up in all three of his campaigns. He was vague, but to his credit, he was also contrite. "There's no question that mistakes

were made, and as CEO, I have to accept responsibility for those mis-
takes," he told the *St. Petersburg Times* in 2010. "I learned hard lessons,
and I've taken that lesson, and it's helped me become a better business
person and a better leader."

Rick Scott is a Republican. I'm a Democrat. Still, viewed in a cer-
tain light, I find his tale uplifting: a man made a mistake, he admitted
he was wrong, and now he's better and wiser for the experience. Not
every Floridian agreed that Scott was qualified to represent them—in
all three of his elections, his margin of victory was less than 1.5 per-
cent. But still, a candidate made his case to the people. They, in turn,
put their trust in him. It's an inspiring story.

Or at least it would be an inspiring story if it were true. Rick Scott's
redemption relied only in part on winning his fellow Americans' votes.
To understand how exactly a disgraced CEO became one of the coun-
try's most successful politicians, we need to put his story aside for a
moment and consider the story of a very different Florida man instead.

We know much less about Ricky Scott than we do about Rick
Scott. In fact, in Ricky's case, all I could find were a few court records.
He was born in 1964. He lived for a time in Wilton Manors, just north
of Fort Lauderdale. And in 1986, he was convicted of a felony.

The crime Ricky committed, grand theft, sounds monstrous but
probably wasn't. In Florida, "grand theft" means stealing anything
worth more than $300 and less than $20,000. You can also be charged
with grand theft for taking a single fire extinguisher off a wall, for ab-
sconding with a farm animal (regardless of its value), or, in the words
of the criminal code, for stealing "any amount of citrus fruit consist-
ing of 2,000 or more individual pieces of fruit." It's unlikely we'll ever
learn whether Ricky Scott stole a Palm Beach socialite's diamond ear-
rings or just a large crate of oranges. In any event, he was sentenced to
nineteen months' probation.

Which leads us to the final thing we know for certain about Ricky
Scott. Unlike Rick, Ricky never got a chance to seek his fellow citi-
zens' forgiveness and run for governor. He didn't even get a chance to

vote for governor. The moment he was found guilty of a felony, he was barred from casting a ballot in Florida—not just for one election, as John Smith had been, but for the rest of his life.

The details of Florida's voting laws have gotten a fair bit of attention in recent years. But we haven't paid enough attention to exactly what those laws reveal about our democracy. In today's America, you can run a company that steals hundreds of millions of dollars from taxpayers, learn your lessons, embark on a second act, and become one of the country's most influential people. Or you can run off with 2,001 tangelos and be permanently stripped of one of your most fundamental rights.

How did we end up with such a lopsided arrangement, a system where Rick Scott runs our government and Ricky Scott has no say? The short answer is "On purpose."

The typical tale of enfranchisement in America—the story I summarized just a few pages ago—is one of constant progress. Sometimes we stride toward universal suffrage, sometimes we take baby steps, but we're always moving forward. But the truth is more complicated. Yes, at decisive moments in our history, we've extended the ballot to those who never had it. But at other decisive moments in our history, we've snatched the ballot away. Disenfranchisement is an American story, too.

Consider what happened to the women of nineteenth-century New Jersey. As a born-and-raised New Yorker it's hard for me to admit this, but Jersey at the dawn of our republic was a remarkably enlightened place. African-Americans could vote, which immediately put the Garden State in the open-minded camp. Even more notably, women could vote as well. That's not to say Jersey was a bastion of feminism— the state had property requirements, and wives couldn't own property, which restricted the ballot to unmarried women who possessed at least some wealth. Even so, in extending the franchise beyond white males, New Jersey set itself apart.

At first, politicians treated female constituents the way they would treat any group of up-for-grabs voters: they pandered. In *The Petticoat Electors*, professors Judith Apter Klinghoffer and Lois Elkis recount the eager if clumsy attempts by the two major parties at the time, the Republicans and Federalists, to court the women's vote. In Bloomfield, for example, one party grandee gave a toast to "the Republican fair. May their patriotic conduct in the late election add an irresistible zest to their charms." So long as both parties thought women were persuadable, both parties did their best to persuade them.

But around the turn of the nineteenth century, New Jersey's women stopped being swing voters. Instead, they became a reliable Federalist bloc. As "the Republican fair" deserted the Republican Party, Republican lawmakers found women voters' charms less irresistibly zesty than before.

It was, of course, theoretically possible for politicians to win back their lost constituents. They could have presented new ideas, come up with new messages, or both. At the very least they could have tried a less condescending toast. But for lawmakers who could no longer count on women's votes, another tactic was both simpler and more politically effective: they could take women's voting rights away.

That's exactly what happened. In 1807, the Federalists were on the cusp of flipping New Jersey for the first time in years. Meanwhile, for reasons too complex and petty to be worth explaining, North and South Jersey Republicans were barely on speaking terms. With a presidential election looming, Republican lawmakers rushed a restrictive new voting bill through the legislature. Among its many provisions, it banned all women from the ballot box.

There are two things to keep in mind here. First, while the Republican politicians who disenfranchised women were almost certainly sexist, so were their Federalist opponents. What ended America's first experiment with women's suffrage was not prejudice, but politics.

Second, the politicians restricting voting rights never admitted their motivations. Instead, Lewis Condict, the chairman of the committee that wrote the New Jersey bill, blamed women (and African-Americans, among others) for election fraud. The idea that white men are New Jersey's anticorruption champions will be strange to anyone who has heard of New Jersey. It was ridiculous even then. But politicians trying to shrink the pool of voters weren't looking for a well-reasoned argument; they were looking for an excuse. "Fighting fraud" worked well enough, and their bill easily passed.

When politicians couldn't disenfranchise voters outright, they got creative. This was especially true in the South during the decades following the Civil War. Thanks to the Fifteenth Amendment, lawmakers could no longer ban all non-white people from voting. But unwilling to allow former slaves into the electorate, public officials nonetheless came up with a series of bank shots to target voting rights.

One of the most audacious, and successful, was a two-part plan executed by Florida Democrats beginning in 1868. Step one was to put in place the rule that would ensnare Ricky Scott more than a century later: anyone convicted of a felony in Florida was barred from voting for life.

Step two was to charge as many Black Floridians with felonies as possible. In the post–Civil War years, the state's criminal code was completely transformed. Florida residents could now be charged with felonies for being disobedient, behaving impudently, or "wandering or strolling about." Writing for the Brennan Center for Justice, the nation's premier democracy reform organization, law professor Erika L. Wood noted that theft of any "agricultural production or fixture" could result in a felony charge. By that standard, today's 2,000 citrus-fruit minimum is positively benevolent.

In theory, any impudent wanderer or disobedient stroller, regardless of race, could be incarcerated and stripped of his rights. In practice, within a decade of Florida's new voting laws, 95 percent of the state's convicts were Black. Without running afoul of the post–Civil War amendments, the white Democrats who ran Florida had hobbled the potential emergence of African-Americans as an electoral bloc. Even better, they had done it in the name of high-minded principle. As noted lawyer Roger Clegg put it, "if you won't follow the law yourself, then you can't make the law for everyone else."

Except he didn't say that in 1868. He said it nearly 150 years later, in 2016. Clegg has a long and distinguished résumé in Republican legal circles—he served as a deputy assistant attorney general in the Reagan and George H. W. Bush administrations. Today he's the president of a conservative think tank that, among other things, defends restrictive voting laws.

"Sound policy reasons," Clegg writes, "support both the disenfranchisement of felons and cautious, individualized consideration when refranchising them."

I don't know Roger Clegg personally—we both attended Yale, but missed each other by twenty-three years—so I can't say if he's making a good-faith argument or an alibi in the manner of New Jersey's Lewis Condict. But to be generous, let's assume it's the former. In that case, one thing Clegg fails to note is that in America, felonious behavior is not at all uncommon. According to reputable estimates, 70 percent of Americans have done something that would technically warrant jail time, mainly involving drunk driving or possession of marijuana. Most of us just never got caught.

In other words, Clegg's argument—that no one who has done something illegal can be trusted with self-government—is shaky at best. If you disenfranchised all those who "don't follow the law," there wouldn't be many voters left.

What's more, just as it did 150 years ago, the definition of "felony" varies wildly by state. Florida, for example, still has one of the strictest criminal codes in the nation. As Ari Berman, the dean of American voting rights reporters, has pointed out, "Florida counts 533 different infractions as felonies, including crimes like disturbing a lobster trap and trespassing on a construction site." Even Floridians who avoid lobster traps and construction sites must tread carefully, because the Sunshine State also has some of the country's strictest drug laws. You can be charged with felony possession for holding just twenty-one grams of pot. (That's about sixty joints, or, if memory serves, slightly less than the amount required to sustain a college improv comedy group on a weeklong tour.) In many cases, a felony record isn't about what you've done. It's about where you've done it.

Of course, all this is just argument and counterargument. What we really need is a real-world test of Clegg's theory, a way to find out whether allowing felons and former felons to cast ballots weakens our society as a whole. Luckily, we have not one test case, but two: Maine and Vermont. In that small slice of the region called New England (thanks, John Smith!), it's not only former prisoners who can vote. Current prisoners can vote as well. You can rob a Birkenstock factory or stab someone at the L.L.Bean store and still cast your ballot from jail.

If Roger Clegg is right, and allowing felons to vote undermines society, Vermont and Maine should be dystopias. But they're not. Apart from a tendency toward crunchy, condescending lifestyles in the former and a surplus of tacky lobster merchandise in the latter, both states are doing fine.

Perhaps Clegg's theory would have been plausible in 1776, when John Adams was first sounding the alarm about the slippery slope of expanding voting rights. But today we can confidently say that Roger Clegg is incorrect. There's no sound policy reason for disenfranchising felons, any more than there was a sound anticorruption reason for disenfranchising women more than two centuries ago. Banishing Ricky Scott from democracy has done nothing to protect us.

It has, however, done a lot to protect Rick.

In the most recent presidential election, thanks to Florida's laws and laws like them, the number of people legally barred from voting because of a felony conviction stood at 6.1 million. Only one-quarter of these non-voters were actually in prison. Half of them—a population roughly the size of Iowa—weren't even on probation or parole. They had done their time. Their taxes were going toward schools and roads and fighter jets and everything else. Even so, these three million people could not cast a ballot.

If you're the kind of person who's reading this book, it's possible you already knew these numbers are very big. What you may not realize is that these big numbers are very new. In the forty years before Donald Trump was elected president, America's population grew by 50 percent. But the number of Americans barred from voting because of a felony conviction grew by *500* percent.

The demographics of the disenfranchised have changed as well. Specifically, they've become less white. This is not, I hasten to add, because nonwhite people are especially felonious. Instead, it's because "tough on crime" policies that began in the 1970s had very different impacts on different racial groups. Just as the lion's share of nineteenth-century Floridians arrested for wandering and strolling were Black, African-Americans are more likely to have been caught up in the war on drugs and its aftermath.

Mass incarceration has led directly to mass disenfranchisement. When Ronald Reagan was first elected president, nine states disenfranchised more than 5 percent of their Black populations because of a past felony. When Donald Trump was elected president, twenty-three states did. In Rick Scott's Florida, more than 20 percent of African-Americans could not vote in 2016. (Mitch McConnell's Kentucky was even worse. Forty years ago, the Bluegrass State barred just 3 percent of African-American voters from the ballot. In the last presidential election, more than 25 percent of Black Kentuckians were not allowed to vote.)

Taking voting rights from the current and formerly incarcerated hasn't just changed the electorate's racial composition. It's changed the electorate's economic composition as well. The average person convicted of a crime has a far lower income than the average American—a disparity that, unfortunately, only widens upon their release. In other words, by making it illegal for Ricky Scott to vote, we help ensure that the electorate will be far wealthier than the population as a whole.

Unlike our Founders, we live at a time when most Americans view the ballot as a right and not a privilege. Yet somehow, over the past four decades, lawmakers took that right from millions of Americans—Americans disproportionately belonging to a particular race and social class—who had previously possessed it. It seems so obviously tragic.

Unless, of course, you know that Ricky Scott would have cast his ballot for your opponent. In that case, the tragedy seems more like a lifeline.

In 2010, when Rick Scott first ran for governor, fewer than one-tenth of African-American voters supported him. He prevailed by just 61,000 votes. It's not hard to see how adding 1.5 million disproportionately Black and lower-income Floridians to the electorate might have made a difference. In fact, if just 25 percent of those disenfranchised voters had actually participated, and just two-thirds had supported Scott's opponent, Florida would have elected a different governor. Rick Scott's entire political career depended on Ricky Scott not voting.

Which certainly explains what happened next. Under Florida law, governors can restore voting rights to any disenfranchised constituent. Scott's predecessor, a fellow Republican, had wielded this power about 39,000 times per year, re-enfranchising citizens who had served their time and demonstrated their commitment to rehabilitation. Then Rick Scott took office. During his eight years as governor, he restored voting rights to just 3,000 people, cutting the rate of restorations by 99 percent.

In 2018, Rick Scott left the governor's office to run for Senate against Democratic incumbent Bill Nelson, and won by just 10,033 votes. In the wake of his victory, journalists focused on Scott's not inconsiderable political skill: his relationship with the state's Hispanic communities; his strict message discipline; the sheer sum of money he spent on ads. Yet the coverage almost entirely ignored Scott's most important political decision. If Rick Scott had restored his fellow citizens' rights at the rate of his predecessor, he would not be a senator today.

One Senate seat out of a hundred may not seem like much. But it turns out that Rick Scott's isn't an isolated case. The sociologists Christopher Uggen and Jeff Manza found that between 1978 and 2000—a period when we withheld voting rights from a far smaller percentage of Americans than we do today—felon disenfranchisement gave one of our two parties a major advantage. Stripping citizens of the ballot flipped seven Senate seats, all of them from blue to red. Among those lucky senators was Mitch McConnell, who won his first term in a nail-biter. If Kentucky hadn't made it illegal for so many Kentuckians to cast a ballot, a different person would be leading the Republican Party today.

Even more consequential than the effect on the Senate was the effect on the White House. If Florida had allowed former felons to vote, George W. Bush would never have become the forty-third president of the United States. In fact, Uggen and Manza estimate that instead of losing by 537 votes, Al Gore would have won by more than 80,000.

Before we go any further, I want you to stop and think, really think, about what this means. The Iraq War. Guantanamo Bay. Trickle-down tax cuts. Inaction on climate change. The seeds of a financial crisis. If you're an American, you are living in the most successful, most powerful democracy on earth. But you are also living in a country, not to mention a planet, shaped by just one state's decision to not let former prisoners vote.

This is usually where the modern story of American disenfranchisement ends: with the approximately 3 percent of us who, due to mass incarceration, are barred from the ballot box. There's no question this is an important group. But there's an even larger segment of the population being kept from the electorate. Unlike Ricky Scott, members of this group have not had their voting rights taken away. Instead, politicians are going to great and unprecedented lengths to make sure they never get their voting rights in the first place.

I am referring, of course, to immigrants.

☆

How many states have, at one point or another, allowed noncitizens to vote? Take a moment. Guess the answer. Now guess higher.

The real number is thirty-eight. Nearly 80 percent of states once extended voting rights to immigrants, whether they became citizens or not.

At the dawn of American history, immigrant voting wasn't even controversial. In John Adams's 1776 broad harrumph against expanded suffrage, you'll recall that he was determined to keep most people from the electorate: women, teens, the poor. But noncitizens voting didn't worry him.

In our modern political climate, Adams's lack of concern might seem strange. How can you be in favor of restrictions on voting and not care if newly arrived immigrants vote? Yet at the time, this attitude made perfect sense. After all, when your country is brand new, everyone is brand new to your country. Moreover, as political scientist Ron Hayduk points out, the revolutionary slogan "no taxation without representation" applied in reverse. It was widely accepted that anyone who paid taxes deserved a say in how their money was spent; their birthplace was irrelevant.*

For these reasons, nearly all the original thirteen states allowed new immigrants to vote. A few of them changed their minds as populations grew. (In fact, the same New Jersey law that disenfranchised women took the ballot from noncitizens as well). But these older states were offset by newer ones, which offered noncitizens voting rights as enticement to move west. In 1848, for example, the new state of Wisconsin permitted all "declarants"—immigrants who publicly expressed a wish to become citizens in the future—to cast ballots.

---

* Hayduk's research is also the source for the figure of thirty-eight states cited earlier. Others haven't reached numbers quite as large, but Hayduk has done more digging.

So why can't noncitizens vote today? The answer depends on the state, but generally speaking, a combination of factors was at work. The number of immigrants arriving in America gradually increased, which spooked those already here. Newcomers often moved to cities, and as we'll see in future chapters, state legislatures favored the countryside. There were also the usual accusations of fraud as recent arrivals became associated—not always unfairly, it must be said—with corrupt political machines. Finally, don't discount good old-fashioned prejudice; as immigrants began showing up from places other than England, Americans became less eager to enfranchise them.

Yet despite all this, it wasn't until 1926 that noncitizen voting in America ceased completely. To put it slightly differently, every president prior to Herbert Hoover was elected with noncitizen help. And for many decades after, nothing prevented states from welcoming immigrants back into the presidential electorate if they chose to. Congress didn't officially ban noncitizen voting for federal offices until 1996. *Friends* has been around longer than that.

I don't mean to suggest that states were eager to give recent immigrants the ballot before Congress stepped in and stopped them. Throughout my lifetime, and yours, voting has been restricted to citizens. What has changed, however, is the impact of those restrictions on our country.

To understand why, let's start with green card holders, or "Lawful Permanent Residents," to use the technical term. Like the declarants of the 1800s, these immigrants arrived here legally and have publicly committed to staying. They pay taxes. Nearly all of them have a spouse, child, or parent who's an American citizen. If a president leads us into a dumb war in the Middle East, green card holders in our military will fight and die on our behalf. They very clearly have skin in the game. Yet in only in a handful of places—the hippie mecca of San Francisco, a few small slices of Maryland—can green card holders vote, and then only in local elections.

This is almost certainly a bigger deal than you think. Unless you work in immigration policy, you are likely underestimating just how many green card holders live in the United States. The current number? 13.2 million. America is home to more green card holders than Alaskans, North Dakotans, South Dakotans, Delawareans, Montanans, Vermonters, Rhode Islanders, Mainers, New Hampshirites, Hawaiians, and West Virginians, combined. If green card holders were their own state, they'd have more electoral votes than Ohio.

And based on historical trends, the number of Lawful Permanent Residents actually ought to be even higher. The main reason it's "only" 13.2 million is that modernizing our immigration system—once a bipartisan priority—has hit a wall. We haven't updated our quota numbers for green cards since 1991, which has increased the backlog of applications. As part of its effort to cut legal immigration, the Trump administration has made this already difficult process even more painful. As a result, there are millions of "missing" Lawful Permanent Residents—people who would love to become Americans, meet all qualifications to do so, but are stuck waiting years or even decades to apply.

Now add to these 13.2 million the undocumented immigrants who, despite President Trump's best efforts, aren't going anywhere. I'm not talking about seasonal workers or tourists who overstayed a visa. I'm talking about people who broke the law to get here, but who have lived in the United States for ten years or more. In 1995, this population of long-term undocumented immigrants was just 1.8 million. It's now 7 million—roughly the size of Massachusetts. Today, the average unauthorized immigrant arrived in America around the time *Finding Nemo* arrived in theaters.

The long-term undocumented may have come here illegally, but America is now their home. Their careers and families are here. Our Constitution requires that they be recorded in the census. Like all immigrants, they pay taxes—well more than $10 billion in taxes each year. They're part of this country. They're just not part of the part of this country that can vote.

I don't believe we should allow unauthorized immigrants—even those who have been here a long time—to cast ballots. But I also don't believe the alternative to noncitizen voting should be mass disenfranchisement. The alternative to noncitizen voting should be mass citizenship.

Historically, that's always been our approach to immigration. In 1929, almost the exact same time immigrant voting ceased, Congress allowed any unauthorized person to retroactively gain legal status. We legalized large groups of immigrants again in 1958, and again in 1965. We legalized 2.7 million undocumented immigrants under Reagan and a million more under Clinton.

And then we stopped. Throughout the last century, noncitizens have at times found themselves in limbo between reforms. But unauthorized immigrants have never gone this long without being given a chance to earn their citizenship. What changed?

The two most common explanations for America's nativist resurgence are economic anxiety and racism, and both of these surely played a role. But if you want to understand why opposing immigration became a right-wing obsession, you need to look at the way new citizens alter—or would alter—our electorate.

For most of the twentieth century, immigrants didn't favor one party over the other. "As recently as the 1970s," writes political scientist Thomas Holbrook, "naturalized citizens used to 'look' a lot like the native-born population." But in the decades that followed, the immigrant population became less white, and non-white people became more closely aligned with Democrats. Today the correlation is clear: the higher the foreign-born percentage of a state's inhabitants, the more likely that state is to go blue. Like New Jersey's women centuries earlier, newly minted citizens are no longer considered up for grabs.

As immigrants began to favor one party, immigration stopped being bipartisan. Consider the following policy proposal, delivered by Rush Limbaugh on Fox News in 2018. "I would be willing, right here, to support an effort to grant permanent citizenship to whatever number of illegal immigrants there are in the country tomorrow," he declared, "if you will make as part of the deal they can't vote for fifteen or twenty-five years."

What a remarkable admission. According to one of the most venerable right-wing populists, the problem with immigrants isn't economic or cultural at all. The problem with immigrants is that they threaten his party's hold on power. The real jobs lost to immigration, Limbaugh argues, would be those held by Republican politicians.

Strangely, I'm more optimistic than Rush Limbaugh is about the future of his party. It's true that, if all America's noncitizens were naturalized tomorrow, Donald Trump would be in trouble. So would some of his right-wing allies. But politicians are nothing if not flexible. Allowing immigrants to become citizens wouldn't mean Democrats win every election. It would mean Republicans have to listen to them.

So long as large groups of Americans remain legally barred from voting, however, politicians don't really need to care about those groups at all. Growing up, I was taught that "People who don't vote have no right to complain." But in fact, in tens of millions cases, it's exactly the opposite. People can't complain because they have no right to vote.

The total number of Americans legally prohibited from casting a ballot is hard to measure precisely. But when you add up disenfranchised felons and ex-felons, green card holders, and long-term undocumented immigrants, you get about 22.5 million adults. That's a lot of people without voting rights. It's also a lot *more* people without voting rights than there used to be. In 1980, when Ronald Reagan was first elected, about 3.5 percent of the population was legally disenfranchised. Today it's about 8.8 percent.

During an election year, you'll often hear that "America goes to the polls." But this is no longer true. Nearly one in ten adults in America— people whose lives are affected by their representatives, and who would have been allowed to cast ballots in the past—is barred from the electorate. And the main reason they've been barred from the electorate is that barring them helps certain politicians win. Without mass disenfranchisement, America today would be a very different place.

I find that rather encouraging.

No, that's not a typo. And yes, I'm appalled that so many of our fellow Americans have had their voting rights taken away. But consider the alternative—that Donald Trump and Mitch McConnell accurately reflect our values. If a clear majority of the United States had indeed developed a taste for incompetence, white supremacy, and corruption, I might well be writing these words from my cozy new home in Ontario or Quebec.

In fact, however, our values remained steady; it's our political process that changed. Our politicians changed it. And I find that encouraging as well. Because it means that We, the People, can change it back.

I didn't write this book because I came up with brilliant new ideas to fix our democracy. I wrote this book because other people did. The solutions are already out there—what we need to do is put them into action.

Restoring voting rights would be an excellent place to start. And an excellent place to start restoring voting rights is with people who committed felonies, went to prison, and have since been released. In our polarized country, one where common ground seems always to be shrinking, Americans still agree with the following principle: if you've paid your debt to society and rejoined your community, you should be allowed to vote.

This was the principle an unlikely band of bipartisan allies came together in 2018 to defend. In Rick Scott's Florida, as in many other states, you can put certain proposed amendments to the state constitution directly on the ballot for voters to reject or approve. In Florida, such measures need a 60 percent majority to pass, a high bar to clear. Yet the same night Rick Scott won his Senate seat by just

10,000 votes, an amendment to restore former felons' voting rights passed by 2.3 million.

Unfortunately, that's not the end of the story. Deprived of one way to disenfranchise their constituents, Republican politicians in Florida's legislature are trying another. Under a new Florida law, passed in the wake of the 2018 amendment, former felons can have their rights restored only after they've paid all fines and fees associated with their arrest. Thanks to another set of defects in Florida's justice system, these fees can easily run into the tens of thousands of dollars, making them essentially unpayable.

As I write this, details of the new Florida law are being tussled over in court. It's quite possible that, in the short term at least, many former felons will remain disenfranchised. But even in a worst-case scenario, the Florida electorate has been forever changed. For the first time since his conviction thirty-four years ago, there's a good chance Ricky Scott will be able to cast his ballot. That's a major step forward.

In states that allow voting rights to be decided directly by voters, we should continue to put Florida-style measures on the ballot. But not every state permits such proposals. That's why the single most effective way to expand the electorate going forward is to win elections right now. Politicians have broken our politics. Politicians can help us fix our politics, too.

Consider the case of former Virginia governor Terry McAuliffe. In Democratic circles, McAuliffe has long been known as a human supernova, the kind of man who is referred to in public as "the Macker" and does not seem to mind. I encountered McAuliffe for the first time, very briefly, in 2004, when he was chair of the Democratic National Committee and I was a high school intern. I had never met anyone with that much energy before, and wouldn't again until I got to college and made friends with people who did cocaine. In 2013, when the Macker was elected governor of Virginia, quite a few people, including plenty of Democrats, rolled their eyes.

The doubters were wrong. McAuliffe did an absolutely fantastic job. And among his many impressive achievements, he says the one he's most proud of is re-enfranchising Virginia's former felons.

What's important, for our purposes, is not just what Governor McAuliffe accomplished, but how he accomplished it. He didn't go looking for an ally in the Republican-controlled state legislature, which he knew benefited from the very laws he was hoping to undo. Instead, he went to his own lawyers, asking them how far he could go on his own. On their advice, he issued a sweeping executive order, using his powers as governor to restore voting rights to everyone with a felony record in the state—206,000 people in all.

As McAuliffe expected, this was just the beginning of the fight. Republican leaders sued, and in a 4–3 ruling, their conservative allies on the state supreme court declared that Virginia's governor did not have the power to re-enfranchise entire groups. Voting rights had to be restored one former prisoner at a time.

A different governor might have admitted defeat. But not the Macker. "Let's get out all 206,000 petitions and bring boxes of pens, and I'm going to sit there and sign every damn one, even if it takes me a week," he recalled saying. That's exactly what he did. Republican officials sued him again, this time for contempt of court, but he won easily. Across the state, newly enfranchised Virginians received an envelope with a signed letter from their governor, a voter registration form, and a self-addressed, stamped envelope. It was one of the largest registration drives in Virginia's history.

I ran into McAuliffe at a D.C. fundraiser in 2019, fifteen years after our first meeting, and toward the end of the evening I cornered him and asked about his voting rights battle. If anything, he had even more energy than I remembered. He went through the saga with so much enthusiasm I thought he might give off sparks. "They took me to court twice! Only Virginia governor to be sued for contempt of court!" When he finished, he leaned in close, as though he were about to whisper something salacious in my ear.

"I loved every minute of it."

We could all use a little more of Terry McAuliffe's happy-warrior spirit. But what I really admire is not his attitude. It's his understanding of power. Not every governor would have devoted so much time to expanding the electorate. Voting laws rarely score headlines. Officials almost always have a more urgent demand on their time. But the Macker understood a basic truth of our democracy: If our political process is broken, then in the long term nothing else matters. The most stirring promises will be little more than wasted breath. The most inspiring policy victories will prove only temporary.

Fixing our democracy is the equivalent of repairing a crack in your home's foundation. It's expensive and time consuming. It doesn't boost your curb appeal. But it's the only way to make every other alteration last. Mitch McConnell understood this. He knew, and knows, that the best way to give your team an unfair advantage is to rewrite the rules. McAuliffe's understanding was similar but in reverse: if we're going to build a fairer, stronger, better America, the foundations have to come first.

McAuliffe also understood that when politicians' hold on power depends on an unfair rule book, they will never be convinced to improve it. The way to restore balance to our political process is not through endless negotiation and the search for a perfect, kumbaya compromise. Reformers can be tempted to think of themselves as cathedral builders, carefully constructing grand edifices over time. These days, though, they're more likely to be Luke Skywalker at the end of the first *Star Wars*. The best they can hope for is a tiny opening in the Death Star and a moment in which to exploit it.

But take advantage of this opportunity, this "Skywalker Window," and everything will change. That's because expanding democracy creates a snowball effect. Allow more people to vote, and more people who support voting rights will get elected. The more successfully we defend our republic, the easier our republic becomes to defend. There are ideas that benefit from years or even decades of nitpicky polish. Fixing our country's foundation is not one of them.

As Governor McAuliffe put it simply in his book *Beyond Charlottesville*: "Action brings change. Do something. Do it now."

Our do-it-now attitude should apply to ideas that traditionally fall outside the category of "democracy reform." For example, most Americans don't support following Maine's and Vermont's examples and allowing incarcerated people to cast ballots, but they do support ending mass incarceration, which would have a similar effect. By reforming the criminal justice system so that we're locking up fewer people, we'll expand the number of people who can vote.

Immigration, too, should be seen as a voting rights issue. In the most progressive pockets of the country, green card holders might gain the ballot in local elections sooner rather than later. But more broadly, providing pathways to citizenship for immigrants—green card holders and the long-term undocumented alike—would close the gap between the people and the voters. In addition to all its other benefits, immigration reform would help ensure that our representatives represented the people they serve.

I shared this opinion recently with a member of Congress. "Interesting," he said, as the full number of disenfranchised sank in. "So maybe we should pass an immigration bill before a voting rights bill?" He was on the right track, but I'd put it slightly differently. We should pass an immigration bill *as* a voting rights bill. And then we should pass another voting rights bill, and another, and another. Do it now. Do as much of it as we possibly can.

The goal, despite Rush Limbaugh's concern, is not to ensure that Democrats seize control forever. Regardless of which party creates it, a one-party democracy would be no democracy at all. Instead, our aim should be to assert a simple principle, a belief that most Americans already hold. If this is your country, you should have a say in how it's run.

If we establish that principle—ensuring that Ricky Scott, and all future Ricky Scotts, can cast a ballot—it will go a long way toward bridging the divide between what Americans want and what our leaders do.

It will ensure that millions more of us are brought into the electorate, and that their voices are heard.

And yet, even if we extended voting rights to every single American adult, the unelectorate would still be enormous. The number of voters would still come nowhere near the number of people. Compared to other democracies, America's turnout would be appallingly low. People who wanted to cast their ballots would still unable to do so.

If we truly want to understand America's non-voters, in other words, we have a lot more exploring to do.

3

THE SASQUATCH HUNTERS

The Unofficially Disenfranchised

My life of crime begins in Taco Cabana. For the uninitiated, that's a chain of fast-casual restaurants with outposts across the American Southwest, known for patio seating, pink signage, and serving alcohol. On a sweltering Sunday in 2019, I arrive at a northwest Houston location, order a Shiner Bock and two hearty fajita tacos, and make my way to a high-top.

Richard has been waiting for me. Approaching middle age, he sports the kind of gray beard that suggests an obsession with something other than beard trimming. Even more gray hair spills from a visor on his head. He's sitting in the very back corner of the restaurant, facing the door, like a Mob boss. Within a minute he's talking to me about apartments.

Houston is large. At last count the city was home to 2.3 million people, spread out over more square miles than Los Angeles, and dotted with at least 2,000 apartment complexes. Richard knows them all. He's spent a decade scoping entrances and exits. He custom-makes digital maps with layers upon layers. He knows which buildings are easy to access and which bristle with security. Richard looks at a multi-family dwelling the way John Dillinger once looked at a bank.

He can't put his plan into action alone, however. He needs accomplices, and soon they arrive. Tracy moved to Houston after her long career as a Detroit autoworker came to an abrupt, recession-era end. If Richard is the mastermind behind the Taco Cabana Gang, she's the face of the operation, the kind of smooth talker who can charm her way out of anything.

Next to arrive is Leah, mid-thirties and yoga fit, from the tony neighborhood of River Oaks. She's the logistics wiz, and as the table grows crowded—a nerdy twentysomething with the ironic T-shirt, a twitchy lady with a hard-to-place accent, a quiet older man with khaki cargo shorts and a floppy hat—Leah hands out gear. Then she goes through the legal risks. One wrong move, and any member of our crew could wind up in jail.

And with that stern warning, it's go time. Tracy sorts us into strike teams. Leah double checks a few details on the map. As we head toward the parking lot, Richard can't contain himself.

"Go storm the castle!" he growls. Our voter registration drive is under way.

In Texas it's hard—confoundingly hard, devilishly hard—to register your fellow citizens to vote. In most states, you just grab a clipboard and ask around. It's the procedure I followed with Slowpoke Dale, and despite the occasional oversize canine launching itself toward your tasty ankles, it's easy.

Not so in Texas. To sign up a voter in the Lone Star State you must first be deputized, like a member of a sheriff's posse. This means going to an in-person class led by your county tax assessor. You sit through a lecture. You take a test. Only after you pass do you get a "certificate of appointment" with your name, address, and a five-digit number identifying you as an official Volunteer Deputy Voter Registrar, or VDVR.

Some counties run VDVR classes regularly and post materials online. But others schedule their trainings for odd and inconvenient windows, with no online preparation, so that the course lasts between four and six hours. Coincidentally, that's about the same amount of time it takes to earn a concealed-carry license. In the opinion of the State of Texas, openly wielding a voter registration form is as dangerous as secretly wielding a Glock.

Actually, that's not fair to the Glock. Because where a Texas gun license lasts five years and can be easily renewed online, a VDVR card expires every two years and must be renewed in person. The rules governing voter registration rarely change. There's nothing new to learn. Nevertheless, if you register voters for a midterm election and a presidential election, and you fail to take a refresher course in between, you're a criminal.

As it turns out, there are lots of ways helping people vote can make you a criminal in Texas. As a non-Texan, if I so much as handle a completed registration form—not fill it out, not alter it, just touch it—I'm breaking state law. Even qualified deputy registrars face the constant threat of legal repercussions. Fail to submit your registration forms on time? Take a photo of a completed form, even with a voter's permission? Register a voter who lives outside the county in which you're deputized? You could go to jail.

The last crime on the list—the one restricting VDVRs to individual counties—is yet another way registration forms are more carefully managed than guns. If you take a concealed-carry course in El Paso, you can tote your Glock to Forth Worth without incident. A deputy registrar card, however, is valid only in the county where it's handed out.

And Texas has a *lot* of counties; 254 of them, the most in the nation by far. Even accounting for the state's square mileage, nowhere else has land been so exuberantly sliced up. It's very easy to accidentally cross a county border in the Lone Star State, and in nearly every case there's no penalty for doing so.

When it comes to voter registration, however, those county lines might as well be made of barbed wire. A licensed deputy registrar in Dallas, for example, can legally sign up a voter at 4010 Midway Road. But if she crosses the street and registers a voter at 4013 Midway, she's committing a crime. This isn't an isolated example. Dozens of Texas cities and towns belong to multiple counties. Even apartment complexes can be split down the middle by county borders—you'd need multiple VDVR licenses, or multiple VDVRs, to operate there.

Barring the Taco Cabana Gang from crossing county lines does nothing to protect the integrity of Texas elections. It does, however, make registration drives vastly more difficult. Take Houston Community College, which has seventy thousand students. It ought to be a gold mine for registrars, the school is located in Harris County, and a large number of its students commute from somewhere else. If you're a VDVR from Harris, and an unregistered young person from Liberty or Montgomery County asks you to sign them up, you are legally obligated to turn them away.

The VDVR requirements make it equally difficult to travel in search of unregistered voters. In Frio County, about one hundred miles from the Mexican border, just 18 percent of voting-age adults cast a ballot in 2016. Frio is a forty-five-minute drive from San Antonio, and plenty of eager volunteers would be thrilled to make the short trip down I-35 to help change those numbers. But they can't. It's against the law.

Tracy, the former autoworker, said she briefly tried to overcome this hurdle by getting licensed in multiple counties at once. But almost immediately she ran up against another feature of the Texas registration system: county tax assessors run their offices as they see fit, and some of them go out of their way to be unhelpful. She told me that Fort Bend County, which runs along Harris County's southwest border, is notorious for handing out only ten registration forms at a time. A VDVR from Houston has to drive forty minutes to the county seat of Richmond, pick up the forms, sign up ten voters, drive back with the completed forms, exchange them for blank ones, and repeat the process ad infinitum. Ordinarily, Tracy doesn't take no for an answer. But even she gave up.

You might think Tracy's defeat proves that Texas's voter registration laws aren't working. But in fact, it's the opposite. Texas's voter registration laws are doing exactly what they were designed to. It's no coincidence that signing up a voter in the Lone Star State is so difficult. Nor is it an accident that holding a registration drive, which in most states feels like planning a bake sale, in Texas feels like planning a heist.

As we've already seen, the simplest way to banish your neighbors from the electorate is to rescind their voting rights. But if you can't make voting illegal, you can make voting impossible. And that's what countless officials—not just in Texas, but across the country—are working hard to do.

While most of my writing life is spent in a small home office with sub-par A/C and a litter box, every so often I get a moment of literary glamour. That's how I found myself on a cobblestone street an hour north of Venice in 2018. I'd been invited to a book festival in the mountain town of Pordenone, and my Italian editor, a warm and knowledgeable woman named Sabrina, took me on a tour that ended with *aperitivi* at a café. It was a perfect European moment—highly civilized with just a touch of classy pretension—until Sabrina pursed her lips and sighed through her nose. It's an expression I'm familiar with, and I'm sure you are, too. First introduced in 2015, it's the universal sign for "Now we're going to talk about Trump."

But to my surprise, that's not where Sabrina took the conversation. Instead, she fixed me with a look of deep and bewildered dismay. "Is it true," she asked, "that in America people have to 'register' to vote?"

More than the question itself, it was her tone that stunned me. I had worked in and around politics for more than a decade. Yet it never occurred to me that voter registration was anything less than essential.

I was totally naive. In the United States, we're proud of our place as the world's oldest democracy, a shining city on a hill. Yet as researchers Jennifer Rosenberg and Margaret Chen have helpfully detailed, when it comes to compiling lists of eligible voters, hardly anyone follows our lead. In England the government pays door-to-door canvassers to collect voters' information, much the way we hire census workers in the United States. In France, they take information you supply for the military draft and port it over to a voting database. In parts of Canada, they do the same thing, but with motor vehicle records.

To understand exactly what it's like to be a voter in another democracy, I called my friend Meg. She's originally from Little Rock, but she married a Swede and now lives in a storybook coastal village full of picturesque views and herring. How, I wanted to know, did voter registration work in her new home?

Meg is a director with the Moth, an organization that produces live storytelling shows around the world. Yet this time, even she had no story to tell. "It's crazy efficient," Meg said, sounding almost embarrassed. She explained that when she signed up for the Swedish equivalent of a green card, she received a *personnummer*, essentially her new Social Security number, and that her *personnummer* information was automatically entered into the voter rolls. That was it. She was registered.

Then again, in Sweden every summer, otherwise sane adults gather to dance around a pole shaped like a leaf-covered phallus while singing a song that includes the lyrics "The small frogs are funny to look at," so perhaps they don't have it all figured out. And besides, who cares if our own country's traditions aren't for everybody? Registering to vote is part of what makes us American.

Except it's not. When our Constitution was ratified, there was no such thing as voter registration. Not a single registered voter cast a ballot for George Washington or John Adams. The concept of "registered voter" simply didn't exist. Even when voter lists did arrive, at the beginning of the nineteenth century, they were mostly limited to New England, and they resembled modern-day Sweden far more than modern-day America. There were no forms to fill out. Volunteers didn't have to canvass a neighborhood in search of sign-ups. Adding every eligible name to the voter rolls was the government's responsibility.

Even these early, unobtrusive attempts at voter registration, modest though they were, proved highly controversial. That controversy came to a head on April 4, 1831, in the Seventh Ward of Boston, when a man named Josiah Capen arrived at his polling place to vote.

Capen had no reason to expect trouble. He was a longtime resident of the area, had voted before, and met all the property requirements then in place. Yet for whatever reason, his name wasn't on the list. He demanded to be allowed to vote anyway. The local official, a gentleman named Samuel Foster, refused. Capen never got the chance to cast his ballot, and after the election was over, he sued.

The lawsuit's target wasn't Foster personally, but voter registration in general. After all, any time you keep a list of eligible voters, you run the risk of leaving qualified people off that list by mistake. Unlike the U.S. Constitution, the Massachusetts Constitution specifically protects voting rights, and Capen argued that these rights had been violated by voter registration's very existence. *Capen v. Foster* went to the state Supreme Judicial Court, where it was heard by Chief Justice Lemuel Shaw.

In paintings and old photographs, Shaw looks a bit like the late actor Alan Rickman, with a stout, jowly dignity and skeptical glare. In thirty years on the court, he wrote 2,200 decisions—only one of them a dissent. Supreme Court justice Oliver Wendell Holmes called Shaw "the greatest magistrate which this country has produced." (Emory Washburn, a distinguished Harvard law professor, offered a very different kind of praise, once remarking that he would rather lay his head on a railroad track than argue a case before the chief justice.)

Shaw's legal legacy was enormous, although not always for the better. His most regrettable decision laid the groundwork for the "separate but equal" doctrine that would eventually underpin Jim Crow. But to-day, Shaw is best remembered for creating the legal foundation of the coming industrial age.* One of his decisions allowed workers to form unions. Another allowed the government to regulate businesses for the sake of public safety.

In its own way, *Capen v. Foster* also laid the foundation of the modern, industrialized state. Shaw agreed that Josiah Capen had been unfairly blocked from voting. Yet he recognized that as urban populations grew, and workers moved more frequently in search of employment, some sort of voter list was needed. Ruling in favor of Foster, Shaw wrote that while the *right* to vote was protected, the increasingly complicated *logistics* of voting were up to lawmakers to decide. "It is clearly within the just and constitutional limits of the legislative power, to adopt any reasonable and uniform regulations, in regard to the time and mode of exercising that right," he declared.

Let me translate into English. If you're a voter, lawmakers can't intentionally discriminate against you. But they're *allowed* to create new election rules, even if those rules accidentally block you from the polls.

Election law is dazzlingly complex, and it's undergone generations of changes since Capen lost his suit. But Lemuel Shaw was the first to explicitly uphold voter registration as constitutional. More important, the principle he laid out is still in use today. We'll call it the Shaw Test: so long as politicians believe, or can plausibly claim to believe, that they're protecting the integrity of our elections, they can pass laws making it harder to vote.

Almost immediately, laws that passed the Shaw Test were used to block eligible voters from the polls. In 1836, just four years after *Capen v. Foster*, Pennsylvania lawmakers set up the state's first registration sys-

---

* Shaw is also reasonably well known, at least in some circles, for rewriting the legal definition of insanity. It's possible he took a particular interest in the subject because of the erratic behavior of his son-in-law, a customs officer and struggling writer named Herman Melville.

tem, which relied on assessors to collect information door-to-door. The new law applied to Philadelphia—and nowhere else. "Although the proclaimed goal of the law was to reduce fraud," writes Alexander Keyssar in *The Right to Vote,* "opponents insisted that its real intent was to reduce the participation of the poor, who were frequently not home when assessors came by."

Rural Whigs (and nativist "Know-Nothings," who gained momentum in the 1850s) came up with other ways to reduce urban turnout. New residency requirements targeted city dwellers, who moved around more than those in the countryside. In Louisiana, for example, you were removed from the voting rolls if you left your home parish for longer than ninety days. In other states, lawmakers devised literacy tests to weed out the poor and uneducated, or English-language tests to block recent immigrants from the polls. The impact of the new laws was obvious, but because they were theoretically fraud-fighting measures, they passed the Shaw Test. They were upheld in court.

Along with reducing turnout among the foreign born and city dwelling, Shaw Test–approved legislation created a blueprint for Jim Crow. After the Civil War, literacy tests and residency requirements were easily repurposed to target Black voters. To these, southern lawmakers added repressive new tools of their own, including one so pernicious and well-crafted it would take a constitutional amendment to defeat it. It was known as the poll tax.

In fairness, poll taxes existed long before politicians weaponized them. The word "poll," which derives from Middle English, originally meant "head." The poll tax, then, was initially a small fee paid by every head of household, and had nothing to do with elections. But in the 1890s, a populist revolution brought together Black and lower-income white voters throughout the South. In response, the ruling Democrats changed the meaning of poll tax. What once meant "tax paid by everybody" now meant "tax paid in order to vote."

Poll taxes were not wildly expensive. In Texas the initial cost was $1.50, or about $40 today. But in an economic system designed to keep nonwhite incomes well below average, these relatively modest fees were enough to shut many minority voters, not to mention lower-income whites, out of the system.

Moreover, in some states the tax accumulated, making it harder and harder to pay. If you went a decade without voting, you had to pay ten years' worth of tax to cast a single ballot. Imagine being told that participating in the next election would cost about as much as a sixty-five-inch TV. All but the wealthiest Americans would be sorely tempted to stay home.* (In the rare cases when the cost of the poll tax failed to deter minority voters from participating, the political establishment could always turn to selective enforcement.)

The poll tax's effect on the electorate was obvious—far more obvious than the effects of the registration systems that targeted urban voters decades before. But as opposed to, say, Florida's felon disenfranchisement laws, the poll tax wasn't technically stripping anyone of their voting rights. And thanks to the Shaw Test, southern Democrats could defend the tax in court. In *Breedlove v. Suttles*, a 1937 Supreme Court case, poll tax supporters argued that the tax's goal was to raise revenue, and that preventing voting was merely a side effect. Clearly this wasn't true. But legally, it was true enough. The poll tax was upheld.

If Jim Crow Democrats had gotten their way, the poll tax would never have fallen out of fashion. By the middle of the twentieth century, however, the Civil Rights Movement was gaining momentum, and segregationists' most effective turnout-shrinking tool was under attack. As a result, in 1949 Texas lawmakers passed a kind of insurance policy. As long as the poll tax existed, nothing would change. But if for any reason the poll tax fell, a new voter-targeting system would automatically spring up to replace it: statewide voter registration.

---

* Some people have compared Florida's new requirement that former convicts pay fines and fees to regain their voting rights (a requirement we covered in the previous chapter) to a poll tax. As you can see, that comparison is wrong. The economic burden imposed by the Florida law is substantially worse.

Which brings us back to present-day Houston. If you want to know why Tracy finds registering voters so difficult, or why Leah has to warn her fellow volunteers about all the ways they could wind up in to jail, just remember this. In Texas, voter registration wasn't designed to keep track of the electorate. It was designed to keep people out. The ghost of Jim Crow still haunts the Taco Cabana Gang.

Nor is Texas the only place where voters, and those who would help them, are today under attack. In the Trump era, our country's air quality is decreasing; the number of people with health insurance is falling; our standing in the world is slipping. But when it comes to keeping eligible Americans from the ballot box, we are living in a new golden age.

☆

Voter fraud is real and don't let anyone tell you otherwise. Voter impersonation—people filling out multiple ballots, or voting in places they're not registered—is real, too. It is highly likely that in the coming presidential election, people will arrive at polling places, slip past officials, and knowingly cast illegal votes.

But the total number of these people will almost certainly be fewer than six. According to the most recent, nonpartisan studies, impersonation tarnishes approximately one ballot out of every 32,250,000. Imagine a human chain of voters, starting at a polling place in New York City, stretching across the country to Seattle, dropping down to Los Angeles, and returning back east as far as New Orleans. Of all the voters in that five-thousand-mile line, chances are that exactly one of them—just one—is committing fraud. The odds that this illegitimate vote will decide the election, rounded to the nearest one-hundred-thousandth of a percent, is zero. (For fans of very small numbers, it's .0000017 percent.)

At our current rate, we can expect in-person fraud to swing a presidential race sometime around the year 120,000,000. By that time, though, we might not care much, since humans will probably be extinct.

In short, voter fraud is real, but it's also incredibly rare. Worrying about voter impersonation swinging an election is like worrying about how you and Emma Watson will share custody of your four children after your whirlwind romance and subsequent marriage ends a decade later in bitter divorce. There are better ways to spend your time.

Yet the fact that voter fraud is essentially nonexistent hasn't stopped some of our country's most powerful people from obsessing over it. Before he became president, Ronald Reagan cautioned that letting Americans mail in completed voter registration forms would trigger a surge of phony applications. In the 1990s, Mitch McConnell warned that fraud would sweep the nation if registration was permitted at the DMV. As it turns out, these predictions could not have been more wrong. We've now been able to register by mail and at the DMV for decades. The total number of states reporting an allegation of widespread fraud as a consequence is zero.

If you were playing the stock market or performing a heart transplant, Reagan and McConnell's brand of confident wrongheadedness might be a problem. For politicians hoping to pass the Shaw Test, however, delusion is practically essential. In our current legal scheme, the only thing an official cannot do is knowingly discriminate against voters. If you believe you're doing the right thing (or, more accurately, if no one can prove you believe you're doing the *wrong* thing) there is almost no legal limit to how far you can push our voting laws. It's as though you're allowed to clear-cut a forest so long as you insist there's a Sasquatch inside.

Which explains why, despite ever-mounting evidence that voter fraud doesn't swing elections, panic over voter fraud remains. In fact, the panic's gotten worse. From the end of Jim Crow until the turn of the twenty-first century, the goal of most self-proclaimed anti-fraud crusaders was to make sure voter registration didn't become too easy. "It takes a little work to be a voter," Regan explained. "That's a small price to pay for freedom."

But starting around the year 2000, the Sasquatch Hunters took a bold new step. For the first time, or at least for the first time on a nation-wide scale, they broadened their focus beyond unregistered Americans. They began booting registered Americans from the electorate as well. This they accomplished through something called a "voter purge."

A voter purge, in case you're unfamiliar, is a voter registration drive in reverse. The former adds people to a list of eligible voters. The latter takes that list and combs through it, hoping (in theory, anyway) to remove ineligible voters from the rolls. The other important difference between a purge and a drive is that in America, getting voters signed up is the responsibility of civic-minded volunteers, while kicking them off is done at taxpayer expense.

In fairness, all states must occasionally scrub their voting lists. People move. People die. Election Day runs more smoothly when the names of the dearly departed aren't clogging up the rolls. But it's not very difficult to figure out who is no longer with us. A variety of government agencies, from the Postal Service to the Social Security Administration, do it all the time. Nor is there any great danger in being ever so slightly messy. There's plenty of evidence to suggest that leaving a few ineligible voters on the rolls is unwieldly, but absolutely no evidence that anyone impersonates those voters to cast a ballot. To put it quite simply, no one steals elections by taking advantage of an untidy list.

The far greater danger is that, in an overzealous attempt to remove the names of the dead or recently emigrated, eligible names will be bumped off the rolls. Conduct too broad a fishing expedition, and legitimately registered voters will be swept up like dolphins in a tuna net.

Like voter registration, voter purges have long been used as an excuse to shrink the electorate. In 1959, for example, the White Citizens' Council of Washington Parish, Louisiana, conducted what it claimed was a routine cleanup of voter lists. As it just so happened, 85 percent of Black voters were kicked off the rolls compared to just .07 percent of whites. But the godfather of the modern purge is a baby-faced lawyer with narrow eyes, prominent teeth, and the remarkably Bond-villainish name of Hans Anatol von Spakovsky.

Nothing about the first thirty-three years of Hans von Spakovsky's life suggested he would reshape our election system. Born in 1951 to immigrant parents, he attended MIT for undergrad, Vanderbilt for law school, and took a variety of bland legal jobs. But in 1992, something big happened: on behalf of his local Republican Party, von Spakovsky signed up to monitor a polling place in Atlanta. It must have been like the moment Julia Child first tasted French cuisine. "The very first time I'm a poll watcher," he later told journalist Jane Mayer, "I walk in and something illegal is going on."

By von Spakovsky's own account, the "something illegal" was election officials asking prying questions, which is not the same as voter fraud at all. So it's curious that fighting voter fraud, and more specifically, fighting voter impersonation, became the cause of Hans von Spakovsky's life. By 1999, the young lawyer had worked his way up to the advisory board of a conservative activist group called the Voting Integrity Project, or VIP. VIP gave its endorsement to a company called Database Technologies, which in turn was hired by the state of Florida to purge its voter rolls for the 2000 elections.

The hallmarks of Florida's purge were breadth, zealotry, and a seemingly fanatical commitment to incompetence. Michael Jones, who lived near Tampa, was mixed up with a different Michael Jones who had committed a felony in Ohio. A gentleman named Willie D. Whiting Jr. was mistaken for a different gentleman named Willie J. Whiting. Lawyers were on the purge list. Even public officials were on the list. The journalist David Margolick reported that "Linda Howell, elections supervisor of Madison County, found her own name on it."

The number of fraudulent ballots prevented by this comedy of errors was almost certainly zero. But the odds that the Florida purge flipped the election to George W. Bush are startling high. A conservative estimate is that 12,000 eligible, registered Florida voters were taken off the rolls, about half of them African-American. Al Gore, as you'll remember, lost by just 537 votes.

To me, the strangest thing of all about this story is that I never learned it growing up. The 2000 election was the first I could remember clearly. The recount that followed dominated conversations for months. Yet at no time did anyone mention that there was a very high probability that our new president had been elected thanks to the forcible removal of thousands of African-Americans from our democracy. The only real indication that something had gone wrong was Al Gore's new beard.

To the genuine if belated credit of the people who worked there, Database Technologies seemed genuinely remorseful about its role in the purge. "We are not confident any of the methods used today can guarantee legal voters will not be wrongfully denied the right to vote," a company spokesman told the *Los Angeles Times*, promising to never again cull voters from the rolls.

But if Hans von Spakovsky had similar second thoughts, he never expressed them. Instead, he moved to Washington, where President Bush assigned him to the Justice Department and put him in charge of protecting our voting rights. Based on his tenure there, it appears that, like Database Technologies, Hans von Spakovsky learned a valuable lesson from the Florida debacle. But the lesson he learned was this: keeping eligible voters from voting helps you win.

Techniques like the one von Spakovsky helped implement in 2000, and would pioneer in the coming years, are now known among many Americans as "voter suppression." As a former speechwriter, I hate this term.

First off, there's "suppression," the kind of formal abstract noun you never hear in conversation. It's like describing a murderer as engaged in "lifespan adjustment." Even worse, voter suppression sounds temporary, as though Americans unable to cast ballots are rubber duckies in a bathtub, nudged under but certain to reemerge.

In a sense I suppose that's true. The voters aren't going anywhere. But the votes are. If you were unfairly kicked off the voter rolls in the

2000 election, you didn't get a redo. That opportunity to select your leaders—the opportunity that defines democracy—is gone forever.

Consider an example from less recent history. In 1888, in Conway Country, Arkansas, masked gunmen entered a polling place in a predominately Black neighborhood, stole a ballot box at gunpoint, and destroyed its contents. What happened to the purged Floridians is less dramatic, in part because their ballots were invalidated before rather than after they cast them. But the effect on our elections is exactly the same. Voters aren't being suppressed. Ballots are being destroyed. What we've termed voter suppression would be more accurately called vote destruction.

The nation's leading vote destruction expert is, in my opinion, an attorney named Marc Elias. He's the first election lawyer to be publicly targeted by Donald Trump on Twitter. To my knowledge, he's the first election lawyer to be publicly targeted by any president, ever.

Stepping into Marc Elias's office, it's not immediately clear why the commander in chief finds him so threatening. Some super-lawyers resemble heroes in a John Grisham movie. Elias resembles the coolest dad in a group of dads where that's not saying much. There's a framed New York Giants jersey on his wall and a box of Quest protein bars tucked under an end table. He wears hiking shoes to work. He wears a fleece.

But looks can be deceiving. Over the last two decades, Marc Elias has taken on nine election recounts, and his clients have won eight. (The exception came when he represented Rick Scott's opponent in the razor-thin 2018 Senate race.) In recent years, he's led a team of attorneys in a game of nationwide legal Whac-A-Mole, suing to overturn anti-voting legislation wherever it pops up. There's been no shortage of unfair laws to go after.

"Basically, you have, up until 1965, voter suppression through two tactics," Elias tells me. (I wish he had used a different phrase, but it's my view that if you win eight of nine recounts you get a pass.) "You had had legal tactics," Elias continues, "i.e., the poll tax, and extralegal suppression, i.e., the Klan. What you saw until 2009 was a falling away of the legal barriers to voting. With the election of Barack Obama in 2008, that all changes."

The reason for the change, Elias explains, was that Obama's coalition was much younger and more diverse than the Democratic base that preceded him. "Newt Gingrich in the nineties said the only thing the Democratic Party has left is to scare old people on Social Security," he reminds me. "Bill Clinton got eighty-three percent of the African-American vote and was called the first Black president." In 2008 and 2012, by contrast, Republicans won the lion's share of senior citizens, less than 10 percent of the Black vote, and shrinking shares of Hispanic and other nonwhite voters as well. Nearly all the fastest-growing demographic groups were now aligned with Democrats. The Obama coalition was an emerging juggernaut.

It was also, however, a coalition of people whose votes were easy to destroy.

When we talk about "the establishment," we generally mean the elites in power, but there's a different kind of establishment that shapes our democracy as well. If you are literally well established—if you own your own home, know the names of your local officials, have voted in the same neighborhood for decades—your vote is fairly difficult to target. To be sure, many established voters supported Obama. But to reach his winning margin, Obama relied on the votes of everyone else.

Indeed, the new Democratic Party is in many ways a coalition of the unestablished. Racial minorities. Young people. Naturalized citizens. Lower-income workers. People who rent instead of own. Add to this group women, who have been drifting away from Republicans for years, and you have nearly every group whose voting rights have ever been attacked.

For Team Mitch, the new calculus was simultaneously grim and promising. On one hand, the GOP base was evaporating like a puddle on the sidewalk. With each passing year, the Republican Party could expect less popular support.* On the other hand, the number of Democratic voters who could be blocked from the ballot box was growing. If Republican politicians could shrink the Obama coalition via new laws faster than your own coalition shrank via natural causes, they could win elections without broadening their appeal.

There was one final factor. "In 2016, Trump takes away the one barrier that was left to Republicans going crazy, which was a sense of decency," Elias tells me.

That's his opinion, of course, but the evidence is on his side. We're unlikely to match the sheer quantity of carnage southern Democrats inflicted during the Jim Crow era. But in terms of quality—the sheer creativity with which some Americans invalidate the fundamental rights of others—my lifetime stands out.

Of all the new vote-erasing tools developed in the last three decades, one has received the lion's share of attention: Voter ID. Before 2006, no state required voters to show photo identification at the polls. Today, seventeen states do. The brainchild of none other than Hans von Spakovsky, voter ID has earned praise and sparked fury in a way that election regulations rarely do. President Trump calls for its expansion. Nearly every Democratic candidate has spoken out against it. Since the end of the poll tax, no vote-destruction measure has so thoroughly captured the public's attention.

Which is somewhat odd, because voter ID is one of the least consequential measures shrinking the electorate in recent years. Don't get me wrong, these laws are not well intentioned. They're designed

---

* This changed slightly in 2016 because the number of white, non-college-educated Americans in the unelectorate is enormous, and President Trump would love to increase turnout among them. But the rest of his party doesn't share his enthusiasm because (a) there's no guarantee the white working class won't revert to supporting Democrats once Trump leaves office, and (b) the GOP's trickle-down economic agenda would be threatened by adding too many populists to the mix.

to target likely Democrats, sometimes in almost comically unsubtle ways. In Tennessee, a registered voter with a gun permit can cast a ballot, but one with a University of Tennessee identification card cannot. In Alabama, you can ignore ID laws if two election observers swear they know you, giving voters in small rural precincts a clear advantage over voters in large urban ones. These are bad laws.

But so far, they don't seem to have destroyed many votes. One study found that in 2014, 2.19 million people cast ballots in Virginia; only 474 were stymied by lack of ID. This appears to be fairly typical. After comprehensively surveying the available evidence, University of California political scientist Benjamin Highton reported, in the tone of someone who knows he will disappoint large groups of angry people, that there were "modest, if any, turnout effects." More recently, a 2019 study from Harvard Business School found that even the most restrictive photo ID laws don't do much of anything. No one really knows why.*

My point is not that we should ignore voter ID entirely. Plenty of politicians are feverishly trying to design more targeted versions of these laws, ones that will have a larger partisan impact, and we can't take our eye off their efforts. But if we equate protecting the right to vote solely, or even mostly, with fighting back against voter ID, our focus will be misplaced. Far more ballots are being destroyed through other means.

Florida-style voter purges are on the rise. Ohio. Maine. Indiana. In state after state where Republicans gained control over the last decade, politicians have cast gratuitously wide nets and begun destroying votes. In many cases, these new purges are even more egregious than Florida's was. That's because states have adopted a new rule they call "Use It or Lose It." If you go for a certain period without

---

* Even if ID laws were made more effective, there's a chance they would affect both parties fairly equally. Younger, nonwhite voters are more likely to lack ID— but so are older, rural ones.

voting—usually six years, sometimes fewer—you'll be taken off the rolls, even if you're an eligible voter who hasn't moved. As you might be able to guess by now, there's no evidence that "Use It or Lose It" reduces fraud. But it passes the Shaw Test.

It's undeniable that the past decade of purges has pushed large numbers of Americans out of the electorate. The only question is how many. Before one recent purge, Ohio took the rare step of allowing volunteers to cross-check the names of those it planned to remove from the rolls. It turned out that more than one in six was on the list by mistake. That may not sound like much, but bear in mind that a single two-year period—between the 2014 and 2016 elections—saw 16 million Americans purged in total. If Ohio's rates are consistent nationwide, more than 2.7 million eligible voters were taken off the rolls.

Nor is there any reason to think Ohio is alone in carelessly removing voters from the electorate. The most aggressive purges, by far, have taken place not in the Midwest but in the South. That's because under the 1965 Voting Rights Act, states and counties with particularly atrocious voting rights records—mostly in the former Confederacy and along the border with Mexico—were put on a kind of probation. Among the new limits was a restriction on overzealous scrubbing of voter rolls.

In 2013, however, thanks to an opinion signed by the Supreme Court's five conservatives and no one else, large parts of the Voting Rights Act were swept away. The result, if you'll pardon the phrase, was a purging binge. According to the Brennan Center, about 2 million additional voters were bumped off the rolls as a result of the Court's decision. Votes disappeared throughout the former Confederacy—in Arkansas, Texas, in Florida yet again, and even in Virginia before the Macker came along.

The undisputed champion of state purges was Georgia secretary of state Brian Kemp. As the official running his state's elections, Kemp cut 1.5 million names from the rolls, many of them under a new Use It or Lose It rule he put in place. If you hadn't voted in the most recent election, you got a notice in the mail; if you didn't respond to that notice, your registration was rescinded. The warning from Kemp's office was printed on a postcard easily mistaken for junk mail, so the percentage of valid names axed from the list was unusually high.

When Kemp wasn't culling voters, he was, as a kind of side job, running for governor. On Election Night he defeated Democrat Stacy Abrams by 55,000 votes. According to one analysis, that's one-seventh the number of eligible voters he purged.

It's worth noting that unlike Slowpoke Dale back in Canton, the Americans purged over the past decade had no idea they wouldn't be voting. They showed up at the polls. If the state required ID, they presented it, expecting to find their names on the list. And when their names couldn't be found, they were handed something called a "provisional ballot."

Provisional ballots were invented by, you guessed it, Hans von Spakovsky. They are not inherently a bad idea. Imagine you're a modern-day Josiah Capen—if you brought your student ID to the polling place instead of your gun license, say, or your name was improperly added to a purge list. Provisional ballots are supposed to allow you to nonetheless cast your vote. Poll workers hand you a special piece of paper. You fill it out in the normal way. After the election, you have a few days to "cure" your ballot by providing proof of eligibility. If your ballot is cured, your vote counts.

The problem is that most Americans have no idea how this system works. In fact, most poll workers have no idea how this system works, which means that most people who fill out provisional ballots don't realize they must also cure them. They think they've cast meaningful votes, when in fact they did nothing of the kind. Marc Elias calls provisional ballots "placebo ballots." You still feel good about voting. You still get a sticker. But you didn't really participate in our democratic process.[*]

---

[*] The exception is California. I won't go into the specifics of its election laws, but California uses provisional ballots differently, and most of them count, so if you live there, don't be afraid to fill one out.

"The problem," says Elias, "is Republicans have weaponized provisional ballots to basically be, 'We give all these people provisional ballots, we don't tell them how to cure their ballot, then they don't count, and they never know.'"

Secrecy is the new frontier in vote destruction. Don't get me wrong, politicians are still attacking the registration process the old-fashioned way. Florida and Tennessee have tried to fine voter registration drives out of existence; Texas lawmakers tried to make incorrectly filling out a registration form a felony, even if you did it by mistake. But the objective of today's Sasquatch Hunters is not just to block Americans from joining the electorate. It's to remove them from the electorate without their knowledge.

In this new crusade, Brian Kemp once again set the bar. In most states, applying to register to vote is like applying for a Target card. Odds are pretty good you'll get it. In Georgia, however, Kemp revamped the application process with a rule called "Exact Match." If you fill out a registration form in an Exact Match state, your information is checked against a government database. If a single letter or number doesn't match—even if it's just a middle initial, or a digit of a zip code scribbled in haste—your application doesn't go through.

Exact Match is particularly unfair because it relies on the person entering your registration form data to get everything right. Intentionally or not, clerical error discriminates against "unusual names." The people doing data entry for Kemp's office were unlikely to have any trouble with, say, Matt Ryan, quarterback of the Atlanta Falcons. But his teammates Takkarist McKinley and Ra'Shede Hageman would be far more likely to have their names inaccurately transcribed. Spanish last names present another opportunity for error, since they are often quite long and don't follow English-language convention.

Three Princeton researchers recently created an algorithm to run through 91,000 valid, legal voter registrations, check them against the government database, and determine how many would remain valid in an Exact Match system. The answer? Just 66 percent. There's a one-in-three chance your own registration would not go through. Many Georgians' registrations didn't. In 2018 alone, more than 53,000 would-be voters had their applications to register put on hold. According to the Associated Press, 70 percent of them were nonwhite.

Nor was the problem limited to Georgia. "Fifty-three percent of the voter registrations submitted in Florida were rejected," Elias says, kicking his hiking shoes onto an ottoman in his office and recapping a 2018 race. "Fifty-three percent of the people who thought they were registered to vote because they filled out a form in fact were not registered." Elias is not the outraged type, but he speeds up and begins clipping the ends of his words in frustration. "The county didn't tell you that you were rejected. You know when you find out you were rejected? When you show up to vote and you're not on the voter roll and they give you a provisional ballot."

For Team Mitch, that's the beauty of Exact Match and systems like it. Almost none of the voters they've targeted knew their votes were destroyed. The first inkling something was amiss would have come at the polling place, when their name wasn't on the list. Many of them then voted with provisional ballots, thought those ballots counted, and didn't bother re-registering for next time, which means the whole process will repeat itself forever. Those who applied for absentee ballots without realizing their registrations had been canceled were similarly out of luck. To this day, they have never been informed that something went wrong.

This is a truly frightening prospect: an unquantifiable but significant number of Americans, mostly supporters of just one party, whose votes never count and who are never given a chance to set things right. And perhaps most disturbing of all, there's another, even more effective vote-destroying technique on the horizon. It's called "signature matching." Odds are you haven't heard of it, but it keeps Marc Elias up at night.

The way signature matching works is as follows: If you send in your ballot by mail, which a growing number of people do, a voting official checks your signature against the signature on file from your voter registration application. If the official decides the two signatures don't match, your vote doesn't count.

Signature matching is terrible for many reasons, beginning with the fact that lots of people don't have consistent signatures. I can vouch for this personally. For the last several years, part of my job has involved signing books, and I promise you no two versions of my name are alike. Older people, who grew up writing cursive, tend to write their name the same way over and over. But younger voters—and many of those for whom English is a second language—do not.

Also, who's to judge if a signature matches? Elias points out that even in court, a trained forensic investigator would never be allowed to compare handwriting using just two signatures. In fact, it would be malpractice to try. Even Hans von Spakovsky once called signature matching "a highly trained skill that cannot be taught in a matter of hours to the average poll worker."

But that was when signature matching was being used in person, as an alternative to voter ID. Now it's being used as a supplement to voter ID, a way of destroying votes after they've already been cast.

Which brings us to the final, and most dangerous, problem with comparing registration forms to ballots: no one ever tells you when your ballot doesn't count. Already, tens of thousands of votes are being discarded each election, without voters' knowledge, because some random poll worker decides the signatures aren't identical. If more states adopt signature matching laws, expect that number to grow.

Add all these things up—not just signature matching, but purges, Exact Match registration, provisional ballots, and a number of other new rules we simply don't have time to cover—and a question may occur to you. It's a question I myself posed to Marc Elias.

Is there a chance that you, the person reading this book right now, had your vote discarded and didn't know it? The super-lawyer does not hesitate.

"Absolutely."

☆

The exact number of votes destroyed across America in a given election is very difficult to precisely count. But the impact of laws blocking eligible voters from the ballot—laws that have exploded in number and aggressiveness in the last twelve years alone—isn't hard to figure out.

As we've seen, the odds that an election will be decided by a single vote are extremely small. But the odds of an election decided by a few thousand votes, or even a few hundred thousand votes, multiplied across fifty states and a dazzling variety of races? There the chances are much, much higher. We also know that in recent years, across our country, elected officials have systematically destroyed votes, votes that would have been cast disproportionately for one party over another.

The conclusion is obvious: A not insignificant number of today's Republican politicians—including senators, governors, and at least one president—hold their offices only because valid votes were discarded. It's a deeply unsettling fact. But that doesn't make it any less factual.

Knowing all this, it's tempting to go one step further and conclude that these elections were "stolen." But that would be a mistake. In some rare cases, politicians really do break the law in order to win. In 1997, the result of a fraud-riddled Miami mayor's race was invalidated. In 2018, operatives employed by Republican Mark Harris collected mail-in ballots from African-American voters under false pretenses and then never turned them in. Those elections really were stolen. (In both cases, the crimes involved absentee ballots, not in-person votes, and were committed by campaign staff, not voters. Hans von Spakovsky's innovations would have done nothing to prevent them.)

In most other cases I've described, however, what happened wasn't illegal; it was extremely unfair. To win a Senate seat and the White House, respectively, Rick Scott and George W. Bush didn't break laws; they took advantage of very bad ones. Even Brian Kemp, the most egregious destroyer of votes in recent memory, is acting unfairly rather than illegally. He's sneaky. He's dishonest. He doesn't represent the will of the people, he has no business running a state, and if you see him at a party by all means refuse to shake his hand. But there's no indication he's a criminal.

The distinction between unfair and illegitimate matters because a democracy is a little bit like Tinker Bell: if people stop believing in it, it dies. If we obliterate the line between the illegal and the merely nefarious, we risk eroding our collective faith in the very republic we're trying to protect.

Rather than try to invalidate past unfair elections, then, we should focus on ensuring fair elections in the future. No eligible American, regardless of party, should have his or her vote destroyed.

It turns out that goal is surprisingly simple to achieve. In fact, we almost achieved it more than forty years ago. In 1977, dismayed by the country's appalling voter turnout, President Jimmy Carter laid out a plan to fix the way we vote. "Millions of Americans are prevented or discouraged from voting in every election by antiquated and overly restrictive voter registration laws," Carter said. In 2015, the writer Rick Perlstein, penning what turned out to be a premature obituary, recalled that Carter's proposal would have made voter registration universal—and that the idea initially had Republican support.

"William Brock, chairman of the Republican National Committee, called it 'a Republican concept,'" Perlstein wrote. "Senate Minority Leader Howard Baker announced his support." Before long, however, the newly powerful right wing began attacking Carter's plan in earnest. RNC Chairman Brock withdrew his support. The bill died. Three years later, Ronald Reagan became president, and the rest is recent history.

But it's worth thinking about how close we came to a very different result—and a very different country. If every eligible adult in America were automatically registered (or could register in person on Election Day, which is effectively the same thing), votes would become nearly impossible to destroy. Texas-style registration laws would be a thing of the past. Unestablished voters wouldn't be blocked from casting a ballot because they hadn't signed up in time. Purges and Exact Match systems would be gone for good, taking provisional ballots with them.

Our leaders would have been different, too. I doubt Carter would have won in 1980, and I can't say that Donald Trump would never have become president. But the hard-right lurch of Republican politicians over the last four decades would almost certainly have slowed. Immigration reform would likely have passed years ago, while tax cuts for the rich would likely have not. Our government, in other words, would have more accurately reflected the will of people it governed. That's the opportunity we missed.

But we can still seize that opportunity today. By a 35-point margin, Americans agree that "Everything possible should be done to make it easy for every citizen to vote." And what was true in 1977 remains true now. Nearly everything about our voting process—from hurdles regarding registration to criteria for a voter purge to the legality of signature matching on absentee ballots—can be changed by a single federal law.

Most of all, we can finish what Jimmy Carter started and make registration universal. This was the centerpiece of a giant reform the House of Representatives passed in 2019. It was called H.R. 1, an exceptionally dorky, lawmakery way of signaling that it was a top priority. Of course, the bill went nowhere in Mitch McConnell's Senate. But one day, we'll get another Skywalker Window—a brief but meaningful chance to pass big laws—and H.R. 1 (ideally with a far catchier name) should be a top priority once again.

In the meantime, states can do a lot on their own. Today, twenty-two of them—including a handful with Republican governors—have passed either automatic or same-day voter registration bills into law. As we gather more data, it's becoming clear that these laws work. In early 2016, for example, Oregon began automatically signing up voters who came into contact with the DMV. By the November elections, 225,000 people had been registered this way, and 100,000 of them had cast a vote.

States can also change the way they approach individual ballots. In Colorado, for example, they've replaced the exact match standard used by Brian Kemp with "substantial match" instead. Essentially, the default there is now to count votes instead of to destroy them. Laws like these could bring tens of thousands of eligible voters back into the electorate each year.

For Richard, Leah, Tracy, and the rest of the Taco Cabana Gang, a good day might be twenty or thirty new registrations. But a really good day—the best day—will be the day they hang up their clipboards for good. Because while there's something fundamentally American about their eagerness to bring strangers into our democracy, there's something fundamentally un-American about the very fact that they have to.

But sadly, even after Tracy turns in her deputy registrar card and Richard moves on from studying apartments, there will still be one final hurdle keeping tens of millions of Americans from the electorate. These Americans will have the legal right to vote. No politician will be able to destroy their ballots. But for them, voting will still be insurmountably inconvenient.

This third group is perhaps the largest portion of the unelectorate. And before you, too, dismiss them as political couch potatoes, let me ask you something:

How long—really, honestly—would you be willing to stand in line?

4

HOW TO PLAN A
FYRE FESTIVAL

The Discouraged

Twenty-three million hours ago, the world was a very different place. For one thing, there was no Netflix. Also, there were no airplanes, no automobiles, no vaccines, no electricity, no English language, no sliced bread, no printing press, no gunpowder, no Roman Empire, no cast iron, and no toilet paper. The year was 605 BC, but that would have been news to everyone, since neither Jesus Christ nor the Gregorian calendar existed yet.

All of which is to say that if someone made you wait 23 million hours, it would be quite the imposition. And yet this is the total amount of time—2,625 years, 7 months, 28 days, and 7 hours—that Americans waited in 2012 to vote.

Of course, not all this waiting was done by one person. Millions shared the burden. But when MIT professor Charles Stewart III delved into the matter, he discovered that the burden was not shared evenly. Long lines, he wrote in a surprisingly poetic flourish for a political scientist, "do not fall like rain, equally on all voters." Some mailed in ballots at their convenience. Others breezed through polling places with no wait at all.

And then there was Blake Yagman. In 2012, on the Saturday afternoon before Election Day, he arrived at an early voting site near the University of Miami, where he was a junior studying political science and preparing to cast his first-ever presidential ballot. He joined the line, which snaked outside the building.

"It wasn't a big deal," he told me years later. "I was happy people were out voting."

His happiness was short-lived. Minutes turned into hours. The queue moved at a snail's pace. The sun beat down. It was 74 degrees, merciful by Florida standards, but still no picnic when it's humid and you're on your feet. Overwhelmed, once-cheerful poll workers grew grumpy. Sometime around 7 p.m., they made an announcement.

"It's gonna be hours," Blake recalled them saying. "You can stay, but we might have to close." So he left.

Blake returned the next day to a different early voting location, in Doral, not far from one of our future president's golf courses. He imagined the line might flow more smoothly there, but his hopes were soon dashed. In fact, his wait was a carbon copy of the one the day before: a long, snaking queue outside the building and the promise of another tightly coiled one inside. Voters got angry. Poll workers got angry. Blake, meanwhile, got nervous. He suffers from severe migraines brought on by low blood sugar, not getting enough protein, or exposure to harsh sunlight. A long outdoor wait in South Florida was a trigger trifecta. Purple blobs undulated through his field of vision. Images grew hazy.

Then came the migraine itself, which felt, in Blake's words "like someone driving an ice pick through my eye." He tried to suffer through it. He had classes on Election Day, so if he didn't vote early, he wasn't sure he'd be able to vote at all. But the ice pick drove deeper and deeper. After nearly four hours, Blaine couldn't take it any longer.

"I just said I was leaving," he tells me. "I was in too much pain." He got in his car and began the drive back to campus, but soon after, he pulled into a Starbucks, ran to the bathroom, and threw up.

I tried to picture it, this twenty-year-old college kid enduring such misery to cast a ballot. What did that say about our country? Determined to peel back the layers, I put on my best NPR voice. "At the moment you were throwing up in the Starbucks bathroom," I asked, "what were you *feeling*?"

"Nausea," he replies.

My own 2012 voting experience was far smoother than Blake Yagman's, and chances are yours was, too. According to Stewart, the MIT professor, the vast majority of Americans who cast ballots that year faced almost no line at all. For an unlucky few, however, voting was seriously unpleasant. One-eighth of voters spent more than thirty minutes at their polling place. A particularly unfortunate slice of the electorate, five million people, waited more than an hour each. This group made up just 4 percent of America's voters. But on Election Day, they did at least 20 percent of America's standing in line.

Your wait time depended in large part on where you lived. In Vermont, the average 2012 voter stood on-line for just two minutes. But the average Ohioan waited for ten minutes, the average South Carolinian for twenty-five minutes, and the average Marylander for thirty-six.

These numbers may not seem awful, but keep in mind that they're just averages. Sandra James, a pastor living ninety miles north of Richmond, testified before Congress that she spent one hour shivering outside her polling place and another two and a half hours shuffling toward the voting booth once indoors. In other words, Virginia's average wait time of twenty-five minutes didn't mean that every voter waited nearly half an hour. It meant that most people waltzed through the process, while a small but significant number, Sandra James included, went through hell.

When it came to sheer nightmarishness, however, no state in 2012 matched Florida. On Election Day, the average wait—the *average* wait—was thirty-nine minutes. Early voting was even worse, and not just for Blake Yagman. In North Miami, some people waited six hours to vote early. In Palm Beach County, they waited more than seven. As best I could tell, the record was set in Aventura, a suburb near Fort Lauderdale, where at least one early voter reported a nine-hour wait.

If 2012 had been an outlier, none of this would matter much. But the only thing unique about the long lines in that election was that President Obama briefly mentioned them in his victory speech. Four years earlier, Americans had actually done 25 percent more waiting—an extra 650 years' worth. We cherish the right to vote. But for millions of us, exercising that right is an absolute nightmare.

Which is one reason so many of us decline to exercise that right at all. Looking at the 2012 elections in Florida, Ohio State professor Theodore Allen to the *Orlando Sentinel* that at least 201,000 Floridians didn't vote because of long lines. "My gut is telling me that the real number deterred is likely higher," Allen added.

He was probably right. For one thing, Allen's figure counted only those people who got in line and then left. It didn't include Floridians who, anticipating chaos at their polling places, didn't attempt to vote at all. The University of Pennsylvania's Stephen Pettigrew has found that for every hour you wait to vote in an election, your odds of voting in the next election drop by about 1 percent. In other words, the mess from the 2008 elections reduced Florida turnout by about 200,000 votes in the 2012 elections, which cost Florida *an additional* 200,000 votes in 2016.

Nor are lines the only hurdles a voter can face. In one MIT study (with the wonderfully kickass title of "A Precinct Too Far"), economist Enrico Cantoni found that increasing the average distance to a polling place by just five blocks reduces turnout by 2 to 5 percent. In a presidential year, that would translate to between 2.6 million and 6.4 million fewer votes.

Put another way, the details of our elections matter. As we've already covered, millions of Americans don't vote because they're not allowed to. Many others try to vote, only to have their ballots destroyed. This chapter is about a third category of non-voters: the Americans who don't cast a ballot because elections are being mismanaged. Despite Mitch McConnell's description, these non-voters aren't "political couch potatoes." They're people with jobs to get to or children to pick up from school or health issues that make it impossible for them to stand for hours on end.

How did voting become so miserable for so many people? How does that affect our elections? And how can we make sure everyone can exercise their fundamental rights—not just in theory, but in real life? That's what I wanted to know. So obviously, I went to Disney World.

☆

If there's a circle of hell below being stuck behind a touring Princeton a cappella group as it goes through the entire *Frozen* soundtrack, I am not aware of it. But that's okay. Two years after spending President Trump's inauguration at the Animal Kingdom, I have returned in order to suffer.

This time, I'm seeking out some of the longest lines in America. I want to spend hours plodding forward; to be packed beside strangers; to wilt in the Florida heat and wonder if my turn will ever come. This is the place Where Dreams Come True™, and my highly specific dream is to experience just a tiny bit of the awfulness Blake Yagman endured.

I head to Flight of Passage, a ride based on the movie *Avatar* that, according to all the Disney fan sites, has some of the most reliably unpleasant lines in the park. I take my place behind the perky a cappellans, a group I can just tell is named The Forget Me Notes or The Ring Tunes. A family on vacation presses forward, locking me in. The line creeps along for a moment, then shudders to a halt. I've been standing less than twenty minutes and my feet already hurt.

The first hours of our line-waiting experience aren't excruciatingly boring. They're excruciating *and* boring. We wind slowly through a series of ersatz caves and into a chamber called, somewhat hopefully, "the bioluminescent rainforest" (basically a dark hallway with some glowy lights). Around the 120-minute mark my feet are swelling, but my ears finally get a rest. The singers move past "Let It Go." For a second of blissful silence, it appears as though they have exhausted their repertoire.

Then two things happen. First, we're informed that one of the ride's virtual reality pods has broken down, and that the already crawling line will henceforth be moving at a fraction of its current speed. Second, the Ring Tunes start in on "Part of Your World." I'll admit it: if I had been waiting on line to vote, this is the moment when I would have seriously thought about leaving. My fellow line-waiters are in similarly dire straits. Parents desperately search their phones for something, anything, to distract their kids. One grown man slumps over, chin on his chest, and simply falls asleep. Every time we move forward, which is not often, he opens his eyes, scooches a few inches, and then immediately dozes off again. This goes on for another ninety minutes, until the broken pod is back online. Even then, we have plenty of line to go.

In the end, we wait approximately four hours—as long as Blake Yagman waited to cast his ballot, longer than it took me to fly to Orlando in the first place—all for a four-minute ride. By the time my turn comes, my ankles ache. My toes have gone numb. I'm exhausted and hungry and in need of a men's room and my attitude toward music now mirrors that of Captain von Trapp. Clearly, there's no way all that waiting could be worth it.

Actually, it was.

I won't spoil Flight of Passage for you, in case you're planning your own trip soon. Instead, let me just say that I'm not the biggest fan of Disney rides, and this one was incredible. During our four minutes—a simulated flight on some sort of Pegasus-type creature—I plummeted and dove and banked sharply and, thanks to the magic of Disney, I literally felt the wind in my hair. When my Pegasus and I traced coastline, ocean spray misted my face. As we swooped through an ancient forest, an earthy, mushroomy scent filled my nostrils and then somehow disappeared the moment we were out of the woods. Stepping from my virtual reality pod, I couldn't stop smiling. If it hadn't been against my new principles, I might have broken into song.

Suddenly, all that waiting was cast in an entirely new light. Rather than focus on everything that made me consider leaving the line, I realized how much work had been put into making me decide to stay. Even before entering Flight of Passage, I had been able to check predicted wait times on an app. I knew what I was getting into, which made it easier to handle later on. The cave system and the bioluminescent forest hadn't seemed like much, but they kept us out of the Florida heat, and there was always some new distraction to look at.[*]

Once I began looking for line management, I saw it everywhere—even on rides far less popular than Flight of Passage. Some of the tools to improve the line-waiting experience clearly cost money, but others didn't. On an outdoor line for the Na'vi River Journey, a separate (and far less thrilling) *Avatar*-themed adventure, I noticed a series of perfectly spaced fans keeping line-waiters cool. It wasn't fancy—you could set up something similar with a trip to Home Depot. All it takes is attention to detail.

When describing his 2012 experience, one Florida voter, Jason Gross, told the *Miami Herald* that "It feels like waiting in line at Disney." But he was wrong. In my lifetime, it has become much more pleasant to wait in line at the theme park. And yet, during those same decades, it's become much less pleasant to wait in line to vote.

To understand how all this happened, it helps to be familiar with a branch of applied mathematics called "queuing theory." I won't go into

---

[*] In fact, had I been just a tiny bit more organized, I could have avoided the lines altogether. Like many theme parks these days, Disney lets visitors reserve their ride time in advance. Show up at the appointed hour, and you can skip to the front.

all the details, in part because I don't understand them. When it comes to voting, there are really only three things you need to know.

The first is that every line has a breaking point, a condition under which it goes from manageable to unmanageable in an instant. Consider your shower. Ordinarily, it works just fine, even if the occasional hair or earring falls down the drain. But the moment water begins flowing into your shower faster than it can be carried away, you're completely screwed. And here's the important part: once this breaking point has been hit, the water will never stop rising on its own. In technical terms, it's "queuing to infinity." When this kind of backup occurs in your shower, you get a steadily rising puddle. When a backup occurs at a polling place, you get a line out the door.

The second thing you need to know is that when long lines are made up of people, rather than H2O molecules, you get what is known as "balking" and "reneging." These are simply fancy terms for not joining a line because it looks too long, or abandoning a line you're already in. After a half hour with an invisible ice pick in his skull, Blake Yagman reneged. Had he not tried to vote at all, he would have balked.

But unlike "leaving," or "quitting" a line, balking and reneging don't place blame on the people who decide not to wait. That's why the distinction is important. We may not realize it, but each of us makes a thousand tiny calculations when we join or remain in a queue. How long will I be stuck here? Will my boss fire me if I'm late for work? Am I excited about the reward at the end? How many times can I hear "Do You Want to Build a Snowman?" without punching someone?

In a recent survey, pollsters asked Americans how long we would be willing to wait to cast a ballot. Forty-one percent of us chose "As long as it takes." But queueing theory suggests that's not true. All of us have limits. There is a point at which any of us will forfeit our chance to vote.

The third and final thing you need to keep in mind about queuing theory, along with backups, balking, and reneging, is that line lengths can be predicted and therefore managed. We may not be able to know what the exact wait time for Splash Mountain will be at, say, 10 a.m. next August 4. But using mathematical models, we can come pretty close. Today, with just a few variables, anyone go online and derive basic estimates of line lengths in milliseconds.

Not everyone takes advantage of these tools. You will likely remember the Fyre Festival, a musical extravaganza planned for a Bahamian Island in 2018. Basic queuing theory could have helped the event's promoters figure out how many tents, meals, and (crucially) porta-potties they needed to serve their thousands of expected guests. Instead, the organizers relied primarily on guesswork and positive thinking, a small army of minor Instagram influencers was left cranky and stranded on a remote island, and Fyre Festival's co-founder, Billy McFarland, was sentenced to six years in jail.

But McFarland is the exception. Today, sophisticated line modeling is used by countless large and small enterprises—not just when you experience a 4-D thrill ride, but when you shop, eat, fly, or dine. Have you noticed the robot who answers your customer service calls telling you your expected wait time, or promising that "Calls will be answered in the order in which they are received?" That's rudimentary queuing theory at work.

You might think our polling places would be similarly transformed by the latest advances in line management. After all, American elections are not just an ongoing experiment in self-governance, an example we hope to set for countries around the world, and a renewal of our faith in the peaceful transfer of power. They're also a massive customer service headache.

Imagine hearing the following pitch on *Shark Tank*: A nationwide mega-chain with no corporate headquarters and no CEO. It will operate eight times as many U.S. locations as McDonald's, serving twice as many customers despite having about half as many employees. Each location will experience nearly double the daily foot traffic of your average Starbucks. Not only that, but every one of these approximately 116,000 stores will be a pop-up, remaining open for a single day and closing for good at night. Oh, and by the way, the more than 900,000 workers will be woefully underpaid. That's Election Day in America.

Given the sheer magnitude of the challenge, it's a minor miracle that most elections run as smoothly as they do. Every November, administrators and poll workers take on a seemingly impossible task, and nearly all of them deliver excellent results. For 80 to 90 percent of Americans, voting is a perfectly pleasant experience.

The problem is that in a democracy, 80 or 90 percent isn't nearly good enough. After all, unlike eating at McDonald's, voting is a fundamental right. When 12.5 percent of Americans wait longer than half an hour to cast a ballot, as was the case in Charles Stewart III's study, it means tens of millions of Americans who might consider casting ballots are under serious pressure to either renege or balk.

Nor is that pressure distributed at random. Instead, Election Day misery has a clear bias. In 2012, for example, white voters waited an average of just twelve minutes. Hispanics waited nineteen minutes. African-Americans waited twenty-three. Forty-seven years after the Voting Rights Act, Black people had to endure nearly twice as much waiting as white people in order to vote. When it came to the particularly soul-crushing lines, the kind that can convince you not to balk in an election but to skip the next one, the situation was even worse. Nonwhite voters were six times more likely than whites to wait an hour or more.

This disparity exists throughout America. In the North and the South, coasts and heartland, red and blue states alike, the less white your neighborhood, the longer you wait. And lines are merely the most obvious symptom of election mismanagement. Professor Cantoni, author of "A Precinct Too Far," has also found that nonwhite voters must travel farther to reach the polls than their white counterparts. Eliminate the gap in distance to polling places, he estimates, and you could reduce the racial gap in voter turnout by nearly 12 percent.

Even if Ronald Reagan was right when he said that voting shouldn't be entirely painless, and that there ought to be a price on freedom, shouldn't that price be roughly the same for everybody? Well, today it's not. People who live in cities pay a higher cost to vote than people who live in the countryside. Americans who aren't white pay a higher cost than Americans who are. And because of the way our political coalitions are currently constructed, these demographic biases become partisan biases as well. The voters most likely to suffer—the voters most likely to balk—disproportionately support just one of our two parties.

Bad customer service, in other words, isn't just an inconvenience. It's a threat to our democracy. If we want to face that threat, we need to make sure our polling places run smoothly. Which also means we need to know all the reasons why they currently don't.

As it happens, I recently experienced a perfect storm of election mismanagement. Technically, I didn't live through it so much as hear about it firsthand, but Jacqui was there, and we're married, so we get to share anecdotes.

Jacqui is a lawyer, and a good one, which is ordinarily quite infuriating. In our household, if the lay-flat-to-dry laundry ends up in the tumble-dry-low pile, what follows can only be described as a cross-examination. But when we volunteer on Election Day, and poll watchers are sorely needed, Jacqui's skills are in high demand. I canvass a neighborhood getting voters to the polls. She makes sure their votes are counted. It's been our routine for years now. On Election Day 2018, we found ourselves in New Jersey, in a county and congressional district that will remain nameless.

That night, when I picked Jacqui up at the polling place where she had been stationed, I could tell right away that something had gone seriously wrong. Driving back to our room at the Hampton Inn, my wife said nothing about the midterm results that were beginning to pour in. Instead, she was oddly quiet, staring blankly at some ever-receding point in the distance. It was as though she'd spent the day in the belly of a whale.

Only later did she explain to me the full cascade of incompetence she had witnessed. It began with a decision made by the state of New Jersey to automatically mail absentee ballots for 2018 to anyone who had requested an absentee ballot in 2016. This was done in a spirt of well-meaning convenience. Unfortunately, New Jersey state officials failed to inform most voters about their plans. They also kept a rule in place that said anyone who received an absentee ballot couldn't vote in person.

The upshot of the state's decision was that on Election Day, tens of thousands of New Jerseyans, including many at the polling place Jacqui was watching, arrived to vote only to be informed that they couldn't. As you'll recall from the last chapter, they would have to vote provisionally instead. Unlike many provisional ballots, these would ultimately be counted—to its credit, New Jersey recognized its mistake and tried hard to fix it. But in the meantime, confusion spread. Across New Jersey, lines hit their breaking points and began to build.

In most polling places, that was as bad as things got. Poll workers sorted out the situation, resolved delays, and the shower drain unclogged. At the school where Jacqui was keeping watch, however, a voting machine went down. That's how everyone described it: "went down," as though it had been bested in a dogfight. In fact, the technical issue was fairly minor, a small glitch any specialist could have resolved. But none of the poll workers knew which specialist to call. None of them even knew there *was* a specialist to call. And Jacqui wasn't allowed to tell the poll workers which specialist to call because the problem was logistical rather than legal. All she could do was watch helplessly as the wait time exploded from nothing to nearly an hour.

The situation didn't improve from there. A supply of emergency paper ballots, the closest thing the polling place had to a backup plan, almost immediately ran out. One of the guys managing the location knew a guy who knew a guy—remember, this was Jersey—and went to pick up some extras. But these new ballots were from a completely different precinct. For all intents and purposes, people were now voting in the wrong place. With no usable emergency ballots, poll workers switched to provisional ballots, because they didn't know that most provisional ballots ultimately don't count. Some voters took a look at the line and balked. Others already in line reneged. Many of those who did vote, meanwhile, cast ballots that were essentially meaningless. This went on for well over an hour before order was restored.

Finally, someone got the machine running, and at my wife's urging, the provisional ballots were put away. The drain unclogged, and the line gradually returned to normal—but not before a least a dozen people in one of the country's most competitive congressional districts were denied the chance to cast their votes.

That's where Jacqui's involvement ended. But even now, years after her long and dispiriting day, it's worth examining what went wrong. No one was deliberately trying to alter the election's result. State officials had set out to make voting simpler. The poll workers my wife encountered took their jobs seriously and did their best. Everyone was hoping that the voting experience would be Disney World, and yet they ended up with a Fyre Festival. How could that have happened?

To answer that question, let's go through the entire process Jacqui witnessed.

We'll start with voter check-in. Crossing people's names off a list doesn't seem like a high-stakes activity. In fact, our elections depend on it. If you have three poll workers, and it takes them sixty seconds each to find a name, they can handle ninety voters per hour with ease. But say there's a snag—for example, a new absentee ballot rule that leaves lots of names off the list—that increases the average lookup time from one minute to two. In that case, ninety voters per hour will be literally impossible to handle. The line will queue to infinity, growing forever until the flow of traffic decreases.

Even when there isn't mass confusion at the check-in table, this first part of the voting process is often where chaos begins. At many polling places, voter lists are still printed out on paper and collected in massive three-ring binders. In sparsely populated areas with just a few hundred voters, that's not so bad. But when the number of voters stretches into the thousands, as it does in many urban precincts, poll workers have to flip through dozens of pages for every check-in. It's no wonder lines back up.

An obvious solution would be to switch from paper voter lists to digital ones. These days, we often thinking of election technology only as a matter of security. But technology is also a matter of convenience. Twenty-first-century innovation has made it easier to order takeout, buy a used car, or sign a legal contract. Why is it that the experience of casting your ballot has barely changed?

The answer is, in large part, Congress. In 2002, the federal government gave states a giant pile of money to switch from hand-counted paper ballots to touch screens and scanners, but they've provided almost nothing since. The last time states could afford to update their voting equipment, Apple was putting out its second-generation iPod and Mark Zuckerberg was a Harvard freshman trying to rate the attractiveness of women in his class. Have you ever wondered why voting machines, even touch screen voting machines, never resemble tablets? It's because when most of those voting machines were purchased, tablets didn't exist.

In recent years, the Trump administration has granted states $380 million to address voting machine obsolescence. This may seem like a lot, but it comes to just 29 cents per American per year. It's about one five-thousandth of what we spend maintaining our highways. It's certainly not enough to create the secure, modern polling places our democracy needs.

Even in the small number of localities that can afford top-notch equipment, those setting up and maintaining that equipment are rarely familiar with how it works. Poll workers have a lot of responsibility: they must open and close a polling place, maintain security, keep a line moving, and adjudicate a tome of election law. To take on all these tasks and more, the average poll worker receives just two and half hours of training. Some parts of America—not tiny backwaters, but major population centers like Philadelphia—require no training at all. As a result, almost no one has practiced dealing with worst-case scenarios. If a voting machine goes down, or a sudden crush of voters sends the line out the door, the best our poll workers can do is improvise.

This lack of a plan B is not a hypothetical problem. In 2016, in Durham County, North Carolina, the new digital voter lists crashed. If workers had trained on the equipment, or learned how to quickly troubleshoot their new technology, they might have been able to get the system up and running. Instead, they switched to the bulky binders full of paper. A queue to infinity ensued.

This error, and errors like it nationwide, don't occur because poll workers are lazy or unintelligent. They occur because most cities and states won't pay to train them. In fact, most cities and states barely pay them for their work. In Phoenix, Arizona, those staffing elections earn $6.20 per hour. In Kentucky, some make less than $4 an hour, barely half the federal minimum wage. These are admittedly two of the more egregious examples, but poll workers frequently make under $10 an hour and almost never make more than $15.

Not surprisingly, America now finds itself facing a poll worker shortage. In 2016, a majority of counties reported having trouble finding Election Day staff. Fewer employees means more overwhelmed polling places, which means more backups that lead to long lines. Given the low pay and long hours, it's particularly difficult to persuade people with full-time jobs to take the day off in order to help manage elections. As a result, an enormous share of our poll workers are retirees. More than half are more than sixty years old. A quarter are over seventy.

In fairness, nearly every poll worker I've encountered, of any age, has been helpful and friendly. There's certainly a place for everyone in our election management, and plenty of senior citizens are quite efficient and tech savvy. The problem is not that there are so many older poll workers. It's that there are so few younger ones. It's hard to speed up the voting process and embrace new time-saving devices when most of your workforce was born prior to the invention of the audio-cassette.

As much as we struggle to hire approximately 900,000 people to work the polls, we are even worse at picking their managers. In the United States, to a degree more or less unique among democracies, supervision of elections is divided among an enormous number of people. As we've already seen, each state sets its own rules, as does the District of Columbia. Not only that, but each county manages its polling places independently, and they are rarely, if ever, audited. To put it in the terms of our *Shark Tank* pitch, our mega-chain has fifty-one chief executives, even they have little authority over what happens at their respective branches, and there's no quality control.

There are some benefits to conducting a cluster of statewide elections rather than a single big one. Most important, it makes our democracy more difficult to hack. But our subdivided process also means we have no data on the tens of millions of customer service interactions that take place between voters and officials every year. With no lines of communication, commonsense standards are surprisingly hard to put in place nationwide. It's quite possible that the Michael Jordan of running elections is out there somewhere, toiling away in a remote Montana corner or modest pocket of St. Paul. If such a person exists, however, his or her election management secrets will most likely remain secret.

Even if our hypothetical polling place guru could share her best practices, it's doubtful they'd apply in all fifty states. In today's America, regional accents are disappearing, but on Election Day local quirks still flourish. Take ballot design. On New York State's ballots, to use just one example, every row of candidate names must be accompanied by an illustration of a pointing hand. (Picture one of those stadium foam fingers tilted on its side.) No other state does this. According to the author Mark Vanhoenacker, even within the Empire State, different places interpret the law differently. New York City has reduced its hand graphic to a tiny, embarrassed dot, while in other counties, the hand drawing is massive, complete with cuffed wrist and fingernails.

It's possible that all these pointy fingers give voters a helpful visual aid. It's also possible that voters find it confusing when an otherwise straightforward list of candidates is decorated with floating disembodied parts. I honestly don't know if New York's law is a good idea. But someone must know. If this were Target or KFC, they'd run tests, identify the most efficient design, and standardize it across the organization. That doesn't happen in American elections.

Instead, poorly designed ballots cost enormous numbers of Americans their vote. If you're my age or older, you'll of course remember the 2000 elections and Palm Beach's "butterfly ballot," whose counterintuitive layout led thousands of elderly liberal Jews to vote for the Trump-y Pat Buchanan when they clearly meant to pick Al Gore. What you may not realize is that ballot design hasn't improved much since. Lists of candidates are frequently chopped into strange configurations of rows and columns. To save space, important instructions are crammed into nooks and crannies where they're hard to find.

Other ballots are in desperate need of an editor. In Ohio in 2010, voters were invited to choose a "set of joint candidates," meaning a governor and lieutenant governor. But many voters, after misinterpreting the poorly worded instructions, voted twice. This was clearly the fault of the person who okayed the imprecise language, not the voters who failed to understand it. The spoiled ballots were discarded anyway. These small mistakes add up. The Brennan Center found that in just two elections, 2008 and 2010, poor ballot design moved half a million Americans out of the electorate.

In other words, design can decide a close race. Rick Scott, our Forrest Gump of election issues, knows a thing or two about this one as well. In 2018, officials in heavily Democratic Broward County, Florida, approved a ballot that squished the Senate race into the bottom right of the page. Most people spotted it anyway. But a few thousand overlooked it. Careful examination of Broward's votes, conducted by

MIT, found that the design flaw cost Scott's opponent 9,658 votes. Had Rick Scott's race been properly situated on the ballot, his margin of victory would have been just one one-hundredth of a percent. That's well within the range where a recount can prove decisive.

Amazingly, 2018 was not the first time that Broward County's elections were marred by gross incompetence. In 2004, approximately 58,000 absentee ballots were never sent to voters. A week after the 2012 elections, workers poking around a warehouse found 963 uncounted ballots in a box.

The person in charge of avoiding these types of errors—indeed, in charge of every Broward election—was named Brenda Snipes. Her performance begs the question: Why did someone who in retrospect was so clearly ill-suited to managing elections choose election management as a career? The answer is that she didn't. Brenda Snipes, just like nearly every other election supervisor in the country, was herself a politician.

No other country runs its polling places this way. The French or German or Argentinian equivalent of our county clerks are appointed managers, not elected officials. Even in America, it's rare to rely on politicians for jobs that are so clearly administrative. Police chiefs, sanitation commissioners, and school superintendents are not directly elected. But election supervisors are. It's as though, in addition to voting for a civilian commander in chief of the armed forces, we also voted for every lieutenant and colonel in the ranks.

One consequence of leaving election management to politicians is that it's not really a profession. There's no ladder to climb, no way to cut your teeth on small-town precincts before moving to chaotic big cities and sprawling, diverse states. There are ongoing efforts to bring such a career ladder into existence. Auburn University offers a fifteen-hour Certificate in Election Administration, and the National Association of Election Officials boasts 1,350 members. But that works out to just one member for every eighty-seven polling places in America. As things stand, if you want to manage elections when you grow up, the best way to do it isn't to become a dedicated public servant and win the job on merit. You win the job by currying favor with your local Democratic or Republican VIPs.

For all these reasons—obsolete technology, underpaid and under-trained poll workers, understaffed polling places, and a management system run by politicians instead of professionals—what Jacqui witnessed two years ago in New Jersey happens nationwide. Even when everyone involved is trying their best, so many things can go wrong. It's very hard to make voting easy.

Which also means that, to put it slightly differently, it's very easy to make voting hard.

Like honeybees and monarch butterflies, polling places have had a rough decade. In 2008, there were more than 132,000 voting locations throughout the country. By the 2012 elections, however, 12,000 of them had disappeared. We lost another 3,000 polling places in the run-up to 2016. Meanwhile, even as the number of places to vote has gone down, the number of people eligible to vote has continued to go up. Between Obama's first election and Trump's, voting-age Americans per polling place shot up by 25 percent.

Like long lines, polling place cuts haven't fallen equally on all voters. Between 2012 and 2016, for example, the number of voting sites actually went up in at least fourteen states. It's just that these gains were more than offset by losses in states like South Dakota, Arizona, and Indiana, which cut more than 10 percent of their voting locations each.

Even within states and counties, polling place cuts were uneven. Consider the case of Manatee County, Florida, home to about 394,000 people just outside Sarasota. In 2011, state senator Mike Bennet, a Manatee native, opposed a bill to make voting more convenient. "Why would we make it easier?" he asked. "I want them to fight for it."

Exactly who Bennet meant by "them" was made clear a few years later, when he left the State Senate and was elected to a new job: Manatee County supervisor of elections. One of his first proposals was to cut the number of voting sites from 99 to 69. White neighborhoods barely noticed the change. But in Black and Latino neighborhoods, polling place counts plummeted. The sole Democrat on the county board of commissioners opposed the plan, but the board's six Republicans approved it. According to a University of Florida study, Bennet's changes lowered Black and Hispanic turnout by 3 to 5 percent.

You might think Mike Bennet's discriminatory cutting should be illegal, and in fact until recently it was. Just as the Voting Rights Act limited certain states' and counties' ability to purge voters, it required areas with a history of discrimination to jump through extra hoops in order to shutter a voting site.

In 2010, however, when the U.S. Supreme Court's five conservatives overturned these restrictions, states where polling places had been legally protected began cutting them with abandon. Writing for *The Nation* in 2016, Ari Berman reported that nearly half the counties formally on probation shuttered polling places between 2012 and 2016. According to a *Vice News* analysis, the chunk of our country once restrained by the Voting Rights Act now has 10 percent more voters per polling place than the rest of the United States. Just as they did in Manatee County, cuts have hit nonwhite neighborhoods the hardest.

It is theoretically possible that Mike Bennet and hundreds of his fellow election officials are simply bad at their jobs. It is also possible that, by random chance, all their mistakes just happen to shove one party's likely voters from the electorate. But the real-world odds of such a coincidence are basically zero. What we're seeing instead is a kind of intentional incompetence. If you had a lot of time on your hands, and a serious grudge against Instagram influencers, you might set out to engineer the next Fyre Festival. It's the same with voting. If you want to prevent certain people from casting ballots, you can mismanage elections on purpose.

Shutting down polling places is only one way to encourage people to leave the electorate. You can also ensure that polling places are poorly run. Here, voter purge champion Brian Kemp makes yet another appearance. In 2018, in Fulton, Georgia, seven hundred voting machines—nearly a quarter of the total—were kept locked up for Election Day. Fulton County happens to include much of metro Atlanta, and voters there supported Stacey Abrams, the Democratic candidate for governor, by a margin of 46 percent. Abrams supporters found themselves waiting two to three hours, while those in areas favoring Kemp faced almost no lines at all. There's no question some Abrams supporters balked and reneged—the only thing that's unclear is how many.

Closed polling places and shuttered equipment mean that some voters are not just waiting longer once they arrive to vote. They're traveling farther, too. In seventeen of eighteen southern counties examined by *Vice*, one or more neighborhoods saw its average drive to the polls increase by more than five minutes.

Perhaps the most audacious polling place relocation was done in North Carolina. There, the number of early voting sites actually went up between 2012 and 2014. But these sites were moved around in a way that nonetheless made it more difficult for likely Democrats to vote. White North Carolinians had to travel, in total, 21,000 more miles to cast their ballots, which comes out to just .004 miles per person. But Black North Carolinians, despite making up just 22 percent of the population, had to travel an extra 350,000 miles to vote early. Put another way, for every additional city block traveled by a white voter, a Black voter was forced to add more than two and a half *miles* to her trip.

Even if you make it to your polling place and get through the line, intentional incompetence can nonetheless cost you your vote. Consider what happens if you show up at the wrong precinct on Election Day. In most states, you can still fill out a ballot. If you're especially far from home, your votes for local offices (city council or school board) might be discarded. But for statewide and national races (senator, governor, president) your vote still counts.

In Texas, however, they do things differently. If you show up at the wrong precinct, your entire ballot is discarded. You can be in the right county, the right city, even the right neighborhood. It doesn't matter. If you show up anywhere other than your assigned precinct, your vote doesn't count at all. This creates all sorts of opportunities for mischief, because Texas is notorious for scrambling precincts. Officials redraw boundaries for no good reason. They cram polling places together. Sometimes they even split apartment buildings in two.

If you're an established voter, you're unlikely to notice any of this. You probably go to the same place year after year, and just to be safe, you might check your polling location in advance. But if you're new to the electorate, or you come from a community that's been historically pushed to the margins, finding your polling place is like playing three-card monte. Lose the game, and you lose your vote.

Not incidentally, at around the same time North Carolina politicians began making Black voters travel farther to the polls, they also adopted Texas's precinct rules. In election management, it's notoriously difficult to share best practices. But worst practices seem to have no trouble catching on.

Once you embrace intentional incompetence, the possibilities really are endless. You can design confusing ballots, or make sure that your party's candidates are listed first. (Social science research shows that ballot order really can give you a small but meaningful edge.) You can cut the number of early voting days to a bare minimum or keep polls open only during working hours. You can force college students to cut through layers of red tape to register on campus. In recent years, the states—certain states, anyway—have become laboratories for undermining democracy. One party's voters are already paying a higher price to vote than the other's. Creative politicians are devising new ways to increase that cost.

Which brings us back to 2012, and a Starbucks bathroom just outside Miami, where poor Blake Yagman is steadying himself against the toilet bowl. We began this chapter by examining how Blake suffered.

Now we can turn to *why* he suffered. His ordeal was no accident. It was the result of an election system doing exactly what politicians hoped it would do.

To understand what happened to Blake—or, more accurately, what was done to him—it will help to try the following experiment. Pull out your phone or check your watch and see how long it takes you to read and comprehend the following block of text.

PROPERTY TAX LIMITATIONS; PROPERTY VALUE DECLINE; REDUCTION FOR NONHOMESTEAD ASSESSMENT INCREASES; DELAY OF SCHEDULED REPEAL.—(1) This would amend Florida Constitution Article VII, Section 4 (Taxation; assessments) and Section 6 (Homestead exemptions). It also would amend Article XII, Section 27, and add Sections 32 and 33, relating to the Schedule for the amendments. (2) In certain circumstances, the law requires the assessed value of homestead and specified nonhomestead property to increase when the just value of the property decreases. Therefore, this amendment provides that the Legislature may, by general law, provide that the assessment of homestead and specified nonhomestead property may not increase if the just value of that property is less than the just value of the property on the preceding January 1, subject to any adjustment in the assessed value due to changes, additions, reductions, or improvements to such property which are assessed as provided for by general law. This amendment takes effect upon approval by the voters. If approved at a special election held on the date of the 2012 presidential preference primary, it shall operate retroactively to January 1, 2012, or, if approved at the 2012 general election, shall take effect January 1,

2013. (3) This amendment reduces from 10 percent
to 5 percent the limitation on annual changes in
assessments of nonhomestead real property. This
amendment takes effect upon approval of the voters. If
approved at a special election held on the date of the
2012 presidential preference primary, it shall operate
retroactively to January 1, 2012, or, if approved at the
2012 general election, takes effect January 1, 2013.
(4) This amendment also authorizes general law to
provide, subject to conditions specified in such law,
an additional homestead exemption to every person
who establishes the right to receive the homestead
exemption provided in the Florida Constitution within
1 year after purchasing the homestead property and
who has not owned property in the previous 3 calendar
years to which the Florida homestead exemption
applied. The additional homestead exemption shall
apply to all levies except school district levies. The
additional exemption is an amount equal to 50 percent
of the homestead property's just value on January 1 of
the year the homestead is established. The additional
homestead exemption may not exceed an amount
equal to the median just value of all homestead
property within the county where the property at issue
is located for the calendar year immediately preceding
January 1 of the year the homestead is established.
The additional exemption shall apply for the shorter of
5 years or the year of sale of the property. The amount
of the additional exemption shall be reduced in each
subsequent year by an amount equal to 20 percent
of the amount of the additional exemption received
in the year the homestead was established or by an

amount equal to the difference between the just value
of the property and the assessed value of the property
determined under Article VII, Section 4(d), whichever
is greater. Not more than one such exemption shall
be allowed per homestead property at one time. The
additional exemption applies to property purchased on
or after January 1, 2011, if approved by the voters at a
special election held on the date of the 2012 presidential
preference primary, or to property purchased on or
after January 1, 2012, if approved by the voters at the
2012 general election. The additional exemption is not
available in the sixth and subsequent years after it is first
received. The amendment shall take effect upon approval
by the voters. If approved at a special election held on the
date of the 2012 presidential preference primary, it shall
operate retroactively to January 1, 2012, or, if approved
at the 2012 general election, takes effect January 1,
2013. (5) This amendment also delays until 2023, the
repeal, currently scheduled to take effect in 2019, of
constitutional amendments adopted in 2008 which limit
annual assessment increases for specified nonhomestead
real property. This amendment delays until 2022 the
submission of an amendment proposing the abrogation
of such repeal to the voters.

The monstrosity you just tackled was a proposed amendment on the Florida ballot in 2012. (I think it has something to do with lowering property taxes for first-time home buyers, but honestly, I'm not sure.) In my case, reading from start to finish took me three minutes and six seconds. Assuming I'm about average, getting through it would have taken Florida voters in 2012 a combined forty years.

As a writer, I believe that the type of paragraph Floridians were subjected to should be illegal. In fact, prior to 2012, it *was* illegal. There were limits to the number and length of proposals you could put on the Florida ballot. But with Obama's reelection looming, Republican lawmakers in the Sunshine State tried something new. First, they removed the rules meant to keep elections user-friendly. Then their political allies larded up the ballot with proposals designed to be as long and clunky as possible.

For the scheme to work, you didn't need every Florida voter to try to read the entire ballot. A small fraction of voters, each taking just a few more minutes in line, was enough to overwhelm stressed polling places, launching queues to infinity and leading voters to renege and balk.

That's the difference between the chaos Jacqui witnessed in New Jersey in 2018 and the chaos Florida went through six years earlier. In the first instance, an election went haywire despite everyone's best efforts. In the second, an election went haywire *because* of everyone's best efforts. Blake Yagman's migraine is proof that intentional incompetence works.

At the same time, however, Blake's migraine is also proof that intentional incompetence has its limits. In the days and weeks after the election, as journalists began printing horror stories from across the state, Floridians grew angry. Rick Scott—then serving his first term as governor—had been a champion of the bill that made voting harder. But in the face of a statewide outcry, he was forced to reverse his position, signing a reform bill that undid many of the worst changes from 2012. In 2016, Florida's voter turnout increased, putting even more strain on polling places—yet the average statewide wait time fell from thirty-nine minutes to just twelve.[*]

---

[*] Wait times in 2016 were also shorter than in 2012 nationwide. The reason I focus on 2012 and 2008 in this chapter is that in 2016, those shorter lines were at least in part due to lower Black turnout, which reduced the pressure on some of the polling places most likely to be targeted by intentional mismanagement.

What's notable here is that the grassroots coalition that forced Rick Scott to change his mind—or at least his behavior—included many people who had voted for Rick Scott. Among politicians, election management is an increasingly partisan issue. In places like Manatee County, Republican officeholders fight to make voting harder and Democratic officeholders fight to stop them. But among voters, competence is popular across party lines. We all want our DMVs to be efficient and our mail to be delivered on time. For the same apolitical reasons, we want our elections to be well run.

Moreover, the vast majority of Americans—regardless of which party we tend to support—don't want to see eligible voters pushed out of the electorate. Some Florida lawmakers may have felt that torturing Blake Yagman was a small price to pay for maintaining their grip on power, but the rest of us don't share their view. We believe that in a democracy, voting is a fundamental right. By extension, we believe our leaders should make exercising that right easier, not harder. And fortunately, despite all the intentional incompetence out there, many of our leaders still agree with us.

Who's your state secretary of state? What's the name of your city's supervisor of elections or your county clerk? Don't feel bad if you don't know the answer. After more than a year spent researching our political process, I still had to google it.

In a more perfect democracy, however, these people would be famous. After all, they're the ones in charge of our elections. Without them, the right to vote would be nothing more than a concept. They make your power real.

We've already seen how a few election managers—Georgia's Brian Kemp, Broward County's Brenda Snipes—have done this important work badly. Now it's time to see what happens when our elections are run well. To understand just how much of a difference it makes to have the right person in charge, consider the case of "Rogers's Law."

Today, Mike Rogers is a CNN contributor and conservative radio host, but in 1999, he was a state senator representing Michigan's Livingston County. There he wrote a highly specific piece of legislation, one requiring the address on a voter's registration form to match the one on his or her driver's license.

To most Michigan residents, the new rules made no difference whatsoever. Their drivers' license addresses and registration addresses were already identical. But for one group of voters—college students who grew up in one part of the state and went to school in another—"Rogers's Law" was a disaster. For all sorts of reasons, many students prefer to maintain their legal address in their hometowns until they graduate. Even those willing to change their legal residences were left with the impression that registering to vote was illegal unless you first made a time-consuming trip to the DMV. (Technically, you could register on campus and your driver's license would be automatically updated—but that part of the law was barely, one might say incompetently, publicized.)

As it just so happened, the year after his law was passed, Mike Rogers ran for Congress in a district that included East Lansing—home to Michigan State University and its approximately fifty thousand students. On Election Day, campus turnout was abysmal. Rogers won his race by just 160 votes.

Remarkably, Rogers's Law outlasted its author's political career, which ended with his retirement in 2014. What finally killed Rogers's Law was not a massive public outcry or a change of heart in the legislature, but the 2018 election of a former law school dean named Jocelyn Benson as Michigan's secretary of state.

Benson is a Democrat, but that's not the important thing about her. The important thing about Jocelyn Benson is that before taking on her new role, she wrote the book on it. I can't promise that every reader will find *State Secretaries of State: Guardians of the Democratic Process* riveting. But for a very particular audience, it's the *You Are a Badass* for election managers we've been waiting for. Benson's book is divided into ten chapters: "The Secretary as Election Reformer," "The Secretary as Enforcer," "The Secretary as Certifier," and so on. It was in one of these capacities—The Secretary as Voter Advocate—that Benson took on Rogers's Law after taking office in 2019. Rather than ask the Republican-controlled state legislature to reverse its policy, she struck a very favorable deal with Michigan students challenging the law in court. Under the new agreement, Benson promised a new, major publicity campaign designed to help students vote on campus. Rogers's Law has been transformed from a tool to keep young people from voting into a catalyst for a registration drive.

Because it happened so recently, we don't yet know what effect Jocelyn Benson's decision will have on turnout. But there's no question tens of thousands of MSU students will find it much easier to vote. So will voters in Houston, where Lina Hidalgo, a twenty-seven-year-old with no prior political experience, in 2018 won a race for Harris County judge. Before her victory, polling places during the early voting period opened at 8 a.m. and closed at 4:30 p.m., making them nearly impossible to get to if you had to work. Thanks to Judge Hidalgo, polls are now open much longer. Even better, Hidalgo created county-wide voting centers where any voter can ensure their ballot will count, regardless of which precinct they're assigned to. A small but important piece of Texas electoral mischief has been rolled back.

If we want to make voting easier, the obvious place to start is by electing more Jocelyn Bensons and Lina Hidalgos, especially in states where elections are likely to be decided by just a handful votes. Yet too often, we overlook these important races. Candidates for state secretary of state or county judge rarely raise millions from small-dollar donors. They don't become heroes among the grassroots. But if we gave election management offices the attention they deserved, we'd be able to fill more of them with people who believe that all Americans, regardless of party, should be able to exercise their rights. Instead of leaders who bump more of us out of the electorate, we would have leaders who bring more of us in.

Other elected officials have a role to play as well. Remarkably, many states have no minimum number of voting machines per precinct, and no maximum precinct size. Local lawmakers and governors can change that. High, clear, statewide standards would help avoid the kind of Fyre Festival that Jacqui encountered in Jersey.*

We should also set high standards for poll workers, coupled with higher pay. Poll workers should spend more time training, they should train on the equipment they'll actually use, and they should practice what they'll do if something goes wrong. In exchange, we should make sure that the people we rely on to help us vote are paid at least a fraction of what they're worth.

If working the polls paid higher wages, more Americans would be eager to do it. But there are other, additional ways states can handle a poll worker shortage. State employees should be allowed time off if they volunteer to help administer elections. So should students. In Cincinnati, for example, high schoolers can skip school on Election Day, provided they help out at a polling place. This eliminates a labor shortage, adds a tech-savvy cohort to the workforce, and gives young people a civics lesson all at once. It's the kind of thing every state and county should do.

There's also a lot we should do as a country. Officially speaking, the federal agency that deals with election management is the Election Assistance Commission, or EAC. Today, the EAC collects some valuable data, delivers a bit of federal money to the states, and runs a surprisingly good blog. The people who work there clearly care about what they do.

The problem is that from its birth in 2002, the EAC has been

---

* It's worth noting that one way to get rid of polling place lines is to get rid of polling places entirely. In 2020, four states—Colorado, Hawaii, Oregon, and Washington—will conduct their elections entirely by mail, and voters seem to like and trust the new arrangement. I doubt in-person voting will be completely replaced by mail anytime soon, which is why I don't focus on it in this chapter. That said, I suspect more states will consider making the switch.

chronically underfunded and under attack. The inaugural batch of commissioners arrived a year late thanks to congressional squabbling. In 2007, the EAC's chairman, an election administration expert named Paul DeGregorio, was ousted for being insufficiently partisan and replaced by a member of the Republican National Committee. Sources told *Roll Call* magazine that the ringleader behind the ousting was, not altogether surprisingly, Hans von Spakovsky. Within a few years of its founding, the EAC was issuing dubious warnings about voter fraud instead of doing its job.

Under Obama, Republicans went further, refusing to confirm a full slate of commissioners, and it was only when President Trump was elected that the EAC returned to full strength. This was something of a mixed blessing. To the commission's credit, under Trump, it's done a good job distributing limited funds for new technologies and election security. But the EAC has also joined the pointless voter ID crusade, and chairwoman Christy McCormack has called claims that Vladimir Putin interfered with the 2016 election "pure B.S."

In other words, the Election Assistance Commission has strayed quite far from election assistance. Instead of weaponizing the EAC (or abolishing it entirely, as some Republican lawmakers have sought to do), we should give it a more clearly defined, strictly nonpartisan set of responsibilities.

But reforming existing agencies is just the beginning. If we ever get our Skywalker Window, Congress could declare Election Day a federal holiday so that more people have time to vote. In recent years this idea has caught fire among progressives, sometimes to the exclusion of all other reforms, and it certainly wouldn't make our elections any worse.

That said, an Election Day holiday is more effective as a statement of values than as a real solution. Public-sector workers already get time off to vote; many private-sector workers have to work on federal holidays; even if people have the day off, that doesn't mean they'll be willing to wait in a four-hour line. If we're really serious about changing the calendar, the best thing to do would be to move our elections to a

Sunday, and require states to allow in-person early voting on Saturday. That would effectively replace Election Day with Election Weekend, giving far more people an opportunity to vote.

Even then, however, it would be a mistake to assume that a single reform will fix the voting experience. Instead, Congress should create its own set of nationwide standards to supplement the standards set by states. In much the same way that rules for interstate highways influence county and city road systems, federal elections can set the bar for local ones. At the very least, Congress should make it illegal for local and state officials to manage elections in which they themselves are running. If the Patriots are playing in the Super Bowl, do we allow them to referee?

Congress can also spend money. True, we can't put an unlimited sum toward better elections. But we don't have to. For sixty cents per American per year, we could pay poll workers more than adequately. For only a little bit more than that, we could replace outdating voting technology nationwide. When it comes to elections and technology, the goal shouldn't just be to make voting unhackable—although that's certainly important. The goal should be to make voting convenient. Imagine a dedicated voting tablet, unconnected to any larger network, that's easy to use and creates a verifiable paper trail. That's the gold standard. And it wouldn't take a fortune to create.

In fact, there are all sorts of ways technology can help us deliver excellent customer service at a reasonable price. Better digital polling books could dramatically reduce voter check-in times—especially if states could afford spares in case one went down.[*] By crunching data from tens of millions of anonymized customer service interactions we could figure out exactly how and when problems occur, and train poll workers to be able to prevent a backup before it starts.

---

[*] Of course, as Democrats learned the hard way when a results-reporting app for the 2020 Iowa Caucuses failed spectacularly, any technology that doesn't include an analog backup plan should be regarded as virtually useless.

If we were willing to get creative, we could not only improve Election Day but transform it. Here's just one example. Imagine you could go online, fill in a sample ballot for your precinct, and have a QR code texted to your phone. When you arrive at your polling place, you scan your code. In an instant, you're checked in and your ballot is uploaded to a machine—all you have to do is confirm your choices. The whole process would take less than a minute. And you wouldn't need everyone to adopt the new technology to see its benefits. Queuing theory tells us that even a small reduction in time-per-voter can be the difference between an hour-long line and no line at all.

Ultimately, regardless of exactly which steps we take, we should dedicate ourselves to a very achievable goal: the entire voting process—getting to your polling place, casting your ballot, and resuming your day—should take no more than thirty minutes.

Put another way, in America, if you have the right to vote and the desire to vote, you should be able to vote. That doesn't seem like too much to ask.

☆

We began this section with the story of Shelly Simonds, a tied election, and the 2017 drawing of lots. Two years later, Shelly faced David Yancey in a rematch. But this time the outcome was never in doubt. She prevailed by nearly 18 percent, and today she's a delegate in the Virginia Assembly. With a winning margin of that size, we don't need to ask if Shelly represents her district's entire population, or only its electorate. She clearly represents both.

But in that same Virginia election, as in all elections, the non-voters made the absence of their voices heard. Along the North Carolina border, Democrat Roslyn Tyler won her House Seat by 506. In the Richmond suburbs, Republican Roxann Robinson defeated Democrat Larry Barnett by just 191 votes out of about 30,000 cast.

What would these districts look like if everyone who wanted to vote had voted? If the unelectorate became part of our democracy, what kind of country would we be?

It's difficult to say, because it's hard to know exactly what America's non-voters want. But my hope is that now you better understand who they are. Too many of us don't have the right to vote. Too many of us who do have the right to vote nonetheless have our ballots destroyed. Too many of us who can cast ballots are being kept from polls because the cost of voting is simply too high. And in every one of these cases, the people kept out of the electorate are more likely to support one party than the other.

If we changed all that, I don't for a minute think Democrats would hold power forever. But I am absolutely certain that America would be a very different place. In some cases, we would have different leaders. In others, the officeholders might be the same, but their agendas would change as they broadened their appeal.

And yet even if every American voted, it is still quite possible—quite likely, even—that our representatives wouldn't truly represent us. Just because you can cast a ballot, and just because your ballot will count, doesn't mean your ballot will matter. We are all created equal, but our votes are not. That inequality between voters is what we'll spend the next few chapters exploring.

But first I want to tell you a story about my grandfather and some charming profanity from 1946.

PART II

WHOSE VOTES MATTER?

5

TAKE A SHIT WITH IRV LITT

The Geography of Gerrymandering

About eighty-five years ago my grandfather ran for president. Of his public high school in Brooklyn, not of the United States. Still, hearing him tell campaign trail stories more than half a century later, you'd never know the second office was any more prestigious than the first.

"I went through *every* hallway," he'd recall, no less proud than a candidate who visited all ninety-nine counties in Iowa. This was my dad's father—my mom's parents were the ones in Florida with the *Schoolhouse Rock!* VHS—and for most of my life, he and my grandma Dorothy lived in a semidetached condo on the Jersey side of the bridge. It was while sitting in their living room that I most often heard the tale of his presidential run.

"I had *signs* printed," he would say significantly, as though this were valuable information I could use if I myself ever ran for student government in the 1940s. "They said, 'Score a Hit with Irv Litt!' I put them up *everywhere*."

I have no doubt he was telling the truth. Grandpa was a first-generation American—he spoke only Yiddish until age six—and had the bone-deep seriousness common to strivers in a new land. As a candidate, he probably wasn't much of a backslapper, but I'm certain he was a workhorse.

Which made what happened next all the more dramatic, even a bit devastating. Yet this was Grandpa's favorite part of the story.

"I came to school one morning," he would recall, "My main rival had taken down my signs and put up his own signs instead. And they all said, 'Take a *Shit* with Irv Litt!'"

Grandpa was not one for dramatic pauses, but here he couldn't help himself. For a moment, he'd slip below the surface of his memories. Then a small, anticipatory smile would brighten one-half of his upper lip. It was a rare acknowledgment, however slight, that the world was beyond his control and that this was not necessarily a bad thing.

"When we had the election, I was the only person everyone had heard of. 'Take a Shit with Irv Litt!' So I won!"

My grandfather's triumph taught me several important political lessons. For one thing, I learned the value of name recognition in close races, especially when voters are tuning in late. Grandpa also taught me the usefulness of a rhyming slogan, although sadly this wasn't enough to save my 1998 middle school ticket ("Dave and Dave, It's What You Crave"), which lost to our opponents ("Joe and Abby, Not Too Shabby") in a landslide.

But the most important part of the story, and the reason I retell it here, is not what my grandfather included. It's what he left out. Even though he was describing a campaign that took place three-quarters of a century ago, he had never had to explain how the election was conducted. It was the exact same process my middle school employed when Dave and Dave got creamed by Joe and Abby, the same process we use to pick church board presidents and PTA chairs, the same process you yourself have been part of when facing choices large and small. Candidates compete for votes. Whoever gets the most votes wins. It's easy. We take it for granted.

We also take for granted—and this is the really crucial bit—that every vote carries equal weight. No ballot is worth more than any other; no ballot is worth less. This is such an obvious and universal principle that I feel strange mentioning it. It's like reminding you that if we each have a quarter, they're both worth twenty-five cents.

Except for this: Our most important elections—the ones to decide who taxes our incomes; oversees our courts; funds our schools; oh, and by the way, controls an arsenal of more than four thousand nuclear warheads—are conducted in a way that would spark a scandal in student government or a riot at the PTA. In American democracy, ballots aren't worth the same amount at all. It's as though the quarter in your pocket can buy a gumball, while the one in mine can buy a boat.

You may think I'm mistaken or exaggerating. After all, in America, we believe in One Person, One Vote. On inspection, however, that slogan is a bit slippery. It's like saying Dwayne "The Rock" Johnson and I are bound by the principle of "One Person, One Body." Technically that's true. But some bodies, and some ballots, are much stronger than others.

In the first few chapters of this book, we explored the gap between voters and non-voters. In the next few chapters, we'll look at the elections for the House of Representatives, Senate, and White House, and explore the difference between the stronger and weaker voters in each. By the time we're done, you'll see how large the gap is, how rapidly it's growing, and how it changes our democracy. After all, the more that power becomes concentrated in the hands of just a few voters, the more our leaders will lavish their attention on those voters and disregard everyone else.

So what decides whether your vote is a powerful Dwayne Johnson or a paltry David Litt? For most Americans, the answer is simple. It's all about where you live.

☆

Elbridge Gerry was actually a pretty amazing guy. Born in 1744, in Marblehead, Massachusetts, Gerry (pronounced "Gary") got into Harvard at the age of just fourteen. His first eight years after graduation were spent in the family fish business, but after the Boston Massacre he won a seat in his Colonial legislature, where he made war all but inevitable by voting to block shipments of British tea. In 1776, at a mere thirty-two years old, he signed the Declaration of Independence. Only four of the fifty-six signers were younger.

Nor did Gerry stop there. He served in the Continental Congress; attended the Constitutional Convention; advocated for the Bill of Rights; was elected to the first House of Representatives; became governor of Massachusetts; and, as if all that weren't enough, served under James Madison as vice president of the United States. "If every Man here was a Gerry," his friend John Adams once proclaimed, "the Liberties of America would be safe against the gates of Earth and Hell." If history were fair, Gerry would be right up there with Thomas Paine or Alexander Hamilton in the pantheon of our nation's heroes.

But history isn't fair. And today, inasmuch as Elbridge Gerry is known at all, it is for being the founding father of gerrymandering.

In a résumé stuffed with accomplishment, here is the only sliver even a handful of Americans have heard of. In 1812, led by then-governor Gerry, Massachusetts Republicans came up with a devious scheme. They would redraw the lines for state senate districts in such a way that they were guaranteed to win it. One of these new districts was so warped and twisted that when a *Boston Gazette* cartoonist drew it, it reminded him of a salamander. The names of the governor and amphibian were mashed together, the hard *G* sound was gradually softened, and "gerrymander" was born.

Two hundred eight years later, for the sake of a good man's reputation, let's correct the record just a bit. First of all, Elbridge Gerry was not the first to draw maps in his party's favor. Back in 1788, in the run-up to America's very first congressional election, Virginia's Patrick Henry carefully arranged his own state's districts in an attempt to keep James Madison out of the House of Representatives. If anything, the *Boston Gazette* should have complained about Henrymanders.

Also—and this is hardly consequential, but it really gets to me—it appears the editors of the *Boston Gazette* had absolutely no clue what a salamander looks like. The creature depicted in the famous cartoon had the wings of a dragon, the talons of an eagle, the neck of a python, the beak of a vulture, and the teeth of a piranha. Beneath all this ran the following caption. "O generations of VIPERS! Who hath warned you of the wrath to come?" The entire image was a crime against herpetology.

There's one final thing you should know about Gerry's gerrymander. It didn't last. Gerry lost the 1812 election for governor, his party lost the State House of Representatives, and when the opposition took charge, they undid the changes to the map. There was even a follow-up cartoon, one featuring the evil salamander's skeleton. "Hatched 1812," read the caption. "Died 1813."

As we know now, the *Gazette* couldn't have been more wrong. Gerrymandering—both the word and the tactic—far outlived both the governor and the paper that created it. The last major book about Elbridge Gerry came out in 1976. It was titled *Elbridge Gerry: Founding Father and Republican Statesman*. Yet the cover did not feature its subject's historic signature on the Declaration, or even his portrait. On the cover of Gerry's biography, there was only the cartoon monster that bears his name.

If anything, Gerry is even more loathed today than he was when that book came out. Of all the topics you'll read about in this book, none has garnered more attention—or more outrage—than gerrymandering. Presidential candidates condemn it. Activists deplore it. My friend Ben Sheehan sells gerrymandering jewelry, necklaces and earrings with shiny replicas of twisty districts. (Proceeds go to a civics nonprofit.) There's even a custom font called Gerry regular,

COBBLED TOGETHER FROM THE UNSIGHTLY PORTIONS OF OUR CONGRESSIONAL MAP.

All this anger is well placed. Gerrymandering is unquestionably a bad thing. But the more you learn about our districts, the more you realize that their problems run far deeper than oddly shaped boundary lines or "politicians picking their voters." Hating gerrymandering is easy. Understanding it is hard.

"I was drawing maps of my neighborhood when I was four," Dave Wasserman tells me, as though this were a normal childhood hobby. At a time when other students polished apples, he was gifting his teachers hand-drawn sketches of his neighborhood in Kendall Park, New Jersey. At age eleven, Dave added a second passion to his repertoire: politics. "I discovered C-SPAN," he explains, as though this, too, were a typical phase of childhood development.

Today, Dave works for NBC News and the Cook Political Report. He has a large and passionate following on Twitter, where he goes by @redistrict. And while he does all sorts of analysis, his specialty, as you might expect, is the intersection of maps and power.

It's a gross understatement to say Dave Wasserman has lots of thoughts about gerrymandering. But if I could boil them down to a single main idea, it would be this: while it's true that some votes for Congress are stronger than others, and that the strength or weakness of these votes gives one party an advantage, politicians rigging the map is only one piece of the puzzle. America does not just have a gerrymandering problem. America has a political geography problem. And it turns out a political geography problem is much more difficult to solve.

Let's start at the very beginning. The Framers of our Constitution had lots to say about what's known as "apportionment," the number of members of Congress allocated to each state. But they had almost nothing to say about the way those members were chosen. It's a little like a wedding planner who obsesses over the number of guests per table but completely ignores the seating chart.

As a result, when the inaugural Congress convened in 1789, different states chose their representatives in very different ways. In Connecticut, Pennsylvania, and New Jersey, for example, no one worried about politicians drawing unfair districts because there were no districts to draw. House members represented their entire state, and were chosen in a single statewide election, just like senators are today. (Political scientists refer to this method of picking legislators as "at-large elections," as though they were serial killers on the loose.)

Even when at-large states switched to creating districts, the number of representatives per district was in constant flux. In 1811, for example, Pennsylvania split eighteen seats among eleven districts: seven with one member, one with two members, three with three. Two years later the delegation grew to twenty-three members, which it split among fifteen districts: nine with one member, five with two members, one with four. It's okay if you can't keep track of all this. I doubt Pennsylvanians could, either.

Yet despite this confusion, states continued to elect at-large representatives, draw multi-member districts of varying sizes, or both. In fact, it wasn't until 1967 that Congress passed a law making congressional districts standard across America. Our current system of House elections—not the lines on the map, but the process itself—was born the same year as the Big Mac.

The modern congressional map is defined by three features. First, districts must be "contiguous." They can be carved into strange shapes, but they can't be divided into multiple pieces (except by a lake or other body of water). Second, districts must be "single-member." As you've likely inferred, this means each district has exactly one representative.

The third feature is optional, but near universal: elections for representative are what is known as "first past the post." The phrase comes from horse racing. To win the Preakness or Kentucky Derby, you don't have to run the race under a certain time; all you have to do is finish faster than the second-fastest horse. A first-past-the-post election is the same thing, but for politics. Let's say you're running against three other candidates for Congress. To get elected, you don't need to break 50 percent. You simply need more votes than whoever comes in second.

Contiguous, single-member, first-past-the-post districts have much to recommend them. They're simple. They're clean. They ensure that all parts of a state are represented in Washington, and that the system of picking winners is instantly familiar to anyone who's watched an episode of *Jeopardy!* or participated in a hundred-yard dash.

Yet for all their virtues, our congressional districts have one glaring flaw. They are perfectly designed to waste your vote.

In 2018, in a forty-thousand-square-mile expanse of Texas starting in the panhandle and running along the Oklahoma border, William McClellan Thornberry, a Republican better known to his constituents as "Mac," was reelected to Congress with 82 percent of the vote.

This sounds like quite an achievement, but it really wasn't. One of Dave Wasserman's employers, the Cook Political Report, ranks House seats based on their "Partisan Voting Index." If a district has a PVI of "D+2," that means it's two percentage points more Democratic leaning than the country as a whole. "R+2" means the same thing but for Republicans. Mac Thornberry's district is R+33. In other words, in a typical year, with completely generic candidates, you could expect a Republican to win Texas's 13th district (TX-13, for short) by a 66-point margin. According to the Partisan Voting Index, TX-13 is the least competitive GOP-held seat in the country.

Clearly, this was good news for Mac Thornberry. In November, as his colleagues made frantic appeals to constituents, he had nothing to fear. But what does the lopsided nature of TX-13 mean for the people who live there? It turns out that even for Mac Thornberry's supporters, their district's one-sidedness comes at a very high cost. If you want your vote to make a difference, the Texas panhandle is one of the worst places in America to live.

There are several ways to think about the strength of a ballot. We'll discuss only two of them here, but still, there's some light arithmetic ahead. That's why I'm bringing in a special guest. My friend Ben Orlin is a teacher and author who runs a blog called "Math with Bad Drawings," wrote a book of the same name, and generously provided the illustrations you'll see sprinkled through the next three chapters. For example, these are his highly realistic depictions of my grandfather's race for student body president, and of mine.

Here we see a key difference between a close and lopsided election. In the first example, where my grandpa beat some jerk, he needed 100 votes to win, and that's exactly how many he got. Every single vote was essential. When Joe and Abby thumped Dave and me, they too needed 100 votes to win, but they received 150. In other words, fifty people could have switched their support to Dave and Dave without changing the result. In election jargon, we would say that fifty of Joe and Abby's votes were "wasted."

Here's another way of looking at it: an Irv Litt's supporter's vote in 1946 was stronger than a Joe-and-Abby supporter's in 1998. To figure out just how much stronger, we can start by dividing the minimum number of votes my grandpa needed in order to win (100) by the number of votes he actually received (also 100). My grandpa's voters had what we'll call a "strength score" of 1. When we do the same math for Joe and Abby voters, we divide the 100 votes needed to win by the 150 votes actually received, for a strength score of .67. Compare the two scores, and we see that Grandpa's voters were about 1.5 times stronger than Joe and Abby's.

With all this in mind, let's return to the Texas panhandle. Out of approximately 169,000 votes cast for Mac Thornberry in the 2018 election, about 67,000—nearly 4 in 10—were wasted. Compare that to the most competitive 2018 House election, the race for Georgia's 7th District. There, Republican Rob Woodall won with just 208 wasted votes out of more than 140,000 he received—less than .002 percent. A person in Texas's 13th District had one vote. So did a person in Georgia's 7th. But when you compare their strength scores, a Thornberry supporter was about 40 percent weaker than a Woodall supporter. The two votes weren't really the same at all.

How did we end up with so many wasted votes in Mac Thornberry's district? Who, or what, is robbing Republicans in the Texas panhandle of their power?

Gerrymandering has nothing to do with it. After all, Texas's 13th District isn't shaped like a salamander or a letter of the alphabet. The GOP legislators drawing the state's map don't want Republican ballots to be wasted—they would love to make panhandle voters very powerful indeed. But they can't. The five districts that border TX-13 have

Partisan Voting Indices of, respectively, R+18, R+18, R+27, R+28, and R+32. Mac Thornberry's district is a sea of red inside an ocean of red. What saps Republican voters in TX-13 of their strength is not partisan mapmaking. It's the fact that they live near so many other Republicans.

The author Bill Bishop calls places like Thornberry's district, where neighbors overwhelmingly vote alike, "communities of sameness." In a 2009 book, *The Big Sort*, he found that more of us are calling these communities home than ever before. In 1976, Bishop wrote, three in four Americans were from counties that split their vote 60–40 or even closer. "By 2004," he concluded mournfully, "48.3% of voters lived in communities where the election wasn't close at all."

Like most things written about the Bush years, those problems seem quaint and delightfully manageable today. By 2016, the proportion of Americans living in counties where the election wasn't close had risen to 59 percent—a more than 10 percent increase in just eight years. Put another way, six in ten of us now live in areas less politically competitive than Mississippi.

In fact, our political divide is even starker than this six-in-ten figure suggests, because the same patterns we see among counties also exist within them. Take Mahoning County, Ohio. Looking at a 2016 election map, you'd think Mahoning was a near-perfect blend of red and blue. Clinton won 50 percent of the vote, Trump won 46.

But using a *New York Times* analysis of results at the precinct level, we can find communities of sameness the typical map doesn't capture. In Mahoning's rural areas and exurbs, Trump won every precinct, often with as much as 70 percent support. In the county seat of Youngstown, meanwhile, the story was exactly the opposite. In one unbroken block of eleven urban precincts, Clinton racked up a victory margin of 89 percent. Despite being a "swing county," this is not a place where Democrats and Republicans live together in harmony. From a purely partisan standpoint, Mahoning County is a patch of rural Arkansas with a tiny piece of Oakland jammed inside.

After the shock of the 2016 elections, you often hear a certain sort of guilty liberal bemoan the fact that Democrats live in a political bubble. But that misses the point. Most liberals live in bubbles because most *Americans* live in bubbles. Regardless of who you plan to support in the next election, odds are higher than ever that your neighbors agree with you.

As Bill Bishop's big sort grows bigger, America's congressional districts are becoming more like Mac Thornberry's safe seat and less like Rob Woodall's nail-biter. Back in 1997, when Dave Wasserman was delivering hand-drawn maps to his teachers, America was home to 165 swing districts—those generally decided by ten percentage points or less. By 2012, the number of swing districts had fallen to ninety. By 2016, it was down to just seventy-two. Your odds of living in a competitive House district—that is to say, your odds of living somewhere where your vote is strong—have been cut by more than half in twenty years.

Partisan maps are partly responsible for that change, and we'll get to them shortly. But for now, it's important to know this: even without gerrymandering, America would be wasting more votes than at any time in recent history.

And here's something else you need to know: even without gerrymandering, Democrats would be wasting more votes than Republicans. That's because while Americans of all parties live in bubbles, blue bubbles look different than red ones.

First, as you're probably well aware, blue bubbles tend to be found in cities. In 2016, of the twenty most populous metro areas in the country, Clinton won fifteen. In metros with more than one million people (a list that includes not just New York and Los Angeles, but megalopolises like Grand Rapids and Rochester), she beat Trump by 16 percent. Population density matters as well: the more people per square mile, the larger the percentage of those people who tend to vote Democrat.

Finally, while there are both blue and red bubbles, voters in the most extremely lopsided pieces of America—the bubbliest bubbles— are more likely to support Democrats.

We can measure this by looking at 2016 results from what I'll call "landslide counties," those that went at least 80–20 for the winner. While more than 500 of the 530 landslide counties went for Trump, these reddest-red bubbles tend to be sparsely populated. King County, Texas, for example, gave Trump a whopping 94 percent of the vote. But with only 159 voters total, that didn't matter much.

Clinton, meanwhile, won just 25 landslide counties. But those counties were packed with people. They included Manhattan, San Francisco, Philadelphia, St. Louis, New Orleans, Seattle, and plenty more. In the country's 80–20 counties, Clinton beat Trump by 2.5 million votes—almost her entire popular vote margin. There are a lot more people living in the very bluest bubbles than in the very reddest ones.

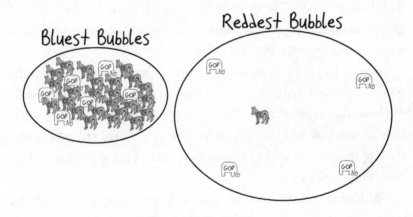

All three of these defining characteristics of blue bubbles—population size, population density, and a tendency to be a particularly dark shade blue—result in more wasted votes for one party than the other. In city after city, Democrats find themselves surrounded by other Democrats. Remember how Mac Thornberry, of TX-13, holds the least competitive Republican seat in the country? Well, 17 Democratic-held districts are *less* competitive than Thornberry's. Of the 30 most lopsided districts in America, 25 are solidly blue.

The Fifteen Districts with the Weakest Voters

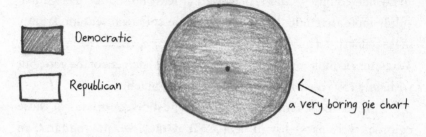

Democratic

Republican

a very boring pie chart

We're almost done with the math bit, I promise. But first, we need to understand what the disproportionate number of deep-blue House districts means for America as a whole. To do that, imagine a House of Representatives made up of just five seats, with PVIs of D+10, D+6, R+1, R+2, and R+3. The *average* district PVI would be D+2. At first glance, that seems good for Democrats, but as we now know, all it means is that Democrats waste more votes.

The *median* district, meanwhile, is R+1. (You'll recall from middle school math that "median" simply refers to the number in the middle of a lowest-to-highest range.) To win control of the House, Democrats have to win this R+1 district, or "tipping point district," plus everything to the left. Republicans have to win the tipping point district plus everything to the right.

While the scale is different, America's real Congress is essentially the same as our imaginary five-seat one. The tipping point district seat changes slightly from election to election, but at the moment, it stands at R+3. The GOP can win a House majority even if it doesn't win every red-leaning district. Democrats face the opposite situation. Even if they win every blue-leaning seat *and* every neutral seat, that's not enough to take control of the House. As of this writing, they have to win at least seventeen Republican-leaning seats as well. In other words, even when Democrats hold a majority, that majority depends on districts, and, by extension representatives, more conservative than the country as a whole.

The average district PVI, meanwhile, while not as bad as our imagined D+2, is still half a percentage point in favor of Democrats. That may not seem like much, but in a country with 230 million eligible voters, it means a huge number of additional wasted votes. When the country is closely divided, Democrats can win a majority of voters and nonetheless fail to win a majority of the House.

That's exactly what happened in 2012. Across the country, by a margin of 1.4 million, Americans chose the Democratic candidate in their local House races. Yet Republicans won control of Congress easily, with a majority of thirty-three seats.

"The American people want solutions," declared then-Speaker John Boehner when the results came in, "and tonight, they've responded by renewing our majority."

Except that wasn't true. The American people had tried to *end* Speaker Boehner's control of Congress, not renew it. The only reason the Speaker retained his gavel was geography: the minority of voters who supported his agenda was more powerful than the majority of voters who opposed it.

As we've seen, much of the strength or weakness of Americans' votes is due to people living in communities of sameness, particularly in cities. But surveying the 2012 results, it's clear that in some states, the number of wasted votes is too large to blame on the big sort alone. In Michigan, where President Obama won 54 percent of the vote, Democrats won just 5 of the state's 14 congressional races. In Ohio, Republicans won 52 percent of the votes but 75 percent of the seats.

Most Americans—even in the states affected—didn't realize how topsy-turvy their elections for Congress had become. But when analysts like Dave Wasserman looked at those numbers, red flags immediately went up. It was a bit like an investigator coming across a clear case of arson in the aftermath of a forest fire. While most of the damage was due to natural causes, this was man-made.

As it happens, we know exactly who the culprits were, because they're very proud of what they achieved. "The Republican firewall at the state legislative and congressional level held," boasts the website of something called REDMAP, which retells the story of the 2012 elections in much the same way my grandpa retold the story of Take a Shit with Irv Litt.

And this is where gerrymandering finally comes in. REDMAP stands for "Redistricting Majority Project," and in the run-up to Obama's reelection, it spent $48 million on an effort to redraw America's congressional lines. REDMAP couldn't have completely reshaped Congress on its own. Bill Bishop had to move to Austin, blue bubbles had to become even bluer, the urban-rural divide had to grow.

Still, REDMAP, and the districts it helped draw, explain why states like Michigan and Ohio were particularly unresponsive to the voters' will. Gerrymandering may account for only a fraction of what has happened to American democracy. But in a country this politically divided, with stakes this high, a fraction is still a lot.

In retrospect, REDMAP was one of the most successful power grabs in American history. For less than it cost to make *Mamma Mia!*, politicians were able to warp our government for a decade.

I never liked Ronald Reagan more than when I learned he pronounced "gerrymandering" the old-fashioned way. "To ask men holding office, elected from districts, to change the lines of that district to fit the new population?" he said incredulously during an Oval Office interview. "I think gerrymandering is what takes place." Only, he said it with a hard "G," Gary rather than Jerry, just the way Elbridge himself had two centuries prior. Be still, my beating, dorky heart.

On a slightly more important note, Reagan went on to call gerrymandering "a national disgrace." And he was not staking out some lonely position in his party. Prominent Republicans opposed gerrymandering at least into my late teens. "I think it's wrong," Newt Gingrich declared in 2006. "I think it leads to bad government."

So what changed? How did Team Mitch stop worrying and learn to love drawing district lines?

Part of the answer lies with the calendar. Like a cicada hatch or a Spice Girls reunion, drawing news maps doesn't happen often: just once every ten years. In a few places, that work is done by the courts or by a nonpartisan committee. But in most states, districts are drawn at the beginning of the decade by whichever party happens to be in charge.

To put it another way, if your party is going to have a good year, you really want it to be a year that ends in a zero. And 2010 was a truly amazing year for the GOP. It wasn't just that a red wave swept the House and Senate. Republicans won eleven new governorships. They flipped twenty state legislative chambers from blue to red. When new maps were made in 2011, the GOP held what pollical operatives call the "trifecta"—control of all three branches of government—in an unprecedented number of states. As Wasserman explains, "Republicans had the ability to draw four times as many districts as Democrats."

Compared to Democrats, Republicans also could gain more electoral advantage from each district they drew. The same geographic trends that weaken Democratic voters by accident make it easier to weaken them on purpose, in much the same way that when a forest fire is raging, arson is (I'm assuming) easier to commit. Across the country, blue bubbles were waiting to be turned into "vote sinks," the political operative's term for uncompetitive congressional districts.

After these vote sinks were in place, the rest of a state could be carved up for maximum benefit.[*] Here, too, Republicans had an advantage in the wake of the 2010 elections: technology. Back when

---

[*] Here's a brief example of exactly how that works: Let's say you're a Democrat drawing three districts. You might draw one R+16 (the vote sink) and then draw two seats that are D+8. This wastes as few votes as possible while ensuring you'll survive any future red wave.

Elbridge Gerry signed off on the original salamander district, even the shrewdest mapmakers were mostly guessing. They knew, in broad terms, who lived in certain areas and which party those people were likely to support. But without any real data to go by, carving up districts was more amputation than surgery.

Today the opposite is true. Modern Gerrys (or, really, Patrick Henrys) can slice districts with a finesse that puts brain surgeons to shame. One company, Caliper, makes a computer program specifically for this purpose. It's called "Maptitude for Redistricting." Draw a shape around a region or neighborhood, and it automatically crunches demographic numbers to tell you, with extraordinary detail, what to expect from a given seat. There's even an "efficiency gap" measurement built directly into the program, so you can measure the exact number of your opponents' votes you're likely to waste.

Such features are occasionally used to give every voter the maximum amount of political power. But as Maptitude's clever tagline, "No Time to Lose," makes clear, its typical customer isn't interested in fairness. Politicians want to know more about their constituents so they can weaken the votes of constituents who don't vote for them.

In 2011, across the country, newly empowered Republican lawmakers rolled out their maps, unboxed copies of their shiny new software, and got to work. From North Carolina (where the vote sinks were Charlotte and Raleigh-Durham) to Ohio (Cleveland and Columbus) to Pennsylvania (Philadelphia and Pittsburgh) to Michigan (Detroit), huge numbers of likely Democrats had their votes weakened. The remainder of each state was then surgically dissected to create the largest Republican gains.

In fairness, my party did some gerrymandering of its own. In the wake of the 2011 redistricting cycle, five state maps were meaningfully skewed toward Democrats. But *nineteen* were skewed toward Republicans. At the moment, to say that both Democrats and Republicans draw unfair districts is like saying that both Michael Phelps and I swim. That's true. We're just in very different leagues.

To measure exactly how different, a 2014 analysis in the *University of Chicago Law Review* looked at each state's "efficiency gap," the same measure of wasted votes employed by Maptitude. Historically, the researchers found, gerrymandering has not consistently favored one party over the other. In the 1980s, gerrymandering slightly benefited Democrats. During the 1990s and 2000s it slightly benefited Republicans.

In the first election after REDMAP, however, the Chicago analysts found that the partisan effect of our 2012 congressional districts was like nothing ever seen before. In a single year, the new map cost Democrats an average of one seat per state. "It thus is clear," wrote the study's authors, "that the scale and skew of today's gerrymandering are unprecedented in modern history." Today, in a way no living American has previously experienced, maps decide who represents us and voters do not.

The Republican Party's big-league gerrymander doesn't mean Democrats will never control Congress. They control it as of this writing. But some simple math suggests that the current shape of America's districts hands the Republican Party somewhere between twenty and thirty extra congressional seats. If the biannual race for control of Congress is a hundred-yard dash, Team Mitch gets a ten to fifteen-yard head start.

It's always possible, in theory anyway, that the GOP head start shrinks of its own accord. If cities became slightly redder, and suburbs slightly bluer, drawing unfair districts would become more difficult. But a more likely possibility is that the big sort continues. If that happens, then gerrymandering, and our political geography problem more broadly, are going to get worse.

To give us a sense of how much worse, consider Wisconsin. In the *New York Times* map of the 2016 results, the Badger State resembles a pair of blueberries, the city of Milwaukee and the college town of Madison, smushed into a light pink carpet. That's a perfect starting point for a gerrymander, and indeed, Wisconsin is among the most gerrymandered places in America today. In 2018, while Democrats won a majority of votes for the State Assembly, Republicans won a 27 percent majority of the seats.

The Assembly's Speaker, a career politician named Robin Vos, offered the following rationale for the fact that voters asked for one party to run things and got another. "If you took Madison and Milwaukee out of the state election formula," Vos explained, "we would have a clear majority."

Well, sure. And if we raptured away approximately 90 percent of America's male population, I would be the country's tallest man. I'm just not sure why either fact is relevant. After all, one important thing about both Madison and Milwaukee, something I'd think would be hard for a lifelong Wisconsinite to overlook, is that people live there. Shouldn't their votes be worth something, too?

Robin Vos clearly doesn't think so. Under his leadership, the state legislature has refused to expand Medicaid, slashed funding for schools, hamstrung the incoming Democratic governor's agenda, and more. Vos has behaved as though the opinions of people who vote against him don't matter. And because of the map he helped draw, he's right.

The great hope of REDMAP is that what has happened in Wisconsin will happen everywhere—America becomes even more citified, cities become even more Democratic, and Democrats' votes become even weaker than they are today. And just in case natural causes alone aren't enough to extend the Republican head start, politicians have some tricks up their sleeve.

The most dramatic scheme involves messing with the census. Our current commerce secretary is Wilbur Ross, an eighty-two-year-old billionaire known mostly for wearing velvet slippers and falling asleep during meetings. Yet in 2018, he made a genuinely dramatic announcement: the 2020 census forms would ask every American if he or she was a citizen.

There are two ways a citizenship question could change the congressional map, only one of which has been widely reported on. First, it could produce an undercount because frightened undocumented immigrants and their families would avoid sending in their forms. This would make the official population of places where immigrants live—which includes many Democratic bubbles—artificially low. The smaller the population of a city or state, the fewer members of Congress it gets. For example, more than one in nine people in New York City are either undocumented themselves or living with someone who is. If they weren't counted in the census, the city would go from twelve to eleven congressional seats.

The prospect of an undercount was well covered as the citizenship question wound its way through the courts. But there's another, even more sweeping way a citizenship question could make congressional maps more Republican-leaning: if you know how many noncitizens there are, and where they live, you can argue that they shouldn't count as people when districts are being drawn.

Let me explain. As it stands, every congressional district must contain a population of about 730,000—not 730,000 voters, or adults, or citizens, but 730,000 human beings. This makes sense intuitively, because representatives are supposed to work on behalf of the people, not just the people eligible to vote. But nowhere in the Constitution does it specifically require that the population be counted this way. States are free to argue that each representative should represent an equal number of citizens, even if that means the total number of *inhabitants* would vary widely from district to district.

The goal here is not just to take undocumented immigrants out of the equation, as an undercount would do. It's to remove *every* noncitizen, including those who came here legally, from the mapmaking process. In some parts of the country, this would transform district lines. In CA-34, which takes up part of Los Angeles, 29 percent of the people living there are noncitizens. In TX-29, on the east side of Houston, it's 24 percent. If you removed noncitizens from the redistricting formula, the official "population" of these deep blue districts would suddenly be way too small. You'd have to expand their boundaries to capture more people, making them even more effective vote sinks than before.

As it happens, there won't be a citizenship question on this year's census. By a 5–4 vote, the Supreme Court threw it out on a technicality. But there's still the possibility that, thanks to the understandable terror sparked by Trump's proposed census change, we'll get an undercount. It is also possible—in fact, it's almost certain—that some states will look for other sources of citizenship data, and will try to use that data to exclude noncitizens when maps are drawn.

When such plans are put into motion, they will end up in court. And while the Supreme Court killed the citizenship question, it's likely that the next time, it won't do anything to stop politicians from weakening your vote. If anything, we can expect the Court to make gerrymandering even worse.

This is a big change for our democracy. It's also a very new one. As recently as 2018, despite the Court's one-vote conservative majority, the justices were willing to accept the possibility that partisan gerrymandering could go too far. If a state were so unfairly carved up that it held elections in name only, the courts could swoop in and demand a fairer map. The biggest concern for Anthony Kennedy, the swing justice in gerrymandering cases, was that such unfairness was hard to measure. That's one reason we have metrics like "efficiency gap" today. The Supreme Court asked Americans to create them.

But in 2018, Kennedy stepped down, Brett Kavanaugh replaced him, and everything changed. Rather than accepting or rejecting the new metrics they themselves had requested, the five conservative justices decided that the issue was simply not worth looking into. "Partisan gerrymandering claims present political questions beyond the reach of the federal courts," declared Chief Justice John Roberts in a 2019 opinion. Cleared of legal gobbledygook, that means that even if gerrymandering is a problem, the federal courts will no longer do anything about it.

☆

I don't want to sugarcoat the new position in which we find ourselves: even in a decade full of body blows to democracy, the Roberts Court's gerrymandering decision stands out. The simplest path to restoring the strength our votes have lost in my lifetime—a path that even a conservative Court seemed willing to provide—is now closed.

But the easy way to fight gerrymandering was never the only way. There's still a lot we can do to strengthen our votes.

One way to get started is in state courts rather than federal ones. Unlike our national Constitution, many state constitutions have clauses specifically protecting the rights of voters and the fairness of elections. In recent years, lawyers have successfully argued that gerrymandering violates these clauses. In Pennsylvania, for example, courts in 2018 threw out what was at the time the most blatantly partisan map in the nation. Courts in North Carolina did the same the following year.

In other states, voters have used ballot initiatives—the same tool that restored voting rights to Florida's ex-prisoners—to strip politicians of their mapmaking power. In California, for example, lawmakers can't weaken your vote even if they want to. Districts are drawn by a citizen commission explicitly prohibited from taking partisanship into account. Similar commissions are used in Washington State, Idaho, Arizona, and New Jersey.

Like many measures that would make elections fairer, independent redistricting has broad bipartisan support from voters. Just look at Ohio. It's one of the most heavily gerrymandered states in the country, and you might think Republican voters there would want to maintain their party's grip on power. But a ballot measure to shift a great deal of district-drawing power to a commission passed with 75 percent of the vote.

Of course, not every state gives its residents the chance to directly demand fairer maps. But even when ballot initiatives aren't a possibility, Americans can use their votes, slightly weakened though they may be, to undo some of gerrymandering's worst effects. It simply requires caring a lot more about local elections.

I write these words as we head into another election year that ends in zero. In some states—Indiana, Arkansas, South Carolina—the Republican hold on all three branches of government will not be broken in 2020. Voters in those states are in for another decade of unfair districts and wasted votes. But in other states, trifectas hang in the balance.

The most significant of these is Texas. If just nine state house seats flip from red to blue, something entirely possible given the suburbs' shift toward Democrats under Trump, Republicans would lose control of the chamber. Any new map in 2021 would need bipartisan support to pass. According to the FiveThirtyEight "Atlas of Redistricting," a map accurately reflecting Texas's partisan leanings would still be highly favorable to the GOP. But it would lead to a six-seat swing in Democrats' favor—and a lot fewer wasted votes among all Texans.

One of the secrets to the GOP's success ten years ago was the careful targeting of elections. REDMAP's operatives didn't try to flip everything. They worked hard to make sure every dollar spent on a candidate maximized the chances of either breaking a blue trifecta or establishing a red one. Those of us who want to see fair maps can do the same thing but in reverse. If you're ready to take a break from reading, and you're feeling generous, go donate a few bucks to a state legislative candidate who could make or break congressional maps for the next ten years. (If you don't know which candidates to support, google an organization called All On the Line, which was launched in order to help exactly answer those kinds of questions.)

As I write this, it's far too early to predict who will be in charge when 2021 redistricting gets under way. But seeing as how 2010 was historically awful for the Democratic Party, it seems quite possible that at least some of the maps drawn by Team Mitch will be replaced with maps that reflect both parties' input.

It is also certain that Democrats will have new trifectas of their own. The drawing of lots kept Shelly Simonds and her fellow Democrats from controlling all three branches of Virginia government in 2017, but they won them two years later. Which raises an important philosophical question: in blue states, where Democrats have full control of district-drawing power, how far should they go?

There is no easy answer. Some would argue Democrats should maximize their advantage this time around as ruthlessly as Republicans did ten years ago. But that approach seems destined to produce a Pyrrhic victory, undermining democracy in order to save it.

At the same time, the alternative—modeling good behavior by drawing districts that don't give the ruling party an edge—is equally unsatisfying. It's not even fairer. As an example, let's say Georgia maintains its current partisan gerrymander, which according to the FiveThirtyEight atlas gives Republicans about four extra seats. Let's also say that Virginia Democrats draw a perfectly non-partisan map. The new Virginia map would indeed close the power gap among voters within the state. The average Democratic vote and average Republican vote would be worth the same. But at the same time, by not balancing out Georgia's Republican lean, Virginia would be helping to maintain the partisan power gap in the nationwide election for congressional control.

The real question, then, is which election matters more, the local one to decide who represents a district, or the national one to decide who runs the House? And with all due respect to individual members of Congress, the answer is clearly the latter and not the former. As we'll see in a future chapter, even the savviest legislator can't get anything done when the other party is in charge.

That's why states of roughly equal size should hold hands to draw fair maps together. Virginia should offer a deal: we'll create completely nonpartisan districts so long as Georgia does the same. But if that deal is turned down, Virginia mapmakers, like mapmakers across the country, should do their best to create balance at the national level.

The closer we bring the tipping point district from red-leaning to truly neutral, the more representative America will be.

Of course, just as gerrymandering is only part of our political geography problem, ending gerrymandering is only part of the solution. We need to consider the broader map-skewing effects of the big sort— and we need to do something about them before they make fair maps even more difficult to draw than they are today.

Over the long term, the single best solution to the bubbling of America might be to switch to an electoral process known as "multimember districts with proportional representation." I don't know what it is about political reformers—whether they try to make ideas sound as dense as possible, or whether it's just habit—but in fact this tongue-twister of a system is fairly easy to grasp.

For an example, let's turn to the city of Los Angeles, which is currently represented by ten different members of Congress. Imagine that instead of ten districts represented by one member each, we switch to one district represented by ten members. On Election Day, each voter in this new megadistrict casts 10 votes. But here's the twist: each of those votes counts both for the person *and* the party who receives it. Let's say Democrats win 70 percent of the vote and Republicans win 30. In that case, the top seven Democratic vote-getters are sent to Washington, along with the top three Republicans. The percentage of seats matches the percentage of votes.

Megadistricts are the perfect solution to the Big Sort. Because they're proportional, there are almost no wasted votes. The bluer or redder your bubble, the more seats your party gets. At the same time, megadistricts give voice to the handful of people who live in a community of sameness but don't share its views. New York City would send at least one Republican to Congress. The Texas panhandle would send a Democrat. In both cases, we might be reminded that our country is less politically polarized than we might think.

Lest you dismiss these megadistricts as a purely theoretical exercise, you should know that several states already use them for their local legislatures. It seems to work. And even if, in the short term, most of us are still stuck in lopsided, single-member districts, there's still another electoral reform that can increase our votes' power.

In our current system, where five in six districts are uncompetitive, the winner of the November election is really chosen in a party primary months before. This is unsatisfying for lots of reasons. Turnout in primaries tends to be low. (Ted Cruz, for example owes his Senate career to a primary where just 9 percent of Texans showed up.) Those who do participate tend to hold more extreme views than general election voters. The parties themselves often go to great lengths to discourage turnout, and a few have rules that help candidates bypass primaries altogether.

You might think the solution would be third parties, which could challenge the Democrats and Republicans in charge. But in America, with our first-past-the-post system, independent candidates almost never have a chance. The best they can hope to do is serve as a spoiler, siphoning off enough votes from the Republican that the Democrat wins, or vice versa. The upshot of all this is that millions of voters have the following two options: vote for a nominee you didn't help pick in an election where the outcome isn't really in doubt, or throw away your vote on a third-party candidate. It's a deeply dispiriting choice.

Except in Maine. Because Maine uses something called "ranked-choice voting," and it's a way of making sure you can vote for the candidate you like most, and support whichever party you desire, without wasting your vote.

Rather than using a real-world example of how ranked-choice voting works, let's hold a mock election between the following four members of my household: our two tabby cats, Harry and Maisie; Florence, our goldfish; and Jacqui, my wife. When voters fill out their ballots, they'll start by picking their favorite candidate, just like you do on a typical ballot today. But they won't stop there. Next, they'll rank the remaining candidates in order—second choice, third choice, and fourth.

When the polls close, the first-choice votes are counted. If any candidate gets more than half, it's over. They win. But say an outright victory doesn't happen. Say that out of 100 voters, Harry gets 40, Jacqui gets 25, Maisie gets 20, and Florence gets 15. (She is a goldfish, after all.) In that case, anyone who voted for the last-place finisher—Florence—automatically gets to have their second choice count instead of their first.

Let's say that once voters initially on team Florence are redistributed, Harry has 41 votes, Maisie jumps up to 30, and Jacqui has just 29. Since there's still no candidate with a majority, we repeat the process with our new last-place finisher, Jacqui. And this time, perhaps because voters like Maisie's health care plan, or perhaps because Harry has a decidedly Trump-like tendency to grab people's butts, Jacqui's supporters choose Maisie over Harry by a 15-vote margin. The final count? 52 to 48. Maisie becomes our first female president, and our second orange one.

The beauty of ranked-choice voting (which I'd love to call "majority-rules voting," but the reformers never asked me) is that voters can express their preference without sacrificing their power. Walking into the booth, you don't have to engage in a series of strategic calculations to decide whether your preferred candidate is viable. You can just vote for them. At a minimum that should increase turnout, because voters can cast their ballots for the person who excites them most. In fact, in Maine, that's already happened: in 2018, Democrat Jared Golden lost the initial round of votes, but won a congressional seat after the second-choice ballots were counted. At least some of the voters who picked an Independent candidate first and Golden second would otherwise have chosen not to vote at all.

In 2019, New Yorkers overwhelmingly agreed to adopt majority-rules voting for citywide elections. As more states and cities hop on the bandwagon, and more Americans gain experience ranking their choices, it's not hard to see how third parties could experience a revival as a result. In blue bubbles, democratic socialists could challenge more business-friendly Democrats. In red bubbles, Never Trumpers might square off against whomever the president endorsed in a tweet. Because there's no chance of any candidate spoiling the outcome, voters would be free to choose their favorite.

In some cases, Independent candidates would not just compete, but win. And in all cases, Americans would walk into their polling places and cast votes that really mattered. The direction of our democracy would be decided by the will of the people, not the lines on the map.

Well, not a map of the House, anyway. Even if we rebalance the lower chamber, sanding down its partisan edges, that still leaves us with two other types of federal elections. When we pick our senators and presidents, there are no districts to be redrawn, no vote sinks to be shoehorned into, no Maptitude to carve us up. Yet when it comes to who wins the Senate and the White House, the gap between the strong voters and the weak ones is every bit as large as it is for the House.

There are plenty of reasons for this imbalance of power. And it all starts with a guy who had a booming voice, a silly name, and a serious problem with anger management.

6

MS. CODFISH'S CLASSROOM

The "Great Compromise"

The patriarch of the clan was named Gunning Bedford. His son was named Gunning Bedford, too. In 1747 this second Gunning Bedford fathered a third Gunning Bedford, who became known as Gunning Bedford Jr. despite quite clearly being Gunning Bedford III. Meanwhile, five years before Gunning Bedford Jr. came along, another of the first Gunning Bedford's children had a son whom he named Gunning Bedford, and who became known as Gunning Bedford Sr., even though he never had children of his own.

If this is all a bit confusing, just wait until you learn the names of five of Gunning Bedford Jr.'s cousins. They were named, respectively, Gunning Bedford, Gunning Bedford, Gunning Bedford, Gunning Bedford, and Gunning Bedford. In total there were nine Gunning Bedfords, all of them related, most of them living in the mid-Atlantic and alive simultaneously. It seems not to have occurred to this family that you could name a child Steve.

And yet Gunning Bedford Jr. (who was technically Gunning Bedford III) managed to stand out. He attended Princeton, ran a successful farm, campaigned to abolish slavery, and served as attorney general in his home state of Delaware. But the event that quite literally made his name—the reason Gunning Bedford Middle School in New Castle is named after him and not one of his family members—occurred in the summer of his fortieth year. Gunning Bedford Jr. was a delegate to the Constitutional Convention, and the rest of the Gunning Bedfords were not.

You've been taught that the American Constitution is a remarkable document, an achievement unmatched in human history. That is surely so. But a common mistake is to assume that because the final product was brilliant, the process that produced it must have been brilliant as well.

The truth is messier. Two weeks after the convention opened in Philadelphia, less than half of the thirteen state delegations had shown up. New Hampshire's would take two full months to arrive. Some delegates never bothered coming at all: of the seventy-four men chosen to shape their new nation's destiny, nineteen never attended a single session or debate, and only thirty stuck around from start to finish. (Among those who checked out early were two of the three delegates from New York, leaving a powerless Alexander Hamilton commenting loudly on the action like an asshole shouting at the screen in a movie theater.)

Like Hamilton, Gunning Bedford Jr. took his role as a delegate quite seriously, but unlike Hamilton, he was unenthused about the convention's work. Six years earlier, the Articles of Confederation had organized the thirteen former colonies into a genuine but loose alliance, a goose flock of completely sovereign states. As far as Delawareans were concerned, this was an excellent arrangement.

The alternative, meanwhile, was unthinkable. At the time, Maryland was home to about 300,000 people, and Pennsylvania about 400,000, while Delaware had fewer than 60,000. If the states merged into a single whole, Gunning Bedford Jr.'s teensy homeland would have barely any influence at all.

Hundreds of miles to the south, James Madison journeyed to the convention from Virginia—population approximately 730,000—with exactly the opposite view. He was dismayed by the unwieldly Articles of Confederation. He was determined to leave Philadelphia with a plan for a strong central government. He was also, as it happens, Gunning Bedford Jr.'s college roommate.

The historical record has little to say about Madison and Bedford's Princeton days, whether one of them snored loudly or barged in without noticing a sock on the door. But try to put yourself in Gunning's shoes. Imagine undertaking the most important task of your life, a monumental responsibility entrusted to you by the people of your state. Imagine knowing that the future of that state hangs in the balance, that you are the only person standing between 60,000 Delawareans and a campaign to rob them of their sovereignty. Now imagine that the leader of the crusade against you is a guy who had absolutely no respect for the chore chart. No wonder Gunning Bedford Jr. was pissed.

Most infuriating of all, the Virginians got to Philadelphia early. By the time everyone else arrived to consider whether the country even needed a Constitution, James Madison had already written a first draft. Then, proving that overachievers have been making group projects unbearable for centuries, he offered a suggestion. Seeing as how his proposal was already finished, maybe it would make a useful jumping-off point?

Madison's "Virginia Plan" was everything Bedford feared. Where some delegates wanted to keep a central feature of the Articles—that each state got an equal number of representatives in Congress— Madison proposed a system where power was allotted by population instead. A giant like Virginia would get bundles of lawmakers while a munchkin like Delaware would be left with almost none. Bedford parried and thrusted, offering objections to his former roommate's plan, but his ideas went nowhere.

By all accounts, Gunning Bedford Jr. was not, even under the best of circumstances, the tranquil type. Tall and fleshy with a booming voice, he was a kind of human volcano, and it didn't take much to trigger an eruption. Now here was Madison, with a new Constitution that would not just diminish Delaware's power in Congress but erase it. After a month of debate, this unthinkable idea was growing steadily more popular. Bedford had been pushed as far as he could go, and taking the floor in Philadelphia, he thundered words that would make him famous, or at least Delaware famous.

"You dare not dissolve the confederation! If you do, the small states will find some foreign ally of more honor and good faith who will take them by the hand and do them justice."

Bedford's ultimatum was couched in old-timey language, but this was a serious threat. He was not merely suggesting that Delaware would reject Madison's plan. He was warning his fellow delegates that, just four years after a bloody war to win independence from Britain, his state would leave America behind and seek a new European partner. On its own, Delaware was fairly scrawny. But as a vassal of Spain, France, or England, it could reestablish foreign dominance over the continent.

Fortunately, that didn't happen. Fearful of leaving Philadelphia empty-handed, large and small states made a deal. The House of Representatives would dole out lawmakers proportionally, just as Madison wanted. But in the upper chamber, every state would receive "equality of votes"—the same number of senators, regardless of population.

Your high school history textbook likely referred to this arrangement as "the Great Compromise," a phrase implying enlightened consensus. The delegates set aside their differences, put the good of the new nation first, and came up with a plan everybody was willing to get behind.

Nothing could be further from the truth. The only way the Great Compromise could have been less popular is if it hadn't passed at all.

Of the ten state delegations then present when the compromise was voted on, five supported the deal. Four, including Madison's Virginia, opposed it. By convention rules, a 5–5 split meant a rejected proposal, so everything came down to the tenth and final state. If a majority of its four delegates supported the compromise, it would pass. If a majority opposed the compromise, it would fail.

It's hard to imagine just how different the past few hundred years would have been had three of those four delegates voted no. It's quite likely the Constitution would never have been signed, the United States of America would not exist, and the French protectorate of Delaware would now be massing troops along the Maryland border. Of course, it's also possible that Madison would have brought his fellow delegates around. Power in America today would be entirely tied to population, as it is in nearly every other democracy.

We'll never know. The deciding state didn't endorse the Great Compromise, but it didn't reject it, either. Instead, its delegation split 2–2, resulting in a tie. By a final vote of 5–4–1, Madison's dream of a purely proportional democracy had been shattered. Gunning Bedford Jr. was a very happy man.

And now for a strange coincidence: when the Great Compromise was put to a vote, the deciding state was Massachusetts. And the deciding vote, the one that created the 2–2 split and sprang our current Congress into being? It belonged to Elbridge Gerry. Gerry was not really responsible for upsetting the balance of power in the House, despite the phrase that bears his name. But he was absolutely responsible for upsetting the balance of power in the Senate. Thanks to his vote, every state would receive an equal amount of power in the upper chamber, no matter how large or small its population grew.

To understand the full implications of the Great Compromise, let's leave Philadelphia for just a moment and return to the world of student government. Imagine, if you will, a student body of 100 kids divided among four classrooms. Ms. Apple has three students; Mr. Albright has seven; Mr. Baker has twenty-five; and Ms. Codfish a whopping sixty-five. Now let's say that, when it's time for student government elections, each classroom picks one representative regardless of its population—an "equality of votes" like the one found in the U.S. Senate.

If students were evenly distributed, every classroom would look like Mr. Baker's: it would contain one-quarter of the voters (25) and elect one-quarter of the representatives (1). But the students *aren't* evenly distributed. Ms. Apple's class contains just 3 percent of the children, and Mr. Albright's contains 7 percent, while the densely populated Codfish classroom contains a full 65 percent of the student body. Yet each classroom picks the same number of representatives, despite their large variations in size.

Three People,
One Vote

Sixty-Five People,
One Vote

What does this arrangement mean for our young voters? First, your vote's power depends on the size of the class you're in. The mighty Apple students each elect one-third of a representative, while the lowly Codfish pupils elect only one-sixty-fifth. When the student government convenes, the preferences of Ms. Apple's students will therefore matter about twenty-two times more than Ms. Codfish's.

Second, we can place each classroom into one of three categories, which we'll call "average," "weak," or "strong." Average classrooms look like Mr. Baker's: their percentage of the population is exactly equal to the percentage of representatives they elect. Weak classrooms look like Ms. Codfish's: their percentage of the population is *higher* than their percentage of representatives. Finally, strong classrooms look like

Apple's or Albright's: their percentage of the population is *lower* than their percentage of representatives.

Importantly, our imaginary school contains twice as many strong classrooms as weak ones, yet 65 students—well over half the total—have a vote that is weaker than average, while only 10 students have a vote that is strong. The structure of our government disadvantages the vast majority of voters at the expense of a few.

It was precisely this kind of power gap that none other than Alexander Hamilton decried in Philadelphia 233 years ago. "As states are a collection of individual men, which ought we to respect most, the rights of the people composing them, or the artificial beings resulting from the composition?" he asked. And then, in Hamiltonian fashion, he answered his own question. "Nothing could be more preposterous or absurd than to sacrifice the former to the latter."

Yet that is precisely what the Framers did. In order to preserve equal power among the states, they created unequal power among the people within them. By giving each state two senators, the Convention's delegates ensured that when the Senate was gaveled into order, the voters of tiny Delaware would be the nation's strongest. Madison's Virginia, with thirteen times Delaware's population, would be the equivalent of Ms. Codfish's classroom. The preferences of each Virginian would count far less than the preferences of each Delawarean when the chamber debated laws.

Even as the Great Compromise neared passage, some Framers sounded the alarm. Congress was about to commit "a fundamental and perpetual error," warned Pennsylvanian James Wilson, likening the Senate's structure to a poison that "must be followed by disease, convulsions, and finally death itself."

Was Wilson right? Or had Gunning Bedford Jr. saved his state and laid the groundwork for America's remarkable success? We'll spend the rest of this chapter figuring that out.

But before we turn to the ways the Great Compromise has affected our country, and affects it today, let's not lose sight of how we ended up here in the first place. The two-senators-per-state rule didn't come about because most Framers believed it was a good idea. It came about because most Framers believed they had no choice. A flawed Constitution was better than no Constitution at all. What we refer to today as the Great Compromise should really be called the Bedford Decree: give each state two senators, or Delaware teams up with Europe to vanquish the United States.

Not to sound too self-congratulatory, but if the paragraphs you just read had been published 118 years ago, perhaps Senator George Frisbie Hoar wouldn't have made such an ass of himself. "The fact that a City or State or Town is a moral being, with a life of its own and a quality of its own is one of the great secrets of Constitutional Liberty," the Massachusetts Republican proclaimed in a 1902 speech. "Our ancestors recognized the American States as equals in these qualities, and did not apportion political power according to the mere brute force of numbers."

As we know now, this is nonsense. Our ancestors apportioned the upper chamber in an act of pragmatic horse-trading, not enlightened principle. That said, it's unlikely any amount if historical evidence would have changed George Frisbie Hoar's mind. After all, his fellow Republicans had controlled the Senate for thirty-five of the forty-one years prior to his speech. Clearly, ignoring the "mere brute force of numbers" was working well for Senator Hoar.

I'm not saying Hoar deliberately lied when he lauded the Senate's structure. I am, however, saying that asking politicians to admit they don't deserve their power is like asking a ten-year-old to admit the tooth fairy isn't real. On one hand, it doesn't quite stand to reason that a flying magical beast would break into your house and trade your bones for cash. On the other hand, there's a very powerful incentive to believe.

Seen in that light, Hoar's turn-of-the-century speech was a masterpiece in tooth fairy logic. By rewriting history—replacing the messy reality of the Bedford Decree with the myth of the Great Compromise—the senator wasn't merely sanitizing Delaware's long-ago demand for power. He was justifying a far more recent power grab on behalf of his fellow Republicans.

To fully understand that power grab, we must first examine one of the Bedford Decree's many side effects: it made expanding the union fraught with peril. Newly admitted states contained few people, so in the House of Representatives, their presence was barely noticed. In the Senate, however, new states received the exact same two votes as everyone else. If a territory favored one faction over another, granting it statehood could tip the balance of power to that side.

In America's first decades, the two great factions vying for control were not partisan, but regional. Northern free states were on one side, southern slave states on the other. To stave off conflict and maintain balance in the Senate, new states were generally admitted in twos. Indiana joined with Mississippi; Illinois with Alabama; Arkansas with Michigan.

When a partner territory couldn't be found, in at least one case it was manufactured. In 1819, Missouri wanted to enter the union as a slave state, but America had run out of northern land to use as counterweight. To maintain the balance between slave and free states (and therefore between slave and free senators), Massachusetts detached its large, woodsy, sparsely populated holding to the north like a lizard abandoning its tail. The new territory of Maine was quickly admitted as a free state, and Missouri received statehood the following year.

This delicate balance, which wobbled in the 1850s, collapsed entirely in the run-up to the Civil War. As southern states broke off from the union and took their senators with them, the chamber flipped to President Lincoln's young political party. At the start of 1859, Democrats held a twelve-seat lead over Republicans. By the beginning of 1863, Republicans held a twenty-three-seat lead over Democrats in the Senate, with a similarly massive advantage in the House. The Civil War was many things: great moral reckoning, test of a nation conceived in liberty, tragic loss of human life. But it was also a terrific time to be a Republican in Congress.

Almost immediately—simultaneous to funding the war, long before freeing any slaves—the new legislative majority began strategically creating new states. Three months before the first shots were fired at Fort Sumter, they admitted the free state of Kansas. Soon after, they began slicing West Virginia from its parent. In just four years, notes Barry Weingast and Charles Stewart III, "Congress passed 15 major statutes affecting territorial boundaries or enabling states to enter the union."* Lawmakers carved up America to gerrymander the Senate, in much the same way lawmakers carved up states to gerrymander the House.

I should be very clear here that I'm not on the Democrats' side. If you abandon our republic in an attempt to continue owning human beings, you don't get to complain when the political map becomes unfair. That said, Abraham Lincoln's Republicans were a devious bunch. And there is no better example of their deviousness than Nevada.

As author Mark Stein recounts in *How the States Got Their Shapes*, in 1859, silver and gold were found in the western Utah Territory. Thanks to good old-fashioned religious prejudice, Congress didn't want the Mormons getting their hands on any treasure, so they chopped away the newly valuable chunk of Utah and named it after the nearest mountain range. In Weingast and Stewart's description, the Nevada Territory boasted "virtually no population, a violent and corrupt history, an unstable economy based on mining, and little prospect for the development of a strong military base." By no reasonable measure did Nevada deserve statehood.

Yet Nevada had one resource that Lincoln's allies craved even more than precious metals: Republicans. The miners and outlaws who

---

* You may recognize the name Charles Stewart III from his studies of voting lines, which were frequently referenced in chapter 4.

flocked to the new territory, violent and corrupt though they were, reliably supported the president. With the 1864 elections looking to be a nail-biter, the president needed all the supporters he could get.

More specifically, Lincoln needed all the electoral votes he could get. We'll dig into the Electoral College in the next chapter, but for now, keep in mind that each state gets one electoral vote per senator and one more per representative, for a minimum of three. In 1864, 107 electoral votes were sufficient to win the White House, so a new state could supply nearly 3 percent of the winning total—enough to decide a close race.

By historical precedent, new states had to contain at least as many people as the least-populous state at the time of their admission. The Nevada Territory had less than one-fifth of the requisite number, and in fact would not cross the traditional population threshold until 1970. The Utah Territory, meanwhile, had more than enough people and seemed primed for statehood. But the Utahns were Democrats and mostly Mormon and the Nevadans were Republicans and mostly not. In March 1864, Congress passed an "enabling act" allowing Nevada to enter the union. On October 31, Abraham Lincoln formally recognized the new state. Just eight days later, Nevadans returned the favor and supported Lincoln.

The 1864 election didn't wind up a nail-biter after all—a third-party candidate dropped out, and Honest Abe won in a landslide—but Nevada and its two new senators were here to stay. So were several others. After the war, when southern Democrats straggled back to the Senate, they found a total of six new colleagues, all Republicans, hailing from states that had not existed when they left. At the exact moment when the North-South divide was replaced by a Republican-Democrat one, Republicans started out with a big advantage.

In the following decades, they pressed that advantage further. While Democrats controlled the House for much of the 1870s and 1880s, making admission of new states impossible, in 1888, Republicans won the national version of a state trifecta—control of the White

House, the House, and the Senate. By this point, five territories had crossed the population threshold for statehood: New Mexico, Montana, and long-suffering Utah leaned Democratic; Washington and Dakota leaned Republicans. The gentlemanly thing to do would have been to admit all five, a 3–2 split in Democrats' favor.

Instead, the newly triumphant Republicans offered the following proposal: forget about New Mexico and Utah, grant statehood to Washington and Montana, and turn the Dakota Territory into not one state, but two. This meant a 3–1 split for Republicans. But Democrats, concerned the alternative might be even worse, took the deal. In 1890, Congress added Idaho, and two more Republican senators, to the total.

All of which is to say that in 1902, when George Frisbie Hoar told his audience that every state was a unique "moral being," he should have known better. By the turn of the twentieth century, the Bedford Decree had been flipped on its head. Delaware got two senators because it was a state; North Dakota was made a state so that it could get two senators. "It is a contest for power, not for liberty," complained Alexander Hamilton, when the idea of giving each state the same number of senators was first proposed. America's first century had proven him right.

America's second century would prove him righter still.

☆

"One Person, One Vote" sounds essential and enduring, as fundamental to our freedom as "Life, Liberty, and the Pursuit of Happiness." In fact, "One Person, One Vote" is younger than George Clooney.

Our origin story begins with a shift that took place around the turn of the last century. In 1890, the year Idaho was added to the union to bolster Republican fortunes, 35 percent of Americans lived in urban areas. By 1900 that number had risen to 40 percent, and by 1910 it was 46 percent. The writing was on the wall: cities would soon hold a majority of Americans. In the kind of government James Madison had envisioned, they would have a majority of the lawmakers, too.

Just as Gunning Bedford Jr. had been terrified about the distribution of power among the states, rural legislators became increasingly concerned about the way power would soon be distributed within them. For many incumbents, an urbanizing population was a demographic death sentence. With each redistricting cycle, growing cities would add new seats, squeezing the old guard out.

To which James Wilson, the Pennsylvanian who compared the Bedford Decree to a deadly poison, would have said: Well, yeah! A democracy is supposed to represent the people; when the people move, the centers of power should move with them. But politicians desperate to keep their jobs didn't share that view.

In Tennessee, for example, where the state constitution required districts to be redrawn to reflect the population, lawmakers came up with a novel approach to their obligation. They ignored it. All through the 1900s, the 1910s, 1920s, and so on, the state's legislative boundaries remained unchanged. Meanwhile, the migration to cities continued. Populations of urban districts in Memphis and Nashville soared, in some cases ballooning to twenty-five times the size of their rural counterparts. Yet despite having starkly different numbers of voters, each district elected the exact same number of representatives. The cities had been turned into Ms. Codfish's classroom. The rural incumbents were saved.

You might think Tennessee's blatant disregard for its own laws was an exception. In fact, it was the rule. From 1921 to 1941, there were two redistricting cycles, one per decade, which meant all forty-eight states then in the union were required to drew new maps twice. Only seven actually did so.

Political reformers, with their typical creative flourish, describe this deliberate skewing of district populations as "malapportionment." (The word derives from the Latin "mal," which means "bad," and the English "apportionment," which means "apportionment.") By the early 1960s, most Americans had indeed migrated to cities—but thanks to malapportionment, political power hadn't migrated with them. Maricopa

County, Arizona, which contained the city of Phoenix and more than half the state's population, elected just one-third of the state's representatives to Congress. "One state senator represented Los Angeles County, which had a population of more than 6 million people," write authors Seth Stern and Stephen Wermiel, "while another represented three northern California rural counties with a total population of 14,294." Author Anthony Lewis provides an example from Connecticut: "177,000 citizens of Hartford elected two members of the state House of Representatives; so did the town of Colebrook, population 592."

In the malapportionment sweepstakes that was 1960s America, the grand prize surely went to New Hampshire. There, one assemblyman represented a constituency of—wait for it—three. A vote from a member of this lucky trio was worth *108,000 times* more than a vote from a fellow New Hampshirite living just miles away. New Hampshire's map was ludicrous.

But was New Hampshire's ludicrous map unconstitutional? For most of the century, the Supreme Court declined to say. In 1946, Justice Felix Frankfurter declared that district drawing was a question best left entirely to politicians, and thus was not for courts to decide. That opinion stood for fifteen years.

In 1961, however, a Republican from a Memphis suburb decided to try again. His name was Charles Baker, and he argued that his ballot's strength had been so badly diminished it violated his constitutional right to equal protection under the law.

William Brennan, a liberal appointed just five years before Baker's lawsuit, was eager to side with Baker and his fellow voters. Felix Frankfurter, who was not just the author of the twenty-year-old decision defending malapportionment, but also Brennan's former law professor, was equally eager to side with Tennessee. Each judge convinced three colleagues to join him. The Court seemed destined for a 5–4 split, although no one knew which side would win.

Then something rather extraordinary occurred. To bolster his argument against Charles Baker's claim, Frankfurter asked an ally, Justice Tom Clark, to write about all the ways the people could reclaim political power that didn't require turning to the courts. Clark dutifully went off to compile a list of available remedies.

A few weeks later, a shaken Clark reported his conclusion to Frankfurter: no such remedies existed. The democratic process had been so thoroughly undermined that it could no longer correct itself. Clark switched sides, giving Brennan a majority. The previously undecided Potter Stewart soon signed on as well, and another Frankfurter ally grew so comprehensively stressed from the *Baker* debate that he succumbed to exhaustion and stepped down. Thus, by a 6–2 vote, the Court decided for the plaintiff in *Baker v. Carr.*

Brennan never said what, exactly, was required of legislative districts or the politicians who drew them. He didn't even give Charles Baker his voting power back. All his decision said was that beyond a certain point, making some votes worth less than others violated the Constitution. As Court opinions go, it was extraordinarily vague.

It was also, almost immediately, one of the most consequential judgements in American history. In the months after the *Baker* decision, lawsuits were filed in twenty-two states, and districts were knocked down in a dozen of them. Georgia's "county unit system," which assigned lawmakers by county in order to hobble urban centers like Atlanta, was soon found unconstitutional as well. In 1964, the justices declared that congressional districts must have roughly equal population so that "One person's vote in a congressional election is to be worth as much as another's," and they soon extended this principle to state legislatures as well. As former Bill Clinton speechwriter Michael Waldman notes in *The Fight to Vote*, 93 of 99 state legislative maps were redrawn in just four years. "One Person, One Vote" had swept America.

Even now, when One Person, One Vote is the law of the land and a frequently cited principle, it's important to be very clear about what it does and doesn't mean. As we've seen, politicians can still waste or weaken their constituents' votes through gerrymandering. They can strip those with criminal records of their voting rights or cull eligible citizens from the rolls in a sweeping purge.

What they cannot do, however, is use George Frisbie Hoar's argument that places are moral beings to make some voters' ballots worth more than others'. As Chief Justice Earl Warren rather nicely put it, "Legislators represent people, not trees or acres." While Warren oversaw a slew of consequential decisions, not least the one in *Brown v. Board of Education* that ended school segregation, he later called *Baker v. Carr* the single most important opinion issued by his court.

Yet for all the dozens of legislatures re-formed in the wake of William Brennan's opinion, one legislative body remains stubbornly unchanged. In the U.S. Senate, legislators still represent acres instead of people. One Person, One Vote does not apply. To give Delaware two senators apiece is a perfect example of malapportionment, quite literally a textbook case.

The reason the U.S. Senate has not been changed is that, unlike every other part of the American political process, it is impervious to all efforts to change it. In Article V of the Constitution, the Framers made a final, crucial concession to states like Delaware: they agreed that the Senate's structure could never be undone. The Bedford Decree is the only provision in the entire Constitution that cannot be changed for any reason, not even by amendment. If we wanted to switch to a fully Madisonian Congress, we would have to tear up our bedrock document and start from scratch.

As a result, for most of George Clooney's lifetime, and yours as well, America has been the home of a glaring political irony. Conceived under duress, expanded via backroom cunning, the U.S. Senate is blatantly unconstitutional. Or at least it would be, if the Constitution didn't go out of its way to protect it.

Strange way to run a country.

☆

So how come the Bedford Decree hasn't blown up in our faces the way its early critics predicted it would? After all, if James Wilson was right, and the Senate was a "fundamental and perpetual error," you certainly wouldn't know it from American history. In the 230 years since Wilson's warning, we've done extraordinary things despite, or maybe even because of, our malapportionment of senators. It's true no other democracy organizes its upper chamber quite the way we do. But no other democracy can boast our centuries of success. It appears Wilson's doomsday prediction never came true.

A closer inspection, however, reveals a rather important qualifier: Wilson's prediction hasn't come true *yet*. If you look at the way the impact of the Bedford Decree has in recent decades, it's hard not to reach the distressing conclusion that a worked-up, long-dead Pennsylvanian had it right. Malapportionment in the Senate is a ticking time bomb. And after more than two centuries without an explosion, time is running out.

To understand why the Bedford Decree now puts our democracy in such danger, we should start with something rather obvious: our country has more people than it used to. For every American alive when the Constitution was ratified, there are ninety-two of us alive today. But that growth has not been evenly distributed. Like a gangly teenager, our country has expanded in profoundly asymmetrical ways.

On one hand, as a percentage of the population, the big states have become much bigger. When James Madison arrived in Philadelphia, the most populous 20 percent of states held 36 percent of the country's people. Today, the most populous 20 percent of states hold more than half. The low-population states, meanwhile, haven't kept up. They've grown, of course. Delaware in 1790 had 59,000 residents; it has more now. But as a fraction of the country's population, Delaware is five times *smaller* today than it was when Gunning Bedford Jr. threatened to join forces with France or Spain.

And don't even get me started on Wyoming. Not to be rude to Wyoming natives—in my limited experience, you're quite generous and friendly—but there are barely any of you. The odds of a random American sharing your birthday are much, much higher than the odds of them living in Wyoming. As a percentage of the national population, rounded to the nearest one-half of one percent, Wyoming doesn't exist. (Neither, for that matter, does Alaska, North Dakota, or Vermont.) If America were a two-hour-long movie, Wyoming would be just twelve seconds.

This gap in state's population sizes—and therefore in voters' relative power—would have surely stunned even Gunning Bedford Jr. When the first Senate was elected, the population of the biggest state was thirteen times that of the smallest. Today that number has gone up to sixty-eight. In the government James Madison envisioned, Wyoming's voters would send less than one-fifth of one senator to Washington, and California's voters would send twelve. Instead, both groups send two.

Nor is it just Wyoming voters who have extraordinary levels of power relative to their state's population. Remember Charles Baker, the man whose lawsuit against his native Tennessee led to "One Person, One Vote"? Under the political map he sued over—a map so insulting to the democratic process that the Court had no choice but to throw it out—60 percent of the state senators were elected by 37 percent of the voters. In America today, 60 percent of U.S. senators are elected by just 24 percent of the voters. Our current democracy is less representative than Tennessee's in 1961.

The Great Compromise always entailed some unfairness. That's not new. What's new is the extent of the unfairness. The power gap between voters from big and small states has never been so great.

Meanwhile, the most persuasive argument in favor of the Great Compromise—that every state's interests are unique, and therefore require their own representation in the Senate—has never been less compelling. It's not that your home state doesn't matter. It's that your home state matters far less than it used to. Local interests are increasingly being replaced by national ones.

This brings us to the subject of roads. We all know cars and planes and highways didn't exist in the 1700s. But we rarely stop to consider how utterly different—how much more stretched and distant—our landscape used to be. Traveling between towns was a headache. Traveling between states was something akin to an expedition.

Even the best American roads were pretty terrible, made of sand, gravel, or clay that turned to mud in the rain. Thomas Jefferson, who obsessed over road conditions the way a modern frequent flyer might rate airport lounges, described one particularly unfortunate byway as "frog-eaten." I have no idea what frog-eaten roads look like, but I can promise that you wouldn't enjoy them. Jefferson certainly didn't. On one occasion he left Philadelphia, and, after six days of hard, nonstop travel, finally arrived . . . in Baltimore. Today that trip takes under two hours.

So when Gunning Bedford Jr. acted as though his state was distant and isolated from its neighbors, he had a point. Everywhere was. For all their imagination and foresight, the Framers could never have envisioned a country as connected as the one we live in today. In less time than it took Jefferson to get from Philly to Baltimore, we can travel to the moon and back.

Nor is it just people who cross state lines far more easily. Information travels instantly, which is one reason Americans increasingly consume national rather than local news. Goods, services, and supply chains snake from coast to coast. Companies have far-flung plants and offices, which mean far-flung political interests, as well. A senator can meet with constituents from her hometown, fly across the country for a fundraiser, be lobbied by a multinational corporation, do a television interview that reaches more than 95 percent of American households, and send out an email soliciting donations from supporters in all fifty states—all on the same day.

As our economy and culture have become more national than

local, so has our politics. As recently as fifty years ago, a (D) or (R) beside a senator's name was only one of many crucial bits of information about them. To guess how they might vote on issues, there was a lot more you'd have to know.

But that began to change in the 1970s. For reasons that aren't worth getting into, the parties went from being bottom-up assortments of state organizations to top-down nationwide ones. Also, for reasons that are very worth getting into but not until a future chapter, ideology began to matter far more than regional or individual quirks where politics was concerned. Today, every single Republican senator is more conservative than every single Democratic one—that's almost never happened before.

One way we can tell that place matters less, and that party matters more, is by looking at the number of states whose Senate delegations have gone entirely red or blue. When I was born, twenty-three states—nearly half—had one senator from each party. Today that number is down to just nine. In the few states that still split their Senate delegations, the Republican and Democrat vote as though they're from completely different places. In a way, they are. Regionalism has been replaced by partisanship as the great American political divide.

This brings us to the third and most important reason James Wilson's doom-and-gloom prediction has begun to look alarmingly accurate. At a time when small states have never been stronger, big states have never been weaker, and national partisanship has never been more intense, the Great Compromise decisively favors one party over the other.

Remember our hypothetical student government election, with its strong and weak classrooms? America is similarly divided. Every state accounts for two of the Senate's one hundred members, or 2 percent. If your state's population makes up more than 2 percent of America, your vote is therefore weaker than average. If your state's population makes up less than 2 percent of America, your vote is stronger.

By a margin of thirty-three states to seventeen, our country is home to more strong states than weak ones. But just as in our school, where 65 of the 100 students were taught by the profoundly overwhelmed Ms. Codfish, the vast majority of Americans live in a place where their votes count less than you'd expect. Weak states account for 69 percent of America's population, but only 34 percent of its senators.

If the weak and strong states voted identically, the Bedford Decree would cause much less trouble (and this chapter would be something of a letdown). But in fact, the two groups don't vote the same way at all. The current Senate split is fifty-three Republicans to forty-seven Democrats. But if the entire country behaved like the weak-voting states do, Democrats would currently hold a Senate majority of fifty-nine to forty-one. That's a swing of *twenty-four* Senate seats. Voters with below-average power, in other words, are far more likely to vote for Democrats.

The reason for this partisan imbalance lies in the same Big Sort that has weakened Democrats' votes for the House. If your city is home to lots of people—if it's the size of say, Atlanta, Chicago, Los Angeles, or New York—then your state is, by definition, home to lots of people as well. The fact that a disproportionate number of Democrats live in America's largest cities also means a disproportionate number of Democrats live in America's more populous states. And thanks to a deal struck more than two centuries ago, living in one of America's more populous states diminishes the power of your vote.

To put this another way, America's states are much more red-leaning than America's people. In the 2016 election, Hillary Clinton prevailed among voters by a margin of 2 percent. But among states, Trump won thirty to Clinton's twenty, a winning margin of 20 percent. In 2016, states were twenty-two points more Republican than voters.

The partisan nature of the Great Compromise is the reason the tipping point state leans Republican. (You'll recall the idea of the political "tipping point" from the last chapter, when we applied it to the House: if Democrats win the tipping point plus everything to the left, they win control of the chamber; the same is true for Republicans if they win the tipping point plus everything to the right.) The current tipping point state has a PVI of R+3. Just as in the House, Democrats cannot win a Senate majority with blue and swing states alone. They must win at the least some red ones.

When you understand this basic fact—that the average senator is more conservative than the average American—many political mysteries suddenly become clear. Why don't we have universal background checks for firearms purchases? Why is beer enthusiast Brett Kavanaugh a Supreme Court justice? Why is it so hard to fight climate change, even during the brief periods when Democrats have full control of government? When Americans want one thing and Washington does another, we tend to blame individual senators. But we'd be far better off blaming the structure of the Senate itself.

The Bedford Compromise has been with us for our country's entire history. But the role it plays in our government today, driving a wedge between the will of the people and the actions of their leaders, makes a centuries-old deal in Philadelphia more damaging now than ever before.

Somewhere, James Wilson's ghost is feeling vindicated. *Tick. Tick. Tick.*

So that's depressing. Even more depressing is that, unlike every other topic discussed in this book, the Senate's underlying structure is impossible to change.

But just because there's no way to completely eliminate the power gap between voters of different parties doesn't mean we're out of options. All we need to do is bring back the idea our ancestors employed two hundred years ago: when the balance of the Senate is threatened, admit new states to even things out. According to the Partisan Voting Index, there are currently twenty-seven red-leaning states and nineteen blue-leaning ones. If we want our country to better reflect the will of the people, we need to close that gap.

The question is where these new states would come from, and history offers at least two suggestions. The first is what I'll call "The Nevada Plan." We could ignore population sizes and admit tiny territories as a way to influence the Senate. Guam and the U.S. Virgin Islands are small by Wyoming standards, but there's nothing in the Constitution barring them from statehood.

The second option is what I'll call "The Massachusetts Plan": An existing state could carve itself into two or more pieces, and Congress could then award statehood to each. The most comprehensive and ambitious of these proposals is detailed by David Faris in *It's Time to Fight Dirty*. He suggests dividing California into seven states, each of them likely to send two Democrats to the Senate.

Here I must admit something. I originally looked into Faris's ideas because I thought they were crazy and power-mad, and I wanted to show you how reasonable I was by rejecting them. Then I ran the numbers. Imagine you added Faris's six new states, plus Guam, plus American Samoa, and that every one of these states was as liberal as California is today. Even then, the Senate *still* wouldn't favor Democrats. The tipping point state would be New Hampshire, with a neutral Partisan Voting Index of 0. That doesn't sound like fighting dirty. It sounds like fighting fair.

That said, it also sounds a bit theoretical rather than practical. Californians don't seem eager to splinter their state into seven blue pieces, and extending statehood to a territory of 100,000 inhabitants would make the overall malapportionment of senators even worse. If, a decade or two from now, the Senate remains woefully biased toward one party, then by all means we ought to consider dramatic measures to narrow the gap. The Massachusetts and Nevada plans are worth real consideration—at the very least, they remind Americans that the Great Compromise is a problem to be solved, not an achievement to be lauded. But ideally, we'll never need to put those plans into practice.

Particularly because D.C. is just sitting there. I'm not exactly objective about the District of Columbia's status, since I've resided there for over a decade. But at the same time, I can tell you from experience how profoundly strange it is to know that you live in America, pay all its taxes, could go to prison under its laws, and yet have absolutely no representation in Congress.

I still go through the motions. Every two years, I trudge to a nearby community center or school. I scan my driver's license. I touch a bunch of buttons on the screen. I get my sticker and post a picture of it on Instagram so everyone can see "I Voted." But when it comes to electing lawmakers, I really didn't. Washington gets one "non-voting representative" and two "shadow senators." Congress allows these people in the building but doesn't officially recognize the offices they hold.

If James Madison and Gunning Bedford Jr. could witness the plight of D.C.'s residents today, the former roommates would surely put aside their differences and roll together in their graves. In 1810, when D.C. was first counted as a separate entity in the census, it had about one-fifth the population of the smallest state. Today, its population is about one-fifth *larger* than that of the smallest state. Disenfranchising D.C. isn't like disenfranchising the U.S. Virgin Islands. It's like disenfranchising Vermont.

Even more vexing to Madison and Bedford would be D.C.'s tax status. As every District resident knows, D.C. license plates read, "No Taxation Without Representation." But for D.C.-ers, unlike their revolutionary forebears, this phrase is less a slogan than a fact of life. Despite having no say in our federal tax laws, D.C.'s residents pay federal taxes. In fact, they pay a *lot* of taxes, contributing more to the Treasury than Oklahoma, Alabama, Kansas, Nebraska, Iowa, Utah, Nevada, Delaware, Rhode Island, New Hampshire, Mississippi, and eleven others.

This arrangement—paying lots of taxes and getting no representation in return—is quite literally second-class citizenship, and people living in Washington have long demanded an end to it. The District of Columbia itself could be preserved. The White House, the Supreme Court, and the Congress would remain on federal land. But the area surrounding the district, an area home to large and growing numbers of people, would be fashioned into a brand-new state.

The that hasn't happened yet fairly simple: most people who would live in that new state aren't white. For nearly all of D.C.'s history, it would have been the first majority-Black state in the union. Even now, after decades of gentrification, D.C. would join Hawaii as the only other state with a white population under 50 percent. Just as Utah was once denied statehood because its residents were Democrats and Mormons, D.C. is today denied statehood because its residents are Democrats and brown or Black.

If you're looking for possible new states, another obvious candidate is Puerto Rico. Puerto Rico's population is far bigger than Washington, D.C.'s. In fact, there are more Puerto Ricans than there are Iowans or Kansans. Nor should Puerto Rico's location prove any barrier to statehood; the island is far closer to the U.S. mainland than Alaska or Hawaii.

When I was a kid learning about the fifty states, I was taught that Puerto Rico didn't want to join them. That was true—when I was a kid. Today the situation's more complicated, but public opinion seems to be trending clearly in the direction of statehood. The final decision should, of course, be up to the Puerto Rican people. But American people who believe in representative democracy should be rooting for, and advocating for, the island to become a state.

Mitch McConnell certainly has no qualms about advocating *against* statehood. To extend voting rights to people living in Puerto Rico and D.C., he recently told Fox News's Laura Ingraham, would be "fullbore socialism." Interestingly that's the exact same objection southern segregationists had to admitting Hawaii as a state in the 1950s. They warned that granting a nonwhite population one House member and two senators was a shady Communist plot. Of course, their real objection was the same as McConnell's now. They were concerned those new lawmakers would vote against them.

This is probably true, at least in the short term (although Puerto Rico frequently elects Republican governors). But after D.C. and Puerto Rican statehood, the new tipping point state would become Florida, which has a PVI of R+2. The average state would still be redder than the country. In other words, Mitch McConnell's great fear is not that the Senate will unfairly favor Democrats. It's that the Senate might unfairly favor Republicans a tiny bit less.

For those of us who aren't Mitch McConnell, however, that's the reason admitting D.C. and Puerto Rico is a logical place to start. It won't create perfect balance, but a more balanced Senate is still better than nothing. And it would indicate that we're unwilling to let our Constitution be undone by just one of its many provisions. If the Gunning Decree threatens the very bedrock of our democracy, then it's time for the rest of us to fight back.

We often hear that our Founders hoped to prevent "tyranny of the majority," and this is true. It's why we have rights guaranteed in the Constitution, and courts that can protect those rights, and much else. But now that we've covered the power gaps that exist in elections for both Houses of Congress, my hope is that you can spot an emerging tyranny of a different type. In today's House and Senate, the minority of voters doesn't just have rights that are protected. A minority of voters rules over the majority. Such a system of government has many attributes, but a respect for the consent of the governed isn't one of them.

So that covers the political geography of Congress. But what about the race for the White House? Is a tyranny of the minority emerging there as well? The answer is yes, but not in the way you might imagine. When we vote for president, we have a system that wastes votes like the House, is malapportioned like the Senate, and is somehow even more random and pointless than both of them.

It's time to talk about the Electoral College.

6¹/²

AN APPENDIX

The Electoral College

On May 23, 2019, an op-ed appeared in *USA Today*. Its author was a gentleman named Trent England, the director of a conservative activist group called Save Our States, and here is how he began: "Should rural and small-town Americans be reduced to serfdom? The American Founders didn't think so. This is one reason why they created checks and balances, including the Electoral College."

I want to be nice about this. I really do. But I honestly didn't realize it was possible to pack so much ignorance into three little sentences. American history, European history, social science, political science, math—Mr. England's opening paragraph is a turducken of ill-informed opinion. And it's not like the author is a crank on Facebook or a high school junior about to flunk a test. This man is paid to be a confident moron in public.

Which frankly makes the Electoral College a good fit for him.

Like our elections for House and Senate, our votes for president are altered, and often weakened, by political geography. But unlike the Bedford Decree, the Electoral College stands on no principle, not even a shaky one. Unlike gerrymandering, our system of electors isn't a clever partisan scheme. Most of the time we forget our two-step presidential-election process is even there. Then, on rare occasions, it flares up and nearly kills us. The Electoral College is the appendix of the body politic.

I don't usually like to call things "stupid." It's so rarely a well-chosen descriptor. That said, to fully understand just how stupid the stupid Electoral College is, we'll start at the stupid end of Trent England's stupid argument and work backward.

Contrary to England's assertion, the Electoral College we currently use is not the one our Founders created. Their Electoral College did have several similarities with today's system: each state received a number of electoral votes equal to its number of senators plus its number of representatives; the winner of the Electoral College won the election. But the process for picking chief executives was totally different. Each elector cast not one vote for president, but two. The person with the most electoral votes became president, and the runner-up became vice president. If we still used our Founders' Electoral College, Vice President Hillary Clinton would be serving alongside President Trump.

Fortunately, it didn't take Americans long to realize that this version of the Electoral College was a mess. In the 1800 presidential election—just the fourth in our history—John Adams's Federalist Party came up with a clever plan. All the Federalist electors would vote for Adams, while all but one would vote for his ally, a South Carolinian named Charles Pinckney. In this way, Federalists could ensure that if their favorite candidate finished first, their second-favorite would finish just one vote behind, handing them not only the presidency but the vice presidency as well.

The scheme would have worked except for one important snag:

Adams didn't win. He finished third, Pinckney finished fourth, and the Democratic-Republican Party won the White House instead. Unfortunately, it was unclear *which* Democratic-Republican had won the White House because Thomas Jefferson and Aaron Burr wound up tied for first. The resulting skirmish between the two men, a stalemate so protracted and divisive it got its own number in *Hamilton*, very nearly tore the country apart.*

Our Founders weren't dumb or careless. They simply assumed that electors would be acting not as functionaries of a political party, but as independent experts, evaluating candidates the way a financial adviser might evaluate investments. Once our two-party system came along, it made debacles like the Jefferson-Burr tie all but inevitable.

To our ancestors' credit, when they realized how unworkable the Electoral College was, they changed it. Under the Twelfth Amendment, which they ratified before the 1804 presidential contest, electors no longer cast two votes for president. Instead, they voted for a party ticket—a president and vice president—and whichever pair earned a majority of electoral votes won both offices. That's the system we have today.

This 2.0 version of the Electoral College is quite different from the one the Founders established. By codifying the two-party system, the Twelfth Amendment ended the brief era of electors as independent wise men whom we rely on for their judgment. From Jefferson's reelection onward, electors have been little more than messengers, conveying the preferences of the states who choose them.

Other developments, which followed closely on the heels of the Twelfth Amendment, moved us even further from our Founders' vision. For one thing, the Constitution doesn't say how electors should

---

* Hamilton, incidentally, was not quite as noble as Lin-Manuel Miranda makes him out to be. He did indeed side with Jefferson over Burr, believing that the former was a man of principle and the latter was not. But he also encouraged his fellow Federalists to use their votes as leverage, withholding support for Jefferson until the new president agreed to a long list of demands.

be chosen, and at first most state lawmakers reserved the privilege for themselves. But it didn't take long for nearly every state to switch to our current model, where voters choose electors directly. Finally, most states quickly adopted a winner-take-all model. If a candidate comes in first in the statewide election, even by a single vote, they get every one of that state's votes in the Electoral College. (The exceptions today are Maine and Nebraska, which choose one elector to represent each congressional district and two to represent the entire state.)

To recap, and excluding the Maine and Nebraska exceptions just noted, here's how the Electoral College works: every fourth November, Americans participate in 51 separate statewide elections. (D.C. gets three electoral votes.) The winner of each state, decided by popular vote, receives all of that state's electoral votes—equal to its number of senators plus its number of representatives. Whichever candidate wins a majority of the electors wins the White House. Whether you think this is a good or bad system, it's not in the original Constitution. It's an attempt to *fix* the original Constitution.

That said, back when Americans ratified the Twelfth Amendment, they chose not to scrap the Electoral College entirely. They could have created a system of direct national elections—whichever candidate wins the national popular vote wins outright—but they didn't. Instead, our turn-of-the-nineteenth-century leaders felt that something about our two-step process was important and worth keeping. What was it?

Trent English helpfully provides an answer: the Electoral College was a form of checks and balances meant to save our rural and small-town Americans from serfdom. This is totally false.

You'll often hear, not just from Mr. English but from other equally confident individuals, that the Electoral College is an extension of the Great Compromise, protecting small-population states from large ones. That's because electors are apportioned in a hybrid system, a mix of James Madison and Gunning Bedford Jr. Most electoral votes— 435 of them—are distributed proportional to each state's population, but the remaining 100 are divided up equally among states. This means that Wyoming once again gets to punch above its weight.

The problem with this argument is that, because the vast majority of votes are doled out proportionally and because statewide elections are winner-take-all, small states are still pretty puny. In the Senate, California and Wyoming are equals. In the Electoral College, the winner of California gets fifty-five votes while the winner of Wyoming gets just three. In fact, if you lose California, you would have to sweep every one of the sixteen smallest states to make up for it. Clearly, big states still matter much more than small ones. (Another easy way you can tell that the Electoral College was never meant to defend small states from large ones: at the Constitutional Convention, James Madison and Gunning Bedford didn't argue about it.)

Similarly, the Electoral College does almost nothing to elevate the voices of rural voters. The ten least urban states in the country— Maine, Vermont, West Virginia, Mississippi, Montana, Arkansas, South Dakota, Kentucky, Alabama, and North Dakota—have 50 electoral votes. The country's ten most urban states (a list that includes not just California and Florida, but low-population states like Utah and Nevada) have 107 electoral votes. If strength in the Electoral College were all that stood between rural voters and serfdom, rural voters would be in serious trouble right now. But of course they're not.

So if the Electoral College isn't a form of checks and balances, protecting the weak against the strong, why do we have it? In *America's Constitution: A Biography*, Yale law professor Akhil Amar sheds some light on the subject. To explain why our Founders created an Electoral College, and why the authors of the Twelfth Amendment kept some version of it in place, he points to three reasons—all of them now obsolete.

The first is logistics. In a brand-new country, one connected by frog-eaten roads, conducting a direct nationwide election was unimaginable. Who would oversee it? How could we ensure a fair and timely result? Far better to hold the election in stages.

The second reason our ancestors wanted an Electoral College is that in early America, as we saw in this book's first section, voting rights varied wildly by state. In a direct national election for president, where every ballot would be counted equally, states like Rhode Island would be punished for restricting the vote to a wealthy few. States like New Jersey, meanwhile, would be rewarded for extending the franchise to Black people and women. By awarding electors based on the size of a state's population, rather than the size of its electorate, states with limited voting rights wouldn't feel pressure to expand them.

Which leads us to the third reason Amar gives for the Electoral College: slavery. When the Constitution was debated, 40 percent of the people living in southern states were enslaved. Those people couldn't vote, so if the president was decided in a direct national election, they wouldn't have counted. But when it came to doling out House seats, each state received credit for three-fifths of its enslaved population. Because electors were apportioned based on each state's number of representatives, not its number of residents, southern states received extra electoral votes. In fact, had electors been apportioned based solely on the free population, John Adams and Charles Pinckney would have defeated Thomas Jefferson and Aaron Burr in the 1800 race.

To his credit, James Madison so firmly believed in proportional representation that he supported a popular-vote process for choosing presidents, even though it would have disadvantaged his home state. "Local considerations must give way to the general interest," he wisely and graciously proclaimed. Not one of his fellow southerners at the Constitutional Convention shared his view.

In other words, the same institution that fails to protect rural Americans or empower small states exists to compensate for dirt roads, old-fashioned voting laws, and slavery, none of which we have today. The Electoral College clearly changes the balance of power in America. But who actually becomes more powerful as a result?

The answer is quite simple. The Electoral College benefits voters in swing states. Just as your vote for the House of Representatives is stronger if you live in a competitive district, your vote for president is stronger if you live in a battleground state.

☆

The terms "swing state" and "battleground state" feel like they've been around forever. In fact, they became popular only in the 1990s. In part that's because the battleground was once a roomy place. In the 1960 presidential campaign, notes Kyle Kondik in *The Bellwether*, John F. Kennedy made it to forty-three states and Richard Nixon made it to all fifty. Not every one of those states was competitive. But twenty were, and they combined for 309 electoral votes. By 2016, however, the number of swing states was down to just eleven, with a mere 137 electoral votes among them. Sixty years ago, your odds of living in a swing state were better than 50–50. Today they're less than one in four.

If you're part of that less than one in four, however, you will be bombarded with ads until you want to blast a hole in your TV, Fat Elvis style. That's because political operatives know there is a very high chance your state will be the tipping point.

You'll recall the idea of tipping point districts and Senate seats from the last two chapters, but it wasn't until 2008 that FiveThirtyEight's Nate Silver popularized the idea of tipping point states. Often, the tipping point state is one that could easily swing to either candidate, but not always.

Consider the 1984 election between Walter Mondale and Ronald Reagan. The *closest* state was Minnesota, which went for Mondale by less than 1 percent. But that was also the only state Mondale won. To get a majority of electoral votes, he would have had to win every state up to and including Michigan, which went for Reagan by a whopping 19 percent. That's what made Michigan the 1984 tipping point—if the election had come down to just one state, Michigan would have been it.

The 1984 Presidential Election

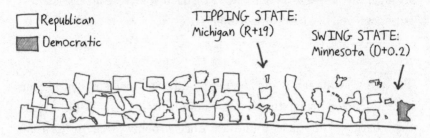

☐ Republican
▨ Democratic

TIPPING STATE:
Michigan (R+19)

SWING STATE:
Minnesota (D+0.2)

In theory, presidential candidates should spend every minute of their time in the tipping point. Mondale and Reagan should have moved their families to Detroit. Speeches in Cleveland or Philadelphia should have been rescheduled for Ann Arbor and Kalamazoo. The main reason this didn't happen in 1984, and doesn't happen now, is that the tipping point state is hard to predict in advance. As I write this, it's likely Wisconsin. But it could also be Arizona, Florida, Michigan, North Carolina, or Pennsylvania. Candidates will have to spend time in all of them, and probably a few more just to be safe.

At the same time, the rest of the states—and the voters within them—will go completely ignored. Whether President Trump wins Arkansas by ten or twenty or thirty points is irrelevant. He gets the state's six electoral votes regardless. The same is true of the Democratic candidate in Vermont or New York. Your margin of victory doesn't matter.

Except in this one way. If you win the non-battleground states by very large margins, and lose the battleground states by very small ones, the popular and electoral votes won't align. The people will support one candidate, and the White House will go to another.

Throughout almost all of our history, that scenario seemed largely hypothetical. The loser of the popular vote became president only three times during the nineteenth century; during the twentieth century, not once did the choices of the people and electors diverge. But we've had more close calls than you might think. According to Kondik, since 1828 (which for a variety of reasons is where those who count these things start counting), about one in five presidential races has come down to a single state. Had the popular vote runner-up in those elections done just a tiny bit better in the tipping point, the Electoral College would have given us a different president.

At one time, both parties recognized that it would be bad for democracy if the people wanted one chief executive and the electors gave us another. In 1968, President Nixon endorsed scrapping the Electoral College and relying on a national popular vote. As part of his 1977 election-reform package, President Carter did the same. Both proposals had bipartisan support in the House. But senators from small states believed (incorrectly, as we've seen) that the Electoral College made them significantly more powerful. They scuttled the reform attempts.

After that, we went five elections where the popular vote winner easily won the Electoral College. When I first learned about the American presidency, in the mid-1990s, I was taught that our archaic two-step process might overturn the people's will. But like sinkholes or killer bee attacks, the danger hardly seemed real.

Young people today view our presidential elections in a very different light. If you're casting your first vote in 2020, two of the three presidents to serve in your lifetime were elected despite the American people choosing someone else. In the case of George W. Bush, the 2000 election was so close—Al Gore won by just .5 percent—that the result could theoretically be written off as a fluke or a coin toss. But 2016, when Hillary Clinton defeated Trump by more than 2 percent yet lost the electoral vote, featured the largest losing–winning margin since 1876. Clinton had a clearer mandate to lead than JFK in 1960, Nixon in 1968, or Carter in 1976. Yet her opponent became president and she did not.

Because the last two presidents to win the White House while losing the popular vote were Republicans, there is now a widespread assumption that the Electoral College favors them. That's why conservative donors pay the salaries of people like Trent England: they think switching to a national popular vote for president would, like ending gerrymandering or admitting D.C. as a state, blunt their party's unfair edge. But they're wrong. We're about to leave Ben Orlin and his illustrations behind, but as a parting gift, here's a graph he's repurposed from his book *Math with Bad Drawings*. (Which is, I should mention, available wherever fine works of literature and cartooning are sold.)

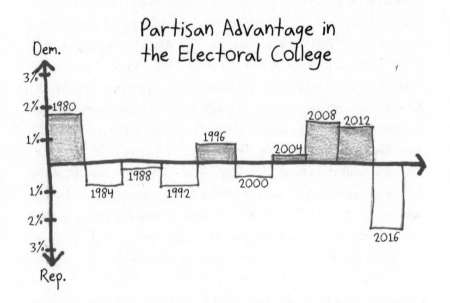

As you can see, as recently as 2012, the Electoral College strongly favored Democrats. Mitt Romney could have beaten Barack Obama by 1.5 percentage points—a margin not much worse than Clinton's—and Obama would still have been reelected.

Going forward, it's entirely possible the Electoral College will favor Democrats once again. In 2016, President Trump's base of white voters without college degrees was overrepresented in states like Michigan and Wisconsin, and that pattern will repeat itself in 2020. Beyond that, however, it's anyone's guess. If Democrats regain their traditional strength with working-class white voters, or if states like Arizona and Texas go from being slightly red to slightly blue, the Electoral College math will make it very hard indeed for a Republican to win.

In other words, not only is the Electoral College useless, obsolete, and unfair to the ever-growing number of voters who don't live in swing states, but its effects are basically random. It's like augmenting a chess match with a round of Russian roulette. Most of the time the outcome will be entirely unchanged. But every so often, for no good reason, you wind up with an awful mess.

In theory, the Electoral College should be easy to get rid of. Since the only states it advantages are the ten or so in the battlegrounds, the remaining forty could team up and pass a constitutional amendment. Such a move would be popular: by a sixteen-point margin, Americans would prefer to have the popular vote elect the president. And switching to a popular vote would benefit neither party over the long run.

Unfortunately, the myths surrounding the Electoral College—the incorrect belief that it protects small states, rural states, and Republicans—are powerful enough that politicians from non-battlegrounds are likely to vote against their own states' interests. If the Electoral College math starts to decisively favor Democrats, I suspect Trent England and his backers will very quickly change their tune, and we might get a constitutional amendment. Until then, we probably won't.

But it turns out that's okay. We don't need a constitutional amendment to perform a political appendectomy. There's a solution, and in the ever-stirring language of political reform, it's called the National Popular Vote Interstate Compact.

The NPVIC (which I'm going to call the "Nip Vic" because the world doesn't need another acronym) is quite simple. A state agrees to pledge all its electoral votes to the winner of the national popular vote rather than the statewide one. But the beauty lies in the timing of the pledge: it takes effect only once states who together hold a majority of electoral votes sign on. If the Nip Vic goes into effect, we wouldn't get rid of the Electoral College. We'd simply alter it so that it automatically agreed with the popular vote.

Right now, the Nip Vic needs the approval of states worth a combined eighty-three or more electoral votes in order to cross the threshold.

Getting those votes won't be easy, but it will be far easier than amending the Constitution. And it would ensure, once and for all, that the American president is the person the American people choose. Democrats might not be better off in the long run. Republicans might not be better off in the long run. But ultimately, our republic would be better off in the long run—which makes the Nip Vic more than worth passing.

Anytime there's an arbitrary power gap between voters, it undermines our country's bedrock principle: that all of us are created equal. Instead, it replaces our founding declaration with a twist on *Animal Farm*. All Americans are equal, but some are more equal than others. And that means our preferences don't matter equally to our leaders. No wonder our government so often does the opposite of what the people would like.

But don't worry. If, after reading about the unfairness of political geography, you're upset that your vote doesn't have enough power, there's something you can do to change that. You don't need politicians to pass a new law. You don't need to move to a small state or a swing district. You don't even need to volunteer in a battleground state. Want to turn your vote into a powerhouse? It's easy.

All you have to do is get really, really rich.

7

OLD SHELDON

The Campaign Finance System

Darla tells me she has two jobs. The first is teaching English to Chinese students via video chat. The second is managing a gentlemen's club on the fringes of the Las Vegas Strip.

I'm surprised to hear Darla say this, in part because I met her just sixty seconds ago. I was sitting at the bar on the casino floor of The Venetian, nursing a scotch and mourning the twenty bucks I had just lost on Willy Wonka–themed slots, when out of nowhere this brunette with an aggressive tan seized the stool beside me and began describing her career arc (or, really, arcs). Now I'm full of questions. Is the time difference a pro or con for her schedule? Does she often tell strangers this sort of thing? Most crucially, are there middle-schoolers in Shenzhen who struggle with the second-person plural but know that "lap dance" is both a noun and verb?

Sadly, I never get answers. As quickly as she appears, Darla mutters something about being late for work, pays for her bottle of water, and hands me a coupon to waive the cover charge if I decide to visit her club.

While I appreciate the gesture, I decline Darla's offer. I've come to Vegas looking not for vice, but for corruption. To me, there's nothing more intriguing than the simple purchase of a bottle of water I've just witnessed.

For her part in the transaction, Darla paid four dollars. Sheldon Adelson, the eighty-six-year-old owner of the Venetian and a small empire of additional casinos, has approximately $33 billion in assets, meaning that his net worth increased by approximately one one-hundred-millionth of a percent. Neither of them is likely to think about the purchase ever again.

But the relationship between Sheldon and Darla is in fact among the most important in America, and quite possibly the world. Because along with being among the planet's richest men, Adelson is the country's single largest donor to Republican campaigns. All these over-priced bottles of water and Willy Wonka slot machines and luxury suites have combined to make him one of the most powerful people in politics today—far more important than most elected officials.

If you feel there's something wrong with that arrangement, you're not alone. According to one New York Times poll, 87 percent of Americans agree our campaign-finance system either needs to be fundamentally changed or rebuilt completely. In another poll taken around the same time, however, 86 percent of Americans said they didn't know much about how our campaign finance system works. If you're part of the vast overlap between those two groups, this chapter is for you. (If you belong to the group I belonged to until recently—you think you know a lot about campaign finance, but actually you don't—this chapter is for you, too.) We'll look past slogans and dig into the convoluted rules our campaigns live by. We'll see what makes money more powerful in politics today than at any time before. We'll dip a toe into the muddy waters of constitutional law.

But ultimately, everything we'll explore in the coming pages comes down to just two simple questions: What can Sheldon do with Darla's four dollars? And what does it mean for the rest of us?

☆

In 1755, an ambitious twentysomething sought a seat in a Colonial legislature. Although the young candidate was quite wealthy, he was determined not to buy his way into office, and instead relied solely on his good character and sound judgment. He got crushed.

Three years later he ran again. This time, however, he bought an enormous quantity of beer and liquor—a half gallon of booze per voter—and gave it away on Election Day. The legislature was in Virginia. The candidate was George Washington. He won in a landslide.

Money, in other words, has influenced American politics since before there was an America to influence. In the wake of Washington's election, scandalized Virginia lawmakers cracked down on candidates buying drinks for voters, demonstrating that campaign finance reform predates America as well.

This cat-and-mouse game, between politicians hoping to spend their way to victory and reformers hoping to stop them, is the underground current that has shaped our republic for centuries. And if you want to understand how Sheldon Adelson—a man who has never run for office or even worked on a political campaign—became one of the most important figures in American political history, then the story of money in politics is a story you need to know.

When the first elections were held in the United States of America, there were no limits on campaign contributions. This was not because our Founders welcomed corruption, but because candidates didn't really run campaigns. Officeholders were expected to be "disinterested," serving the republic out of a sense of duty rather than ambition. To actively seek money in order to win political office—to wear your desire for power on your sleeve—was so classless as to be disqualifying.

The man who changed all that, and kicked off the first major era of campaign finance history in the process, was a strawberry-blond New Yorker known to his admirers as "the Little Magician" and to his enemies as "the Sly Fox." Martin Van Buren would eventually become president himself, and it's for his rather undistinguished single term that he's best remembered. But his real contribution to America came in 1828, when he served as chief political strategist for Andrew Jackson.

Jackson's presidential campaign was the first to resemble the ones we have today. As campaign manager, Van Buren hired staff. He operated campaign offices. He built local organizations to hand out lyrics to pro-Jackson jingles. The Jackson campaign even financed its own newspapers to ensure better coverage. Van Buren's style of politics was more effective and strategic than anything that came before it.

It was also more expensive. In the 1828 race, Jackson and his supporters spent more than one million dollars, the equivalent of $27 million today and a record-shattering sum at the time. To afford the campaigns he pioneered, Van Buren took a set of unwritten rules from his native New York State and expanded them nationwide. The result was known as "the spoils system," and it defined politics for decades.

Provided you weren't overly burdened by ethics, the spoils system was deliciously simple. Upon winning office, a president would fill the government with political loyalists. Each of these new public-sector workers would receive an annual "assessment circular." This was a kind of invoice, asking employees to give a portion of their salaries (usually 2 percent, but sometimes much more) to the president's political machine. Federal employees who declined to donate soon found themselves looking for new jobs. For allies of the president, the spoils system was all upside. The president got a loyal workforce; political hacks got employed; parties got the money they needed to run increasingly expensive campaigns.

For the American people, however, the Van Buren era of campaign finance was less of a win-win. By rewarding political loyalty over competence, the spoils system undermined the government's effectiveness.

Even worse, by giving the incumbent party a massive fundraising head start, the spoils system made it much harder to hold underperforming leaders accountable. In this sense, Van Buren's political wizardry was also a cautionary tale: when you reshape the way campaigns are paid for, you can't help but reshape our entire republic along with it.

What finally ended the Van Buren era of campaign finance wasn't a brave leader or charismatic reformer. It was a nutcase with a gun. In July 1881, a small-time grifter, occasional cult member, and full-on megalomaniac named Charles Guiteau assassinated President James Garfield as he waited to board a train. A motive soon emerged. Guiteau had self-published a pamphlet supporting Garfield's campaign, which he believed entitled him to a post as a minister to France. The Garfield administration denied Guiteau the job, and so, according to Guiteau's account, God instructed him to kill the president as revenge. This was clearly a bit loony, especially the part about divine retribution. But the idea that anyone might be willing to kill for the sake of political patronage turned the public against the spoils system. Chester A. Arthur, who took office after Garfield died, signed something called the Pendleton Act, which made it illegal to demand contributions from government employees and created the merit-based civil service.

Sheldon Adelson was born fifty-two years after Garfield's assassination. Even so, it may have been the turning point of his life. Under the spoils system, political machines short on money could always squeeze more of out state and federal workers. But the Pendleton Act cut off that supply. Campaigns were growing more expensive by the year, and candidates needed a new source of cash to fund them. As if by magic, a new source of cash emerged: corporations and the enormously wealthy people who ran them.

The big-money donor had arrived.

Just like government workers under the spoils system, the new breed of campaign contributors didn't always give voluntarily. As the twentieth century loomed, state and local governments encountered a new phenomenon known as the "squeeze bill." Perfected by

Pennsylvania senator Boies Penrose, but used throughout the country, squeeze bills were proposals introduced during election season and designed to devastate a specific company or industry. Once leaders from said company or industry made a sufficiently generous campaign donation, the threatening bill would mysteriously disappear.

For the most part, however, the relationship between politicians and corporate donors was more symbiosis than shakedown, and no one fostered that symbiotic relationship more expertly than an Ohio businessman named Marcus Alonzo Hanna. With his regrettable comb-over, full-moon face, and elfin ears, Mark Hanna hardly looked like a captain of industry or political power broker. But in 1896, after making his fortune in mining, shipbuilding, railroads, and steel, he brought his business savvy to his friend William McKinley's presidential campaign.

As with the assessment circulars handed out under the spoils system, Hanna financed campaigns via a kind of tithe: he asked corporations and rich people to donate .25 percent of their net worth to the McKinley campaign. The investment thesis, not stated outright but clearly implied, was that once in office, McKinley would help them grow the remaining 99.75 percent

We know Hanna's approach obliterated the old fundraising records. But because the law allowed wealthy donors to give in secret, we have no idea by how much. The best estimate is that in today's dollars, McKinley raised anywhere from $50 million to $300 million more than any candidate before him. Americans didn't know then, and still don't know now, where all that money came from.

Was Hanna's system corrupt? On one hand, the answer is obviously yes. On the other hand, the problem with the word "corruption" is that it's nearly as vague as McKinley's fundraising totals themselves. The essence of Hanna's system—you help us get elected, and once elected we'll help you—is the same bargain politicians offer voters all the time. A quid pro quo between leaders and the people is at the heart of a functioning republic.

Instead of dismissing the Mark Hanna era as corrupt, then, it's worth looking at exactly how it reshaped our government. In the era of campaigns as corporate investments, politicians were still accountable to the people. But there was now a new class of people—the donors—to whom politicians were *extra* accountable. These donors didn't have to live in the same district as a candidate, or even the same state. They might be corporations rather than people. They might be completely secret, so that Americans wouldn't know just how much influence they had. Yet all these groups were now part of the electorate. They helped pick our leaders, too.

A few progressive crusaders, most notably Teddy Roosevelt, felt that siphoning power from voters to corporations was dangerous and un-American, but the reform bills they passed were, as Lyndon Johnson later described them, "more loophole than law." In the Mark Hanna era, campaigns weren't really limited by the amount of money they could raise. Instead, campaigns were limited by the amount they could spend. The Sheldon Adelsons of the 1920s or '30s would get hit up for cash, but there were only so many pamphlets and radio ads money could buy.

It wasn't until the rise of television that political campaigning got really expensive. In 1952, in a preview of things to come, Walt Disney's brother, Roy, produced a minute-long animated commercial. For those concerned that today's campaign ads lack nuance or policy depth, consider that "I Like Ike" featured a cartoon elephant banging a drum with its tail, Uncle Sam leading a parade of dronelike citizens on a march to nowhere, and the sophisticated chorus of "You like Ike / I like Ike / Everybody likes Ike (for president)."

The problem for Eisenhower strategists was that while the "I Like Ike" ad was (and still is) frustratingly catchy, most Americans couldn't see it: 90 percent of the country's households at the time didn't own a TV. By the 1970s, however, 95 percent of American homes had televisions, and We, the People were watching 150 *billion* hours of programming each year. About 38 billion of those hours were commercials. There was now a virtually unlimited amount of American attention to capture, which meant a virtually unlimited amount of money was needed to capture it. The donor class was suddenly more in demand than ever.

The man who ended the Mark Hanna era of campaign finance, and ushered in a new one, was Richard Nixon. Nixon didn't exactly invent a new style of campaigning, but in his 1972 re-election bid, he combined all the old ones more ruthlessly and aggressively than ever before.

Like Boies Penrose, Nixon wasn't shy about squeezing reluctant contributors. The Committee to Re-Elect the President, better known by the acronym CREEP, drew up lists of people and companies who had government business or might want to avoid an IRS audit. Then the campaign sent "pickup men" to shake down its targets for cash.

Meanwhile, just as Mark Hanna had done decades earlier, Nixon went to extraordinary lengths to provide donors with the secrecy they craved. The April before the election, with a deadline looming for a new transparency law, the Nixon campaign took in the equivalent of between $20 million and $120 million in just four weeks. Some donations were laundered through Mexican banks; others were delivered by corporate jet. In the Midwest, contributors handed over checks at a donor's private game preserve. One New Jersey financier, hoping to head off a fraud investigation, sent an emissary to Nixon headquarters carrying an attaché case stuffed with $200,000 in cash.

Even after the transparency law went into effect, CREEP was masterful at hiding the true origins of its money. The Nixon campaign created more than 450 seemingly independent entities, each one sounding like something named by a patriot who'd been lobotomized: "Organization of Sensible Citizens," "Americans United for Objective Reporting," "Supporters of the American Dream," "Committee for Political Integrity." Giant personal contributions (or illegal corporate ones) were sliced into pieces small enough to be undetectable by the IRS and split among these front groups. Thus laundered, the money was rerouted back to Nixon headquarters.

All this cash propelled the president to a landslide win in 1972.

But where the first era of campaign finance had been defined by Martin Van Buren, and the second by Mark Hanna, the third was defined not by Nixon but by Watergate. As Americans began to realize exactly how much secret money had been sloshing around in their elections—and exactly how that secret money had been spent—they were appalled. Even if future presidents behaved more scrupulously, the very knowledge that our elections were essentially for sale would erode public trust in our democracy. Something had to be done.

So something was. Forty-six years ago, Sheldon Adelson was a toiletry kit salesman turned mortgage broker turned tour bus operator with little more than caviar dreams. But even if he had already struck it rich, his wealth would not have made him one of the most politically powerful people in America. In the wake of Watergate, Congress passed strict new limits on campaign fundraising and spending. Those limits didn't get money out of politics entirely. Wealthy people and corporations still had clout. But their power was reduced to its lowest level, by far, in nearly a century. After two centuries of playing catch-up, the reformers had finally prevailed.

Their triumph wouldn't even last two years.

It was late 1973, Watergate had reached a boil, and the chair of the Jefferson County Republican Party was incensed. The object of his frustration was a new local campaign finance law. In the opinion of the thirty-one-year-old attorney, it didn't go nearly far enough. "This ordinance merely applies a band-aid to a cancer," he seethed in an op-ed for his hometown paper. Warning of the "many corrupt—or potentially corrupt—campaign practices involving the raising and spending of money in electioneering," the county chair proposed a bold and sweeping fix.

"Now is the time," Mitch McConnell wrote, "to begin to reconsider the place of the private financial contribution in the political process."

Needless to say, Brother Mitch's enthusiasm for campaign finance reform has waned somewhat since his youth. In fact, where some leg-islative giants display a passion for health care, and others for foreign policy, tearing down the post-Watergate limits on money in politics has been the cause of Senator McConnell's life.

We'll get to the reasons behind that change of heart. But first, we should note that as McConnell's opinion evolved, the way he advo-cated for his opinion evolved as well. As a reformer, County Chairman McConnell appealed to the political process. He hoped to persuade the people, and by extension their representatives, to pass new laws. As a reform opponent, however, Senator McConnell has never really called for those laws to be repealed. Instead, he bypassed the politi-cal process entirely. Rather than reach out to voters or lawmakers, he sought to persuade the Supreme Court.

McConnell's argument was simple: limits on money in politics, including the very limits he once called for, violate the First Amend-ment. How this notion went from legal Hail Mary to unalterable law of the land explains a lot about America today.

"Money isn't speech." For today's campaign finance reformers—those trying to constrain what Sheldon can do with Darla's four dollars—this slogan is often pronounced with a certain smug finality, as if it settles the debate. It doesn't. While money and speech may not be synonymous, they're certainly related. Yeast isn't alcohol. Jet fuel isn't aviation. But when you cross a certain threshold, a restriction on one becomes a restriction on the other.

This was the Supreme Court's ruling in a 1976 decision. The case was *Buckley v. Valeo*, but it might as well have been called *Young Mitch McConnell v. Old Mitch McConnell*. One side argued exactly what County Chair McConnell had argued in 1973: private spending on politics invites corruption and undermines public trust in our democ-racy, and thus ought to be curtailed. The other side argued exactly what Senator McConnell would argue for the rest of his life: private spending on politics is a form of speech, and is therefore protected by the Constitution.

Rather than agree entirely with either McConnell, the Court split the difference. Reducing money's role in politics was in the public interest, it reasoned, and thus limits on campaign donations were upheld. But the Court also ruled that limitations on money were inherently limitations on speech, and therefore risked running afoul of the First Amendment. After Watergate, lawmakers had capped the total amount of money a candidate could spend on his or her campaign. They also restricted the amount a Sheldon Adelson–like figure could spend on "independent expenditures," public advocacy efforts that didn't mention candidates by name. The Court found that these reforms crossed a free-speech line, and overturned them.

Buckley v. Valeo was important for two reasons. First, it turned reformers' post-Watergate win into more of a tie. Wealthy Americans had less influence than they did when crooked businessmen were schlepping briefcases full of cash to Nixon headquarters. But by opening the loophole of independent expenditures, rich people could still spend as much on politics as they chose. Also, by giving candidates a constitutional right to raise as much money as possible, the Court ensured that politicians' desperate hunt for cash would continue.

Buckley v. Valeo also laid the groundwork for the next phase of the fight over money in American politics. Anticorruption would be in one corner, and free speech would be in the other. When the two sides came to blows, the winner would no longer be chosen by voters or lawmakers. Now, the judges would decide.

It's worth noting that other well-established democracies would never pass *Buckley*'s free-speech test. In the United Kingdom, parties can spend only about $25 million per election—and are banned from spending a single dime (or farthing or whatever) on TV commercials. In Germany, each political party is allowed to shoot exactly one ninety-second ad, which it can air in rough proportion to the number of votes it received the last time around. By international standards, the major campaign finance debate in America is not about whether to remove big money from politics. It's about just how much big money to allow.

Over the past half century, the overwhelming majority of Americans agreed with County Chairman McConnell that we should limit, not expand, the power of wealthy donors. Most of us also agreed that the problem with our campaign finance laws was that they weren't strict enough.

Senator McConnell's position, on the other hand, was deeply unconvincing. When he argued that the real threat to the republic was that the wealthy had too little influence, only a handful of Americans agreed. But increasingly, members of that handful were appointed to the Supreme Court.

In hindsight, 1990 was a turning point. *Austin v. Michigan Chamber of Commerce*, a decision handed down that year, was on its face a win for Young Mitch over Old Mitch. The Court ruled that companies could spend money on politics via "political action committees," or PACs, sister organizations set up to donate directly to campaigns. But companies couldn't donate to campaigns directly from corporate treasuries as though they were acquiring a rival or hiring an employee. To most Americans, including six of the Court's nine judges, this kind of restriction seemed quite reasonable.

To the Court's three newest justices, however, this mild check on corporate campaign spending was not merely on the wrong side of *Buckley v. Valeo*'s careful balance. Antonin Scalia, Anthony Kennedy, and Sandra Day O'Connor saw the *Austin* decision as an attack on democracy itself. Scalia called the reform "an Orwellian announcement," and warned that all Americans' free speech was at risk. The idea that corporations had the same political free-speech rights as human beings was a fringe view, one no justice had held for the first two hundred years of American history. But times had changed. A new age of money in politics was on the horizon.

That era took a bit of time to arrive. For most of my childhood, and the beginning of my young adulthood, the push-and-pull created by *Buckley v. Valeo* continued. Reformers passed new laws; those laws were challenged in court; anticorruption squared off against free speech; judges picked a winner. One of *Austin*'s three dissenters, Sandra Day O'Connor, even reversed her old position, deciding that modest restrictions on corporate speech were not so Orwellian after all. But in 2006, O'Connor retired, and President Bush replaced her with Justice Samuel Alito. Americans still felt there should be less money in politics. But a majority of the Supreme Court now felt there should be much, much more.

Which brings us, finally and inevitably, to the present era. "No one formally amended the Constitution," writes University of California, Irvine, law professor Rick Hasen in *Plutocrats United*. Instead, as he puts it, "The Supreme Court decided that what had been constitutional under the First Amendment one day was unconstitutional the next." The year was 2010. We had entered the world of *Citizens United*.

A quick confession: when I began researching this chapter, I was sure *Citizens United* was bad. Yet I wasn't really sure why. What exactly did the Court decide ten years ago? In case you find yourself in a similar predicament, let me do my best to explain.

Technically speaking, our political process was upended by a lawsuit about a crappy movie. In 2008, Citizens United, a conservative nonprofit, produced an anti-Hillary Clinton documentary it hoped to run on TV during the Democratic primary campaign. Thanks to campaign finance law barring nonprofit organizations from "electioneering," the documentary went unshown. Citizens United alleged that this was a violation of its free speech rights.

The Supreme Court could have issued a narrow ruling allowing *Hillary: The Movie* on the airwaves. Instead, the new 5–4 conservative majority issued a sweeping opinion, one that went far beyond a tedious ninety-minute film and took aim at the very heart of our campaign finance system.

In the short term, the *Citizens United* decision had three big effects. Reversing its ruling from 1990, the new 5–4 Court majority ruled that corporations did indeed have the right to speak freely in elections. The Venetian could now take Darla's four dollars and use it to directly fund political ads.

Sheldon Adelson, too, was given new ways to spend Darla's money on politics. Wealthy people had always been allowed to advocate for specific *issues*. But now they could also buy TV ads urging viewers to vote for or against specific *candidates*. The financial entities created for this purpose—entities that could accept unlimited donations—became known as superPACs.

SuperPACs had to disclose their donors, but under *Citizens United*, other types of organizations did not. 501(c)(4)s, nonprofits named after the section of tax code that created them, are known by their fans as "social welfare organizations" and by everyone else as "dark money groups." They've been around for a while, but their current role is brand new. Because dark money groups are corporations, they don't have to reveal who funds them. Sheldon could now dump money into a 501(c)(4), that money could go toward a political issue ad, and no one who saw the ad would ever know Sheldon paid for it.

If *Citizens United* had stopped there, the ruling would already have been huge win for Old Mitch McConnell. Unrestricted corporate political spending, superPACs, and dark money were body blows to the post-Watergate reforms. But *Citizens United* didn't stop there. Instead, the Court reached further.

Not since Mark Hanna first made his pitch to corporations has the relationship between politicians and the public been so thoroughly reshaped. Writing for the one-vote majority, Anthony Kennedy declared that the public's interest in fighting corruption, an interest recognized as valid in *Buckley v. Valeo*, was now limited to cases of outright bribery. Buying a favor from a politician was illegal; buying the loyalty of a politician was not. "We now conclude that independent expenditures, including those made by corporations, do not give rise to corruption or the appearance of corruption," Kennedy further declared. The thesis of McConnell's 1973 op-ed—that private spending on politics was "a cancer" demanding treatment—was summarily dismissed.

Kennedy's opinion was remarkably ballsy. He never argued that allowing more money into politics wouldn't change our government's behavior. Instead, he simply asserted that even if elected officials prioritized wealthy donors over the rest of their constituents, their behavior couldn't possibly be corrupt. "If it looks like a duck, and quacks like a duck, the Court declares it not a duck" is a reasonable summary of Kennedy's view.

Even more audacious than Kennedy's writing on corruption was his writing on the *appearance* of corruption. This distinction is important, and it goes back to the Tinker Bell nature of democracy: if people stop believing in it, it dies. For this reason, the Court had long held that whether or not the campaign finance system actually *was* corrupt, a campaign finance system that *seemed* corrupt threatened our republic because it caused Americans to lose faith in their government.

Citizens United completely reversed that view. In his ruling, Kennedy proclaimed that no matter how much money corporations or rich people donated to campaigns, it would never cause the American people to suspect corruption. How he arrived at his confident prediction about the future beliefs of Americans is a bit of mystery. To borrow from another famous First Amendment case, it's as though Kennedy ruled that yelling fire in a crowded theater couldn't possibly make the audience concerned.

This was the true power of the Court's 2010 decision. *Buckley v. Valeo* had pitted anticorruption advocates against free speech advocates. *Citizens United* didn't just award a round to the free-speechers. *Citizens United* called the fight. Legally speaking, corruption no longer existed. There was therefore no longer any need for measures to prevent it. Overnight, nearly every campaign finance regulation found itself in the Court's crosshairs.

Limits on overall campaign spending are a perfect example. In the first few years after *Citizens United*, there remained a cap on the total that Sheldon Adelson could donate directly to campaigns per year. The limit was what most Americans would consider large—$123,000— but it represented only about .0003 percent of Sheldon's net worth. In 2014, after yet another 5–4 decision, Chief Justice John Roberts wrote that such caps were unconstitutional. "Spending large sums of money in connection with elections, but not in connection with an effort to control the exercise of an officeholder's official duties, does not give rise to quid pro quo corruption. Nor does the possibility that an individual who spends large sums may garner 'influence over or access to' elected officials or political parties."

Let me try to put Roberts's words into English: for American democracy to flourish we are not just allowed, but required, to put our leaders' loyalties up for sale. The more money you invest in our elections, the more influence you should get in return.[*]

As it happens, there's some precedent for the kind of election Roberts envisioned. In a public company, where important decisions are often put to shareholders, no "One Shareholder, One Vote" principle applies. Instead, by purchasing shares, you also purchase influence; the more shares you own, the more power you have.

And that's the simplest way to understand the new era of American history that began a decade ago. Just like Martin Van Buren and Mark Hanna, by changing the way politicians raise and spend money, *Citizens United* changed our republic itself. As of 2010, we are no longer equal owners of American government. Instead, we're shareholders, with our influence explicitly tied to the amount we invest. This is not how most of us think their democracy should function. It's not the campaign finance system we voted for, the system our representatives created, or the system we want. But it's the system we have.

---

[*] By the Roberts Court's logic, it's hard not to reach the conclusion that foreigners— Vladimir Putin, to pick an example at random—ought to be allowed to buy influence in American democracy, too. So far, the Court has reacted to this thorny legal issue by ignoring it.

I should be clear: I don't believe the Supreme Court, or its current chief justice, imposed this system upon us out of malice. I have every reason to believe John Roberts is a good person. He's certainly a smart person. But he's the kind of smart person who doesn't seem to get out much. His is the worldview of a small child who chucks a goldfish from his bedroom window and, with unshakable certainty, announces it is free to fly.

Of course, in Sheldon Adelson's case, the *Citizens United* era has been liberating indeed. According to Rick Hasen, in 2012 Adelson and his wife, Miriam, contributed between $98 million and $150 million of his money to Republican campaigns and superPACs. Because of the new rules allowing secret donations, the exact number will forever remain a mystery, but one thing is very clear: Sheldon can now spend as much of Darla's money on politics as he likes.

Does a return to the pre-Watergate era of campaign finance jeopardize our republic, as Young Mitch McConnell might claim? Or does it make America stronger than ever, as Old Mitch McConnell insists today? There's a lot riding on the answer. And to figure out what the *Citizens United* era has done to our democracy as a whole, it helps to start with a slightly more personal question.

What does Sheldon Adelson's money do to you?

In a modern-looking office tower in D.C.'s Dupont Circle neighborhood, you'll find an organization called the Institute for Free Speech. Like Trent England's "Save Our States" project to defend the Electoral College, the institute is financed by the same wealthy donors who fund Republican campaigns. But it is not itself a campaign organization. Instead, it's a kind of perpetual war room. In the national fight over money in politics, the institute's seventeen men and two women serve as intellectual muscle for Team Mitch.

It's hardly surprising that, with so many experts on the payroll, the Institute for Free Speech puts out reams of material each year. But when extolling *Citizens United*, their arguments usually fall into one of just two categories: first, allowing wealthy donors to spend unlimited sums on politics doesn't make a big difference; and second, even if all this money *does* make a big difference, that's a good thing.

Let's start with the first one. When the institute's research director, Scott Blackburn, recapped the 2018 midterms, his headline began with four magic words: "Money Doesn't Buy Elections." This is the pro–*Citizens United* version equivalent of "Money isn't speech," a mantra for those who believe our democracy is better off when Sheldon can spend Darla's money however he pleases. In case readers missed the point of the headline, Blackburn repeated it like a chorus through the rest of the piece.

"At the end of the day, voters, not money, decide who wins the election . . ."

"It is simply not the case, nor has it ever been, that outspending your opponent can 'buy' the election . . ."

"In 2018, as in every election before it, the voters ultimately decide . . ."

I don't like the Institute for Free Speech. I think much of its work is misleading, including its name, and I can't imagine why anyone would want to devote their limited time on earth to working there. So let me say this about Scott Blackburn's points: they're true. Money *doesn't* buy elections. If Sheldon Adelson taps his fortune to purchase a new electric toothbrush or a private jet, he'll get what he pays for. When he shells out money for a political campaign, there's no guarantee of success.

Adelson has learned this lesson the hard way. In the 2012 Republican primary, he and his wife, Miriam, blew $20 million on a super-PAC supporting Newt Gingrich. For the typical American, such a sum would represent 427 *years* of full-time work. And what did Sheldon receive in exchange for all that cash? A candidate who stupefied audiences reminiscing about the 1970s and took time off from campaigning to visit local zoos.

The *Citizens United* era is full of, or at least dotted with, similarly flush candidates who came up short. In 2018, Beto O'Rourke collected far more money than Ted Cruz. In 2016, Hillary Clinton outspent Donald Trump two to one. No, money doesn't buy elections.

Money buys votes.

This is almost embarrassingly obvious. Politicians would rather not spend their time dialing prospective donors. They don't enjoy sending you emails with subject lines ("Running Out of Time." "Falling short." "I don't know where else to turn, David") that would inspire a wellness check if you received them from a friend. At a town hall, I once heard a seventeen-year-old ask President Obama what he should know about being a politician. "You go to a lot of rubber-chicken dinners," the president replied, "And sometimes the chicken isn't very good." But the candidates make the calls and send the emails and eat the rubbery chicken at fundraisers because they know money helps them win. And the way they win is by getting more votes.

We don't usually acknowledge money's vote-buying power, in part because it's a bit icky and in part because the cost of a ballot is difficult to quantify. Back in 1758, George Washington could tally up his alcohol budget, divide it by the number of voters he'd invited over for drinks, and figure out his per-person costs. Modern campaigns are far too complicated for that. Determining the precise cost of a single vote is a fool's errand.

So let's try it. We'll do our best to estimate the cost of buying votes, and in order to be fair to the "money doesn't buy elections" crowd, we'll set our assumptions in a way that makes those votes as expensive as possible. As it happens, I know the perfect example of campaign spending that garnered relatively few votes in return: me.

In the 2008 Obama campaign, I was a field organizer, the lowest person on the campaign totem pole. It was a presidential race, which meant both candidates had lots of name recognition. I was also in a Republican-leaning area, which meant there wasn't much low-hanging fruit. Instead, hunting for votes in Wayne County, Ohio, was like hunting for truffles in a forest—difficult and extremely expensive. Hiring me was something a campaign would do only if every less pricey option had been explored.

Now for some numbers. Estimating very conservatively, I sent out 800 volunteers to knock on doors over the course of four months, and they talked to about 11 voters each. According to the most optimistic research, that translates into about 628 votes, and for this work I was paid the princely sum of $12,500. To factor in the cost of my health insurance, office space, and the salaries of my bosses, let's double it to $25,000. And then, just to be extra cautious, let's call it 30 grand. Thirty thousand dollars in campaign spending ultimately generated 628 votes, for a final figure of $47.77 each.

For most Americans, that would make vote buying a staggeringly expensive proposition. Even the 537 votes that decided the 2000 election, the closest presidential race in American history, would have cost about $26,000, more than twice the typical American's household savings. For the majority of us, then, donating to politicians is like voting for them, a way to express our values and show support. We do it hoping others will join us. But even if you give several thousand dollars per year, there's essentially no chance that your contributions alone will change the outcome of a race.

Sheldon Adelson, however, is in another league entirely. Forty-seven dollars is nothing to him. Forty-seven million dollars is nothing to him. Even $98 million, the amount the Adelsons spent on campaigns in 2012, hardly put a dent in Sheldon's expansive net worth. Yet using our earlier calculation, that money was enough to buy more than 2 *million* votes. Just to reiterate: votes are almost certainly cheaper than my $47.77-per-vote figure suggests. Yet even by this conservative estimate, Sheldon Adelson was responsible for approximately as many Republican votes in 2012 as the entire state of Georgia.

We tend to refer to the people who take advantage of *Citizens United* as "megadonors." But this describes a means, not an end. Sheldon Adelson is not a megadonor. He's a megavoter. He buys ballots in bulk.

The emergence of megavoters—far more than any novel constitutional thesis or newly created legal entity—is the defining feature of the *Citizens United* era. Since 2010, our country has converted income inequality into political inequality with the ease of a gambler converting casino chips into cash. The American electorate has been split into two groups of very different size. There's the 99.99 percent of us who participate the traditional way, and the .01 percent who can afford to bulk-purchase votes. Not surprisingly, if you're a member of this second category, your preferences matter much, much more than if you belong to the first.

To which the Institute for Free Speech might reply: about time! When pushed to concede that, in fact, money carries quite a bit of influence in politics, the institute retreats to the line of reasoning Chief Justice Roberts employed in 2014. The largest shareholders deserve the most power, they argue. That's a sign our republic is working well.

I don't want to dismiss this argument out of hand. After all, there are plenty of other ways to gain extra influence in our democracy. You could be an activist who knocks on thousands of doors. You could accrue a million Twitter followers. What makes spending money different?

To understand that question, it's important to wrap your head around just how much money Sheldon Adelson has. If you're a regular person, or even a regular rich person, $33 billion is a difficult number to comprehend. It's as though you were asked to consider the number of stars in the universe or cells in a human body. Your brain simply did not evolve to consider the possibility that there might be 33,000,000,000 of anything.

But here's one way to think about it. During my careful perusal of slot machines at the Venetian, the biggest, most life-altering jackpot I could find was for about $9 million. Your odds of winning such a fantastic sum are essentially zero.

But imagine you got really, really lucky. You walked into the casino, pulled the lever at the Megabucks machine, and, astoundingly, won the jackpot on the very first try. Now imagine you came back the next day and did it again. And again. And again. Every day you walked into the casino. Every day, you won a statistically unwinnable $9 million prize. How long do you think your streak would have to last before you passed Sheldon Adelson on the *Forbes* list?

The answer is not months, or even a few years. It's nearly a decade. It would take you nine years and nine months of daily once-in-a-lifetime jackpots to match the wealth of the Venetian's owner.

Bear in mind that Sheldon Adelson is by no means the country's richest person. He doesn't even crack the top ten. Yet unless you belong to a very fortunate handful of people, to say that Sheldon Adelson is richer than you is not like saying a housecat is smaller than a lion. It's like saying a housecat is smaller than three thousand Empire State Buildings laid end to end.

The power gap created by *Citizens United* makes the disparities created by geography look puny. You'll recall from chapter 6, for example, that a Wyomingite's vote for Senate is about sixty-eight times more powerful than a Californian's. But using his spending totals from 2012, Sheldon Adelson's vote is more than *thirty thousand* times more powerful than a Wyomingite's. If the gap created by the Bedford Decree is the width of a credit card, the one created by Sheldon's spending is longer than the George Washington Bridge.

Consider the $20 million he wasted on the 2012 presidential campaign. That infusion of cash—an amount that completely transformed—was, for Sheldon and Miriam Adelson, the equivalent of the average American household spending about forty-five bucks. I'm sure they noticed the money was missing. But it was hardly a devastating blow. It wasn't even the .25 percent of net worth Mark Hanna asked from rich people on William McKinley's behalf.

Ever since 2010, in other words, we have been living through an interesting experiment in democracy: for a tiny group of people, permanently altering our politics involves less financial sacrifice than a typical family's dinner at Olive Garden.

☆

Of course, there is theoretically a big difference between Adelson and a random person from Wyoming, a reason that Sheldon might deserve his newfound clout. Power deriving from wealth is not distributed at random. The Republican Party's biggest donor worked hard to get rich. But is this really true? I'm not saying Sheldon Adelson was lazy—the son of a cabdriver, he's a legitimate rags-to-riches story—I just doubt he's several billion times more industrious than you or me or Darla.

Besides, even if you concede that Sheldon earned every one of his 3.9 trillion pennies purely through merit, does that necessarily make him the best person to decide who leads the United States? It takes a certain set of skills to build new casinos and attract convention-goers to your hotels and name the Italian restaurant at your casino "Casanova's" instead of something less tacky. But do those skills make you uniquely qualified to pick the leader of the free world?

And finally, let's just assume for a moment that Adelson's skills *are* perfectly translatable to politics, that he is wise in direct proportion to his wealth. What about his kids? It seems relevant that so many of the wildly wealthy people who have reshaped our country—Betsy DeVos, Jared Kushner, the Koch brothers, the Trumps, a small parade of others you rarely hear of because they give their money in aristocratic quiet—are heirs. In such cases, the political inequality created by wealth is every bit as random as that created by geography. In *Citizens United*–era America, the easiest way to become wildly powerful is to become wildly rich. And the easiest way to become wildly rich is to have wildly rich parents.

In other words, a decade-old, 5–4 Court majority has split voters into two outrageously unequal groups along largely arbitrary lines. It will not shock you to learn that the results of this experiment thus far have not been promising. In fact, we've seen exactly what the *Citizens United* decision promised we wouldn't: corruption and the appearance of corruption.

Consider two recent events that occurred within just a four-month span. In November 2018, Donald Trump presented Sheldon Adelson's wife, Miriam, with the Presidential Medal of Freedom, the nation's highest civilian honor. In February 2019, President Trump's Justice Department reversed a long-standing policy enabling online gambling—the single greatest threat to Sheldon Adelson's brick-and-mortar casino business.

It is theoretically possible that Miriam Adelson is among the most impressive Americans, living or dead, in our nation's history. It's also theoretically possible that the Justice Department's change of heart had nothing to do with appeasing a man who spent more than $20 million backing the president's campaign. But both explanations stretch credulity. Despite Anthony Kennedy's confident prediction, our system seems corrupt to most Americans. And the very fact that we have to wonder—that we quite reasonably worry that our government's chief concern is satisfying a handful of fabulously wealthy donors—undermines the public trust upon which democracy depends.

Yet even this type of quid pro quo corruption, or potential quid pro corruption, is only the tip of the *Citizens United* iceberg. Today, megavoters don't need to bribe candidates with cash. Instead, they can seek out candidates that come pre-bribed.

Here's what I mean by that. Let's say I have $38 billion in my bank account. Let's also say that my pet issue is (to borrow a genuine conspiracy theory) proving that Justin Bieber is a shapeshifting lizard person sent to enslave the human race. There are a few ways I could get what I want. First, I could explicitly promise campaign donations to a candidate in exchange for an investigation into Justin Bieber's reptilian past once they won. Even under *Citizens United*, that's not allowed. Second, I could do what Sheldon Adelson did with online gambling: bankroll a politician, use my newfound access and influence to lobby that politician, and hope they start to see things my way on the Bieber-lizard issue.

But there's a third option. I could find someone who *already* believes that Justin Bieber is a lizard person, and use my money to single-handedly turn that wackadoodle into a top-tier candidate. This is perhaps the greatest danger of allowing unlimited money in politics—not that successful politicians will be bribed into adopting dumb ideas, but that people with dumb ideas will nonetheless become successful politicians. Under *Citizens United*, power often derives from sharing the viewpoints, however obviously wrongheaded, of people who happen to be absurdly rich.

This leads us to one final difference between private spending on politics and all other types of political activity: money can be used to procure even more money. This is especially true in a democracy as large and powerful as ours. Even in our new gilded age, the amount of wealth possessed by the superrich is nothing compared to the federal budget. If you seized every dollar belonging to the richest Americans on New Year's Eve and used it to fund our government, you'd be tapped out by mid-May. Uncle Sam spends more money each year than even the most powerful billionaire can fathom. One of the most efficient ways to get rich quick—or to get much richer quickly—is to get just a few crumbs of that pie for yourself.

Consider what has happened over the last four years. The eighteen largest donors to Republican candidates gave a total of $205 million in 2016. That's a lot. But thanks to the tax cuts President Trump passed two years later, they are set to receive $68 *billion* in return. That's a lot more. With a return on investment of 33,000 percent, buying votes for Trump in 2016 turned out to be a better bet than buying Apple stock in 2002.

Of course, this works only if you're a rich person who wants the government to make you richer. If you believe that government should be doing more to help all Americans, and that taxes on the rich should be higher, campaign donations are much more like charity than invest-ment. In other words, the *Citizens United* era is lucrative for conserva-tives in a way it isn't for progressives.

And this leads us back to Mitch McConnell's campaign finance change of heart. Dick Lugar, one of McConnell's longest-serving Republican colleagues, was fairly suspicious about the transformation. "He's come to the conclusion that raising money is tremendously important for his own success." That's undoubtedly true. Money, and the television ads it could buy, were the miracle elixir that turned a savvy but awkward striver into a U.S. senator.

But Lugar was almost certainly not cynical enough. In 1973, when McConnell's pro-reform op-ed appeared in the *Courier-Journal*, labor unions frequently matched or even exceeded corporate political giving. By supporting strict campaign finance laws, McConnell hoped to cut off Democrats' cash. In the following decades, however, labor grew far less powerful, and business far more. By 2016, corporate political action committees were giving four times as much money to candidates as unions. Meanwhile, as the GOP became the party of tax cuts for wealthy individuals and regulation cuts for businesses, McConnell could revive the sweeping bargain offered by Mark Hanna a century before: give us a little money now, and you'll get a lot back once we win.

That's not to say Democrats don't raise money. They certainly do, much of it from very wealthy individuals. But like ending gerrymandering or expanding voting rights, campaign finance reform stopped being a bipartisan solution once the problem started giving the Republican Party an edge.

Today, Sheldon Adelson can influence the politicians he funds in whatever manner he pleases, and candidates can become instantly viable simply by pleasing him. He is free to make bargains with the government, both implicit and explicit, that nearly all Americans view as corrupt. And these corrupt bargains are structured in such a way as to massively favor one party over the other.

Congratulations, my fellow goldfish. We're free.

☆

I wish I could tell you a new and brighter era of campaign finance history is dawning. It should be. Had the majority of Americans gotten their way in 2016, Hillary Clinton would have picked new Supreme Court justices, and it's quite possible *Citizens United* would now be on the trash heap.

But that's not the way things turned out. A majority of the Court believes that the wealthiest Americans have a right to spend as much as they want on politics. And while passing an amendment to overturn *Citizens United* is a noble idea, it's also never going to happen. Too many Republican lawmakers have arrived at the same conclusion Mitch McConnell reached decades ago: the exchange of money for power is essential to the modern GOP. For the foreseeable future, the megavoters are here to stay.

Yet there remain quite a few options that fall between "changing the Constitution" and "wailing and gnashing of teeth." We can't end the bulk purchasing of ballots entirely. But we can make the bulk purchasing of ballots a far less lucrative investment.

To start, we could increase each vote's cost. We wouldn't even need new campaign finance rules to do it. We'd simply have to enforce the rules already in place. Even in the *Citizens United* era, superPACs and campaigns are supposed to be fined if they directly coordinate with each other. If dark money groups engage primarily in political work, donations to them aren't supposed to be tax-deductible. Yet in 2015, the head of the Federal Election Commission grimly told the *New York Times* that "the likelihood of the laws being enforced is slim."

Remarkably, the situation has gotten even worse since then. Because commissioners have retired, and because the Trump administration has made no real effort to replace them, the FEC is literally no longer *allowed* to enforce the rules. It's as though a midsize city—Des Moines, say—fired all its police officers. Technically, things like vandalism and murder would still be illegal. But the vandals and murderers might not see it that way. Without anyone to uphold them, laws are just fancy suggestions. (On the rare occasions when then the Trump Administration has tried to nominate new commissions, they've generally been the kinds of people only a Hans Von Spakovsky could love.)

To make ballot-buying more expensive, we should restore the FEC to its full slate of six bipartisan commissioners and give it the tools it needs to get tough on campaign finance crime. Wealthy Americans would still be able to spend millions purchasing votes. But by removing the discount that donors receive when they can break the law with impunity, we could at least force them to pay sticker price.

We can raise the social costs of megavoting as well. The *Citizens United* era has been marked not just by unlimited money, but unlimited *secret* money. Superrich donors have been living by the opposite of the Peter Parker principle: with great power comes no responsibility whatsoever. Yet even the Roberts Court seems willing to accept that free speech is not the same as secret speech. For several years, lawmakers have put forward the DISCLOSE Act, which would require any organization spending money in federal elections to make public the names of its donors. When Democrats get their Skywalker Window, they should pass that bill into law.

Even in the absence of stronger disclosure laws, there are ways to bring the debate over vote buying out of the shadows. It's long been a norm of our political culture that while politicians are "in the arena," and therefore subject to far more public scrutiny than ordinary Americans, the wealthy donors who back those politicians are not. In the *Citizens United* era, that needs to change.

Someone like Sheldon Adelson is vastly more important to our politics than a backbench congressman or the governor of a small state. Like it or not, he's a leader of our democracy. And in a democracy, we should be able to evaluate a leader's fitness to lead.

We've already seen that once campaign finance itself becomes a campaign issue, bulk-buying votes becomes far less enticing. In the 2020 Democratic primaries, not a single major Democratic candidate accepted corporate PAC donations. This is not because Democratic campaigns don't cost money. It's because in Democratic politics, being seen as beholden to big companies is so damaging that it's not worth the extra cash.

The same incentives exist in elections between the parties, not just within them. In 2018, Democrat after Democrat publicly refused to take corporate money. This made it much harder to get ads on the air. But in nearly every case it was the right decision, not just morally but politically. Voters were more likely to vote for candidates who they felt would put their own interests first.

Thanks to the Court's current makeup, there aren't many ways, beyond what I've just described, to increase the cost of buying ballots. But there's another side of the ledger to consider. If you want to blunt the impact of *Citizens United*, you can reduce the benefits of donating enormous sums.

Rick Hasen, the *Plutocrats United* author, calls this strategy "leveling up." Rather than close the power gap between the superrich and the rest of us by making them weaker, we can make the rest of us stronger.

The level-up strategy certainly has three big things going for it: first, it's more likely to survive the Roberts Court; second, the number of us who aren't billionaires is quite large; and third, thanks to twenty-first-century technology, there's more power in numbers than ever. In 2018, for example, an online clearinghouse called ActBlue made giving small donations to candidates even easier than buying shoes on Zappos or pet food on Chewy. It's one reason Democrats raised about $300 million from donations of $200 or less.

Technology even makes it possible for small donors to do what big donors have long been able to: instantly make a candidate viable. In 2015, a platform called CrowdPAC launched what is essentially Kickstarter for elections. A would-be politician promises to run, provided they can reach a certain target in pledge donations. If you make a pledge, and the candidate's target is reached, your credit card is charged. If not, you get your money back. You get the rewards of donating to candidates you believe in without the risk that your money will be wasted if they fail to take off.

Of course, not every voter has money to give, even in small amounts. That's why another way to level up is to use public funds to encourage grassroots donations. In this area, the city of Seattle is a pioneer. Each election season, its residents get four "democracy vouchers" from the government. They're basically twenty-five-dollar gift cards. You can donate them to candidates for local office, in which case they function exactly like cash, or you can leave them in a drawer, in which case the money remains in the city treasury. Your decision is personal and entirely up to you. But taken together, Seattleites now have an additional $3 *million* to donate. Were such a program expanded nationwide, the American people would be able to contribute about $1.6 *billion* more per election cycle. That's more than enough to go toe-to-toe with Sheldon Adelson.

That said, despite the promise of ActBlue, CrowdPAC, or democracy vouchers, we shouldn't overstate small donors' power. Coordinating groups of thousands or even millions of people will always be more difficult than asking a single wealthy individual to write a check. More important, online fundraising really works only for candidates charismatic enough to become internet sensations. There are more than half a million elected officials in the United States. They can't all go viral.

That's why we should consider another, even more straightforward way to level up Americans using public funds: have the government write candidates big checks. This is not nearly as crazy as it sounds. For a long time after Watergate, presidential candidates of both parties took public financing. Not only that, but they agreed to limit fundraising from private donors as a condition for getting their government money. As recently as 1984, both Ronald Reagan and Walter Mondale used taxpayer dollars to hire staff and put ads on the air.

But campaigns kept getting more expensive, fundraising totals kept getting bigger, and the level of government support didn't keep pace. In 2008, then-Senator Obama collected vast sums from both establishment fundraisers and small-dollar donors. He turned down public funds, raised truckloads of cash, and was followed in this decision by both parties' nominees in 2012 and 2016.

I don't blame Obama (or Romney, or Clinton, or Trump) for playing by the rules we have—but I do think that those rules need to be changed. Today, presidential candidates who choose to reject private money and take public funds would receive $104 million. That's a lot of money, but in modern campaign terms, it's nothing. Imagine if instead, candidates could take $1 billion—or, better yet, if the amount of public financing were indexed to the cost of recent campaigns. Suddenly, ditching supervoters wouldn't be so crazy after all.

One way to tell that this idea would be effective is that Mitch McConnell—the savviest campaign finance expert of his generation—absolutely hates it. In his 1973 *Courier-Journal* piece, he explicitly called for public financing. But in a more recent op-ed on a Democratic reform bill, this time for the *Washington Post*, McConnell singled out public financing for attack. "They'd rather use your money to enrich campaign consultants," he warned taxpayers.

Old Mitch's talking points were well crafted, but as you might expect, I'm with Young Mitch on this one. Let's say that by spending a billion dollars on campaigns, we could avoid a trillion dollars in unnecessary tax cuts for the wealthy. That's a return to taxpayers of about 10,000 percent.

There's one final way to level the playing field when it comes to money and political influence, and while it doesn't close the power gap between the superrich and the rest of us, it does close the gap between Republicans and Democrats. When one party's billionaires and corporations spend extraordinary amounts of money on our politics, the other party's billionaires and corporations should try to match them.

This is hardly an elegant solution. I wish we lived in a country where liberal donors like Tom Steyer and Mike Bloomberg weren't allowed to spend hundreds of millions on superPACs.* But *Citizens*

---

* Both men also financed their own presidential campaigns, with little success. While self-funding is clearly an example of the way the superrich and the rest of us play by different rules, Bloomberg's and Steyer's efforts also demonstrate that it's far easier to buy influence over an officeholder than it is to buy the office itself.

United has ruled out all the elegant solutions. In a democracy where Sheldon Adelson has a right to buy as many votes as he pleases, I'm glad that Steyer, Bloomberg, and the like are there to counter him. I have little patience for any wealthy individual who, in order to remain pure of heart and wallet, would surrender our republic to the very people who corrupted it in the first place. You can't change the rules until you win.

I want to be very clear about this. I don't think Democratic mega-voters are inherently good and Republican ones are inherently bad. To me, the crucial distinction involves not allegiance to party but hunger for power. If you're a wealthy person who takes advantage of *Citizens United* to maintain and expand your influence, that undermines our democracy. But if you use your newfound influence to reverse the effects of *Citizens United*, effectively returning your ill-gotten power to the American people, that's not just acceptable but noble. It's the difference between Scrooge at the beginning of *A Christmas Carol* and Scrooge at the end.

It's worth noting that even if we made all these changes—raised the costs of vote buying, lowered the benefits, leveled up the American people, and leveled the playing field between the parties—Sheldon Adelson would still be doing fine. When it comes to picking our leaders, his opinion will carry more weight than the average voter's, not just by a little bit, but by orders of magnitude unprecedented in American history.

But if we can scale back those orders of magnitude by just a little, Sheldon might be encouraged to spend Darla's four dollars on something other than politics. There are yachts to purchase and art to collect. Until the Court changes (and we'll talk about that soon enough), we can't end the *Citizens United* era. But we can hit a kind of national carriage return, signaling a new and fundamentally different phase. We can stop the decay of our republic, our ugly transformation from a government of the people to a government of the few.

And that's what really matters. If our leaders aren't chosen by us, and they don't care about our interests, our republic will remain a republic in name only. That's precisely what earlier generations of Americans worked so hard to avoid. Our ancestors didn't always conceive of "the people" the way we do today. They didn't always succeed at preserving the consent of the governed. But they handed down a representative democracy from generation to generation, and in fact made it more representative over time.

At least, that's the story of the America I grew up in. The story of the America that today's newest voters have grown up in is very different indeed. Over the last couple hundred pages we've explored the many reasons why. Diminished voting rights and dirty tricks shrink the electorate. Gaps in power between voters are caused by geography, money, and the partisan manipulation of both. We've seen how unrepresentative government is flourishing—more and more, our leaders are people whom a majority of Americans rejected rather than endorsed. We've examined the ways we can reverse that trend before our democracy capsizes completely.

But elections are only a first step. Let's say we put in place all the solutions you've read about thus far. We start sending more people to Washington who are accountable to all of us, and who will fight for all Americans, not just a privileged few. What can our elected officials now do with the power they now hold? To find out, it's time to move from our political process to our legislative one—from the way we pick leaders to the way we make laws.

Like Bill in a cartoon musical, we have arrived at the steps of the Capitol. And the remainder of this book is about what happens to us next.

PART III

WHICH IDEAS BECOME A LAW?

8

I'M JUST A DOOMED BILL

The House of Representatives

An asteroid slammed into earth. Not while you were reading this, so no need to panic, but sixty-six million years ago. You probably know the asteroid I'm talking about, because this was the big one. It wiped out the dinosaurs, sent flaming radioactive particles zooming across the planet, and blotted out the sun so that no plant could grow. And here's the thing to keep in mind: according to the latest scientific estimates, a species' odds of surviving the most cataclysmic extinction of the last hundred million years was better—*more than ten times better*—than the odds of a bill becoming a law in America today.

Bills are not just imperiled. They are far more imperiled than they used to be. In the 100th Congress, the first full legislative session of my life, 7 percent of introduced legislation passed both the House and Senate. In the 1990s, Congress approved about 5 percent of bills, a number that dropped to 4 percent in the 2000s. During the 2010s,

Congress approved just 2 percent of new proposals, its lowest rate in half a century. To say today's legislative process turns bills into laws is like saying the veal industry turns calves into cows. We don't pass bills. We kill them.

But let's not tell this to the adorable cartoon scroll gazing up the Capitol Building from its steps. It's easy to imagine a Bill Jr. picking up where his old man left off, but since this is 2020, we'll give our "I'm Just a Bill" reboot a female protagonist. Let's call her Belle. Belle the bill, with her dreams and ambition and her heart full of song, has just arrived in Washington. And she is almost certain to die.

The next few chapters are about exactly how Belle will meet her demise. (If you're an optimist, I suppose you could also say the next few chapters are about how she'll live, but you'll probably be disappointed.) We'll start with Congress—first the House, then the Senate—followed by a look at the people who can kill legislation despite not being legislators themselves.

At every point in Belle's journey, we'll see how the way bills survive directly affects *which* bills survive. The rules of basketball give tall people a big advantage; the rules of soccer favor those with nimble feet. So who do the rules of our legislative hunger games favor? Which kinds of bills will be left standing?

If Capitol Hill were a true meritocracy of ideas, Belle's low odds might not necessarily be a bad thing. Every year, lawmakers propose thousands upon thousands of pieces of legislation that are useless, terrible, or both. Not to be overly callous, but those bills deserve to die. Survival of the fittest would ensure that bad ideas were weeded out while good ones had nothing to fear.

This naturally raises an important question: when it comes to legislation, who decides what "fitness" really means? There's no perfectly objective method for separating good bills from bad. Which is why I'm not going to propose my own criteria. Instead, I'll let Thomas Jefferson and George Washington do it for me. Consider the following tale, the single anecdote most often used to explain the purpose of our two-chamber Congress, which was first popularized in the 1800s by an author and abolitionist named Thomas Wentworth Higginson.

> It is said that when Jefferson returned from France he was breakfasting with Washington, and asked him why he agreed to a Senate.
>
> "Why," said Washington, "did you just now pour that coffee into your saucer before drinking it?"
>
> "To cool it," said Jefferson. "My throat is not made of brass."
>
> "Even so," said Washington, "we pour our legislation into the senatorial saucer to cool it."

Before we get to the heart of Washington and Jefferson's exchange, we should clear up a few things about their conversation, starting with the fact that it probably never occurred. (In the careful language of Monticello record keepers, "There is no definitive proof that the story is not true.") Second, I should explain what Washington meant by "saucer." After all, words' meanings change over the centuries, and I wouldn't want you to picture our Founders lapping up hot liquid from tiny plates.

Except that's exactly what they did. Today, you or I might cool coffee by stirring it. In the late 1700s, you poured a hot beverage from your cup into a shallow dish before taking a careful sip.

Yet there's a reason that, despite the cup-and-saucer story being untrue, and despite the fact that it refers to a beverage-cooling technique no American still uses, this anecdote remains a popular way to explain Congress. The exchange between Washington and Jefferson is a kind of democratic fable, suggesting a two-tiered system for evaluating the fitness of a bill. First, is the bill generally popular—does it have heat? Second, is it responsible—do well-informed experts and respected elites, upon careful, cooling consideration, offer their approval? In the cup-and-saucer model, Congress is a blend of passion and responsibility. In my limited experience with the institution, it's exactly the combination that makes a marriage work.

But the legislature Washington described at his apocryphal breakfast bears little resemblance to the Congress we have today. Ninety percent of Americans support background checks for gun sales. Three-quarters of Americans support the DREAM Act, which would protect undocumented immigrants brought here as children. At least 60 percent of Americans support marijuana legalization, ending mandatory minimum prison sentences, raising the minimum wage for everyone, and raising taxes for the rich. Those who have spent the most time studying these issues tend to share the public's view. Yet for years, these ideas have languished.[*]

Meanwhile, the most significant new bill to pass the House and Senate this decade—the massive tax cut of 2017—was both wildly unpopular *and* considered irresponsible by policy experts. If Belle meets both of Washington's criteria, with public support and elite approval, she should have a better chance of passage than a bill that meets neither. But that's not how our modern Congress works. The fittest are not most likely to survive.

So who is? That's the question the next two chapters seek to answer. We'll get to the Senate's cooling saucer. But we'll start, as good things tend to, with a cup of coffee. It's time to enter the House.

In the spring of 1776, a pair of anxious North Carolinians asked John Adams for advice. William Hooper and John Penn were delegates at the Continental Congress, and their colony was headed toward independence, which meant it would soon need a constitution. Adams was

---

[*] "Elites" has a negative connotation these days, but here I use the word in its traditional sense, to refer to the people who, by experience, knowledge, and temperament, are particularly qualified to weigh in on specific questions of policy or law.

crotchety, abrasive, and from New England, but he was also undeniably brilliant, and before leaving for home, Hooper and Penn sought their colleague's help. In Adams's own, obnoxious words, he agreed to "borrow a little time from his sleep" and lend a hand.

The result was better than anything the North Carolina delegates could have dreamed of. Where a different kind of grumpy wise man might have dashed off a few key principles or a bullet-point list of suggestions, Adams sat down and wrote a three-thousand-word essay. The treatise was eventually published as a pamphlet, *Thoughts on Government: Applicable to the Present State of the American Colonies.*

Even now, centuries later, *Thoughts on Government* bubbles over with giddy possibility, a stark contrast from Adams's usual grouchy tone. "As the divine science of politics is the science of social happiness," he wrote, "and the blessings of society depend entirely on the constitutions of government . . . there can be no employment more agreeable to a benevolent mind than a research after the best." The government that Adams's benevolent mind envisioned for North Carolina had three branches, including a legislature with two distinct chambers. What John Adams wrote as a side gig, the way you or I might help out with a friend's online dating profile, was the first draft of the republic we have today.

As part of that draft, *Thoughts on Government* described the lower chamber, the legislative body that would become the House of Representatives. Even more important, the treatise explained why we'd want such a chamber in the first place. Adams wrote that "In a large society, inhabiting an extensive country, it is impossible that the whole should assemble to make laws. The first necessary step then, is, to depute power from the many to a few of the most wise and good."

It may not appear this way at first glance, but Adam's was expressing an extremely populist view. In his telling, we don't delegate power to a House of Representatives because the mob can't be trusted. We delegate power to a House of Representatives because we have no choice. It's the same set of logistical concerns—brand-new country, slow pace of information, frog-eaten roads—that comes up again and again in the Founders' writing.

If you must have representatives, it's better that they be wise and good than dumb and evil, a fact that *Thoughts on Government* makes clear. But Adams's ideal House was not meant to be better than us. It was meant to be *identical* to us. "It should be in miniature," Adams wrote, "an exact portrait of the people at large. It should think, feel, reason, and act like them."

Nor was Adams alone in this opinion. It's true the Founders worried about ancient Athens, where direct democracy led to disaster, and they sought to avoid a "tyranny of the majority." That's why they placed cooling saucers in every branch. But they also believed those saucers should have something hot to cool—and the logical place for that heat to come from was the House. Alexander Hamilton, hardly a populist, referred to the House as "the popular branch." So did Madison, Adams, and Jefferson, to name just a few.

When our Framers wrote the House of Representatives into the Constitution, they sought to put *Thoughts on Government* into practice, creating the kind of public-in-miniature Adams had envisioned. Members of Congress would face reelection every two years, forcing them to constantly react to conditions at home. The age and citizenship requirements for the chamber would be just twenty-five and seven years, respectively; with the people's blessing, almost any adult could serve. With only sixty thousand constituents per member at the outset, representatives would have fewer interests jockeying for support than their Senate colleagues.

The House of Representative's single most important feature, however, is one many Americans have never heard of. Every two years, it ceases to exist.

I don't mean this literally, of course. As I write this we're nearing the end of the 116th Congress, and when that Congress expires, the Capitol Dome won't go anywhere. If past is prologue, more than 80 percent of members will return to Washington when the new legislative session begins. But technically speaking, those members will not be returning to the same House. The entire chamber will be disbanded, leaving us briefly with no House of Representatives at all. Then, in January, the House will be reborn like a phoenix, or a weed. The 117th Congress, officially a brand-new legislature, will gavel itself into existence.

For most of us, the House's circle of life has little practical effect. But for Belle, the chamber's cyclical nature is a crisis. If she's not approved by Congress before the end of the two-year term, she'll be swept away in a kind of cleansing flood. And while a lawmaker can always introduce a copy of Belle in a future Congress, in the same way a biologist can clone a sheep, her entire legislative journey will have to start from scratch.

That's why most bills that die in the House, good or bad, don't get voted down. They simply run out of time. In the 115th Congress, the last full one as of this writing, members introduced 7,401 resolutions, more than 10 per day. Even if every one of those proposals met Washington's cup-and-saucer criteria, there would be no way to pass them all.

The House's phoenix-like, weed-like nature has consequences for the chamber's rule book as well. You probably think congressional rules are dense and complicated, and all I can say is that you have no idea how right you are. The current edition of the *House Rules and Manual* runs 1,494 pages and weighs 3.2 pounds. That's two *Moby-Dicks* and a midsize ferret, respectively. And unlike Melville's classic tale, the House rules contain no dramatic harpoonings or psychos with wooden legs. Consider a sentence I picked at random:

> After the Speaker has put the affirmative part of the question, any Member who has not spoken before to the question may rise and speak before the negative be put; because it is no full question till the negative part be put. Scob., 23; 2 Hats., 73.

It's like a riddle delivered by a Sphinx on cocaine.

Of the 327 million Americans alive today, only a handful are genuine congressional procedure experts. Fortunately, you don't have to count yourself among them to understand the basics of House rules and why they matter. Imagine an upside-down pyramid. At the bottom, holding everything up, is the Constitution. In just a few words, it proscribes the basic structure of the House—term lengths, age requirements, the apportionment of representatives per state. These things can be changed only by amendment.

The next level of the pyramid is called "*Jefferson's Manual.*" In 1797, Jefferson became vice president, which among other things made him presiding officer of the Senate. "I am entirely rusty in the rules of parliamentary procedure," he fretted, and set about creating a how-to guide for running a legislature. The resulting document covered fifty-three separate categories—everything from questioning a witness to impeaching a president—and put meat on the Constitution's bones. Jefferson's procedures weren't set in stone, but they were so useful that in both chambers of Congress, they remain the platform upon which everything else is built.

In the House, that "everything else" is a truly massive pile of rules, procedures, and precedents. And this is where the lower chamber's bi-annual self-destruct sequence comes in. While the congressional rules might at first seem a kind of legislative stalagmite, built up through the centuries by the steady drip of parliamentary debate, they are technically brand new. When the House collapses at the end of each term, the entire rule book is shredded. When the House is reborn, a completely new set of rules is written from scratch.

Usually that rewriting is more of a copy-and-paste job than a brand-new draft. The rules of the 117th Congress will probably look nearly identical to the ones from the 116th. But they don't have to. If representatives want to change the rules, in ways large or small, they'll get their chance in two years or less.

This procedural flexibility has given us the lower chamber we have today. It's why our current House of Representatives is nothing like the replica of the people that John Adams imagined. It's also, not incidentally, one of the main reasons Belle is doomed.

To understand the full power of rulemaking, consider a slightly different parliamentary tactic, one employed by John Wilson, first-ever speaker of the General Assembly of Arkansas. In 1837, Wilson was overseeing a debate on a bill regulating wolf hunting when a fellow representative, one J. J. Anthony, submitted what the *Encyclopedia of Arkansas* calls a "tongue-in-cheek amendment." Perhaps, Anthony suggested, bounties for wolf pelts should be submitted by the Arkansas Real Estate Bank.

To those familiar with state politics at the time, Anthony's amendment was no mere suggestion. The Arkansas Real Estate Bank was one of the most powerful interests in the state, and Wilson, in addition to being assembly speaker, just happened to be the bank's president. With his cheeky proposal, Anthony was calling his colleague corrupt. Wilson this accusation highly offensive, mostly because it was true. Words were exchanged. Voices were raised.

Finally, Speaker Wilson employed a procedural trick not found in *Jefferson's manual*. He moved briskly from the podium to the assembly floor, unsheathed a bowie knife, and stabbed his fellow lawmaker to death.

(Although expelled from the assembly, Wilson was soon found "guilty of excusable homicide"—a full acquittal—and his first act as a free man was to throw a giant party for the jury members and their friends. It was a simpler time.)

Even in Washington, far from the frontier, political violence was shockingly common. In *The Field of Blood*, historian Joanne Freeman writes of more than seventy violent incidents in the three decades before the Civil War. Her research uncovered "canings, duel negotiations, and duels; shoving and fistfights; brandished pistols and bowie

234 DEMOCRACY IN ONE BOOK OR LESS

knives; wild melees in the House; and street fights with fists and the occasional brick." Lawmakers today worry about losing their seats. In the 1830s they worried about losing their lives.

Some bloodshed was random—westerners in particular seemed to just enjoy hitting people—but violence was often a means rather than an end. Political factions in the early 1800s were organized not unlike today's men's hockey teams, with designated brawlers ready to rumble. Just as elections shifted the balance of power within the country, violence changed the balance of power within a legislature.

Most crucially, violence shifted that balance toward preserving slavery. "By definition," Freeman points out, "a slave regime was violent and imperiled . . . In congressional lingo, most Northerners were 'non-combatants' and many Southerners were 'fighting men,' which gave them a literal fighting advantage." If you were an antislavery lawmaker, it wasn't just your bill that might die in committee.

Yet remarkably, when it came to silencing their abolitionist colleagues, pro-slavery lawmakers possessed a weapon even more powerful than the bowie knife, cane, or pistol: the House rules. In 1836, the chamber passed a ban on all "petitions, memorials, or resolutions" regarding slavery. Soon known as "the gag rule," for nearly a decade it barred abolitionist sentiment from Congress completely. Even those willing to risk injury or death could no longer read antislavery speeches or introduce antislavery bills.

The gag rule was finally scrapped in 1844, but its eight-year run holds two lessons still relevant today. First, just as the rules governing our elections determine who holds power, the rules governing our legislatures determine how they can wield it. Adams had hoped for a perfect barometer of public opinion. But thanks to changes in the rule book at a time of growing antislavery sentiment, the House could not think, feel, or act exactly like the people at all.

Second, procedure is a powerful weapon indeed. The chilling effect of violence—violence that injured dozens of congressmen and, as J. J. Anthony learned the hard way, could cost lawmakers their lives—

paled in comparison to a simple rule change at the start of a new Congress. In a legislature, the rulebook is quite literally mightier than the sword. Over the past two centuries, battles over procedure have warped the body John Adams hoped would be an exact mirror of the people. And each twist has brought with it a new answer to an all-important question:

If the House of Representatives doesn't reflect the public, whom or what does it reflect instead?

I suppose you could say the modern congressional era began on a winter's day at the tail end of the nineteenth century, when Representative Constantine B. Kilgore, Democrat of Texas, kicked down a door in the House chamber and fled. He was one of the lucky ones. Most of his fellow Democrats were caught rushing locked exits or hiding pathetically under their desks.

The reason for this mass panic? A man named Thomas Brackett Reed took attendance.

Everything about Thomas Reed was larger than life. In the late 1800s, when the average American man stood five foot seven, he was six three. He weighed three hundred pounds back when it really meant something. With his enormous, shiny head and beady-eyed, mustachioed face bobbing above his collar, Reed was the kind of man who could go as a walrus to a costume party simply by showing up.

As a lawyer from Portland, Maine, and then as a young member of Congress, Reed was known mostly for his witticisms. "A statesman is a politician who is dead," he liked to say. On another occasion, a colleague sanctimoniously proclaimed that he "would rather be right than be president." "The gentleman need not be disturbed," Reed replied. "He never will be either."

But Reed's lasting contribution to the House—the one that sent Constantine Kilgore running for the exits and that shapes Belle's journey today—came after the 1888 elections, when he became Speaker.

To understand what Thomas Reed did, and why it set off such pandemonium in the House chamber, we need to quickly define a procedural term known as the "quorum." Simply put, a quorum is the number of members of a legislative body who must be present in order for any business to take place. In the House, both then and now, the quorum requirement is half the total number of members plus one. If the House has one hundred seats, and a member requests what's known as a "quorum call," you need fifty-one members present to keep the lights on.

In Reed's day, there were two reasons a quorum was difficult to produce. First, lawmakers missed lots of votes. Imagine being a representative from California or Colorado before cars or airplanes. Traveling to and from D.C. took days if you were lucky, weeks if you were not. Also, antibiotics didn't exist yet; fevers that are today a nuisance could keep a congressman laid up for a month. When the roll was called, lots of members would be marked "absent" for the obvious reason that they were someplace else.

But other members would be marked absent despite the fact that they were standing on the House floor. That's because, under the original rules of the chamber, you were "present" only if you voted either for or against a bill. If you abstained from voting entirely, you didn't count toward the quorum requirement.

This combination of factors—a half-plus-one quorum requirement, sparse attendance, and the marking of nonvoting members as absent—could be used by the minority party to devastating effect. Here's how. As Thomas Reed prepared to take the Speaker's gavel, the quorum threshold stood at 165 votes; Reed's Republicans held just 168 seats. This meant Democrats didn't have to outvote a bill in order to kill it. If Republicans couldn't get 165 members from their 168-person caucus to the Capitol, an impossible task in an age of steamships and gout, Democrats could simply abstain from voting and be marked absent. Without a quorum present, the bill would die.

Today, political scientists call this procedural stunt "the disappearing quorum." But back in the late 1800s, Americans had another name for it: "the filibuster."

Bear in mind that back in the late nineteenth century, Republicans, not Democrats, were the party of activist government. The 1888 elections handed them what should have been a Skywalker Window, with control of the presidency, Senate, and House for the first time in sixteen years. But thanks to the House filibuster, the GOP's ambitious agenda was dead on arrival.

Or so everyone assumed. In fact, as historian Barbara Tuchman recounts in *The Proud Tower*, the human walrus had done some thinking. Reed took seriously our Founders' concern that a legislature's minority party should have rights. That's what debate and voting are for. But when the minority can kill a bill *without* voting, Reed felt it ran counter to everything our Framers wanted. "It becomes a tyranny," he wrote.

So Reed hatched a plan. He did it quietly, without fuss or hand-wringing or an attempt to persuade his harshest critics. He told almost no one what he was about to do—and was willing to live with the consequences if he failed. "I had made up my mind," he later said, "that if political life consisted of sitting helplessly in the Speaker's Chair and seeing the majority helpless to pass legislation, I had had enough of it and was ready to step down and out." When the 51st House kicked off its session, the Speaker was ready.

First, Reed introduced a resolution he knew would be controversial. As he suspected, while the measure had majority support, it fell two votes shy of a quorum. According to the rules, the House filibuster had succeeded once again.

But then Reed announced a roll call. He went through the names exactly the way your third-grade teacher did: the As, the Bs, the Cs. But for the first time in the history of House attendance, he didn't let members decide whether or not they were officially in the chamber. If a lawmaker was standing on the House floor, or sitting at his desk, Reed marked that person present—no exceptions. According to onlookers,

Reed was calm and businesslike, mowing through names like a reaper with a scythe. Finally, halfway through the alphabet, a Kentuckian named James McCreary cried out from the floor.

"I deny your right, Mr. Speaker, to count me as present!" the Democrat thundered.

"The Chair is making a statement of fact that the gentleman is present," Reed replied. "Does he deny it?"

The silenced McCreary watched in horror as Reed made it through the alphabet and announced his ruling: a quorum was indeed present. The resolution had passed. Not that the fight was over. For days, Democrats burst forth in fireworks of righteous objection. One member called the outrage "as violent as was ever witnessed in any parliament." (This was the same legislature, I should remind you, where thirty-four years earlier Massachusetts senator Charles Sumner was beaten to within an inch of his life on the Senate floor.)

But Reed's opponents were powerless to stop him. When Democrats insisted the rules had always allowed a disappearing quorum, Reed pointed to the House's two-year cycle. Because the House was beginning a new session when he pulled his parliamentary gambit, the old rules no longer applied. The Speaker was free to rewrite them however he chose. After four days of angry debate, Reed's opponents finally reached a similar conclusion. It was around this time that Representative Constantine B. Kilgore, terrified of being marked present, kicked down the door. But with his colleagues rounded up and the roll call finished, the fight was over. The House filibuster was dead.

The effect of Reed's maneuver was felt immediately. Instead of accomplishing nothing, the 51st Congress became one of the most significant in history. The Sherman Antitrust Act, which Reed's protégé Teddy Roosevelt later used to defend consumers and workers from monopolies, passed just months after the fateful attendance call. The 51st Congress created the federal immigration system, funded new land-grant colleges for Black students in the South, expanded pensions for Civil War veterans, and laid the foundation for what would become our national parks. Five new states were added to the union.[*]

Critics of the expansive Republican agenda called it "the billion-dollar government." "It's a billion-dollar country," Thomas Reed replied.

Yet the most meaningful achievement of the 51st Congress was not the legislation it passed, but the precedent it set. In 1892, after wresting back control of the House, Democrats tried to reinstate the filibuster. But Reed used the disappearing quorum to torture the new majority in exactly the way the Democrats had once hoped to torture him. In the end, Reed's opponents gave up, adopting the very same majority-rules system they had so recently fled the chamber to protest.

The end of the House filibuster ensured that the chamber would never find itself completely unable to pass legislation. To go back to Washington's famous breakfast, there would always be hot coffee in the cup. Yet the price we paid for adopting what came to be known as "the Reed Rules" was to forever alter the House of Representatives' role. No longer would the lower chamber be, or even pretend to be, an Adamsonian reflection of the people. Instead, the House was a reflection of the majority party. When Republicans control the Speaker's gavel, they rule with an iron first. Ditto for Democrats.

By now it won't surprise you to learn who came up with the snappiest summary of our new legislative process. "The best system," opined Thomas Reed, "is to have one party govern and the other watch." If Belle's going to survive the modern House, she won't just have to be popular with the American people. She'll have to be popular with the party in charge.

Still, if partisan approval was all it took for a bill to become a law,

---

[*] You'll recall from chapter 6 that those states—North Dakota, South Dakota, Washington, Montana, and Idaho—were overwhelmingly Republican. By breaking the filibuster in the House, the GOP also expanded its power in the Senate.

the survival rate in Congress would be far higher than it is today. Once Belle finds herself on the right side of the two-party system, her long journey has only just begun. Any part of the legislative process could prove deadly. And every part of the legislative process will warp our mirror of the people just a little bit more.

☆

Before we continue shadowing Belle on her quest, we need to borrow another term from political science. "Veto point." I'm sure there's a long, academic definition out there somewhere, but for our purposes, a veto point is simple: it refers to any hurdle that a bill must overcome in order to survive. Imagine a fairy-tale bridge with a troll lurking underneath. Veto points are that but for legislation.

In school we learn that a bill must pass three veto points—the House, Senate, and White House—to become a law. Many academics would add to that list a fourth veto point, the Supreme Court. But the reality is much more complicated. The House, for example, is not a single stumbling block. Instead, the House is a meandering ellipses of veto points, a bridge made up of smaller bridges, each guarded by its own unique troll. That's why Belle's survival chances remain poor. She has a lot of death-defying to do.

To understand just how dangerous and unexpected a veto point can be, consider the House "Committee on Rules." We've covered the way the overall House rules are rewritten every two years, but before a bill can be voted on by the full House, it needs its own individual rule as well. A bill's rule governs the amount of time it can be debated, the type of amendments that can be offered, and the number of speakers from each party who can oppose it. Seems innocent enough. But if someone on the Rules Committee wants to sabotage Belle, they can tweak her rule to make it more likely she dies on the House floor.

Even better, at least from the killer's perspective, the Rules Committee can choose not to vote on Belle's rule at all. A piece of legislation can have overwhelming support among the majority party, but without the committee's blessing, it will be held up indefinitely. At the end of the House's two-year cycle, the bill will die.

This was the fate that befell countless proposals during the reign of Howard Worth Smith, who was known to friend and foe alike as "Judge." A bespectacled, plantation-born Virginia conservative, Judge Smith, a Democrat, was first elected to Congress in 1930 and became Rules Committee chair in 1955. He was a lanky beanstalk to Thomas Reed's state fair pumpkin, yet their attitudes toward legislating were largely the same. As the *New York Times* once reported, Smith's self-described approach to his job was simple.

"Grasp any snickersnee you can get hold of and fight the best way you can."

Unlike me, Smith's contemporaries had no internet, and therefore probably had no clue that a "snickersnee" is an obsolete style of Dutch fighting knife. But regardless of the metaphorical weapon Judge Smith chose, they would have been painfully familiar with how he wielded it. As the New Deal was being debated, Smith's procedural poking so vexed FDR that the president attempted, unsuccessfully, to oust him in a primary. Later, Smith held up Alaska statehood for an entire year.

But his real achievement came as chair of the Rules Committee, which became known as "Judge Smith's Graveyard." In 1961, JFK put forth a sweeping plan to improve America's public schools. It would have passed the house easily—if the Rules Committee had released it. Instead, Smith delayed it to death. The following year, a chastened president returned with a smaller education agenda, just ten modest proposals. Smith snickersneed five.

A proud small-government conservative, Smith killed bills of every description. But the judge's specialty—the cause that really brought out his talents—was white supremacy. Even by the low standards of his time he was wildly racist, unwilling to waver even slightly in his defense of Jim Crow. Whenever civil rights bills arrived in Judge Smith's graveyard, he refused to grant them votes. One time he disappeared from the Capitol for days to delay proceedings. On another occasion, he summoned a parade of particularly long-winded speakers to a hearing on a bill. Hours later, when exhausted supporters of the measure briefly left the room for a break, Judge Smith leapt into action and voted down the bill without them.

Fortunately for Belle, the Rules Committee is one veto point we no longer have to worry about. In the early 1960s, Speaker Sam Rayburn was able to pry power from Judge Smith, and the once-feared committee is now an extension of the Speaker's office in everything but name.

Still, the story of Smith's graveyard reminds us that the placement of veto points decides which kinds of bills survive. Take the Civil Rights Act. This landmark bill became law thanks to brave and tireless activism, masterful legislative strategy, and a growing wave of popular support. But the fact remains: had Judge Smith's graveyard lasted just a few years longer, the Civil Rights Act would nonetheless have gone nowhere. The arrangement of trolls and bridges determines what our government can and cannot do.

As Belle begins tiptoeing her way through the House's veto points, it's not certain which one she'll face first. Still, since we have to start somewhere, we'll follow approximately the same route taken by the titular scroll from "I'm Just a Bill." As you may remember, he starts off by bemoaning his "long, long wait, while I'm sitting in committee." But that line undersells the peril he faced back then, or that Belle faces today. Just as the House holds up a warped mirror to the country, congressional committees hold up a warped mirror to the House.

There are two types of committees Belle can find herself in front of. The first is the "select committee," so called because it addresses one specific issue and then closes up shop. Select committees have turned their attention to such weighty subjects as Hurricane Katrina and the Iran-Contra Affair. They've also pursued slightly less urgent missions. "The House Select Committee on Banking Memorials," "The House

Select Committee on the Bible Society of Philadelphia," and my personal favorite, "The House Select Committee on Alleged Abstraction of Books from the House Library."*

The second type of committee, and the type far more likely to decide Belle's fate, is the "standing committee." Every member of Congress is assigned to at least two standing committees, which have no expiration date and oversee a broad range of issues. Lawmakers are defined by these assignments the way some college students are defined by their sorority or frat. If the official question of Washington, D.C., is "What do you do?," the official question within Congress is "What committees are you on?"

The number of standing committees varies from session to session— they tend to accumulate for years, even decades, before embarrassed legislators Marie-Kondo the chamber—but at the moment there are twenty. MIT professor Charles Stewart III (the same one we've encountered measuring voting lines and uncovering the history of our state borders) divides those committees into three groups. First are "constituency committees" (such as Veterans' Affairs), which pass laws primarily affecting individuals rather than industries. Second are "policy committees" (such as Armed Services), which each deal with a specific issue area, such as the military or education, and thus touch on a sector of the economy. Third, and most desirable, are the "power committees." What distinguishes power committees is the sheer amount of government money they control—they affect our entire economy, not just a single slice.

According to Stewart, who analyzed these things with as close to mathematical precision as possible, today there are only three power committees. "Ways and Means" is in charge of our tax code. "Appropriations" is in charge of spending the federal budget. "Energy and

---

* This last one dates from 1861 and refers not to abridgment but to theft. Apparently, congressmen from states leaving the Union were stealing library books on their way out the door.

Commerce" is in charge of whatever it can get its hands on, which given the committee's all-encompassing title is a lot.

Throughout the twentieth century, most lawmakers would gladly donate a kidney for a seat on a power committee. Some would gladly donate two. But plenty of other committees were universally coveted as well. That's because they ran on what's known as the "seniority system"—the longer you served on a committee, the more powerful you grew, with the longest-serving member of the majority party becoming the chair. If you earned a seat on the Armed Services Committee, for example, and you lasted a few decades in Congress, you would find yourself in charge of an entire legislature-within-a-legislature. Your committee might not be among the three most powerful, but you'd make up for it by exercising near-total control.

That has changed in recent decades, and the reason it changed is Newt Gingrich. In 1994, when the baby-faced Georgia Republican seized the Speaker's chair, Democrats had controlled the lower chamber for forty straight years. That meant Republicans had gone four decades without a crack at the House rule book, and when Gingrich took charge, he made up for lost time.

One of Gingrich's most dramatic changes was to dismantle the seniority system. This was not necessarily a bad thing—after all, choosing chairs solely by length of service is what placed Judge Smith atop the Rules Committee—but for better or worse, it redirected power from the committees to the Speaker. This was just fine with Newt. Instead of allowing committees to elect leaders on their own, committee chairs were picked by the "Republican Steering Committee," a group stocked with the Speaker's handpicked allies.

Party loyalty—and personal loyalty to Newt Gingrich—were now the keys to securing a fancy assignment. And the key to *keeping* your fancy assignment was doing what the Speaker told you to do, whether or not you agreed with it. Future Speakers, both Democrats and Republicans, liked this arrangement, and kept large portions of Gingrich's system when the gavel changed hands.

The committee system we have today, in other words, is meaningfully different from the one that existed twenty-five years ago. Before Gingrich took charge, lawmakers informally ranked committees the way *U.S. News & World Report* formally ranks schools. There was a best choice, a second-best choice, and so on, all the way down the line. Today that's changed. There are now just two groups: the three power committees and everything else. It's not that the seventeen non-power committees don't matter. It's that they matter differently to everyone. Instead of looking at the rankings, lawmakers are searching for the best fit.

With college admissions that's probably healthy. Sometimes it's healthy in Congress, too. Congresswoman Lucy McBath, for example, became an anti-gun violence activist after her son Jordan was shot and killed in cold blood. Upon flipping a previously red Georgia district in 2018, she asked for, and received, a seat on the Judiciary Committee, which has jurisdiction over gun laws. Eight years after her son's murder, McBath helped shape the first major gun safety bill to pass the House in more than a decade.

But the "best-fit" approach to committees has changed the House in other, less inspiring ways. One of the main reasons lawmakers seek out an assignment is that they hope to protect their constituents' jobs. There's nothing inherently shady about that. If a large number of my voters work at Pinkberry, why wouldn't I seek a seat on the Tasty Treats Committee, or the chairmanship of the Subcommittee on Frozen Desserts? But imagine a piece of anti-obesity legislation came before us. Rather than reflect the interests of the American people, my committee would reflect the interests of the frozen yogurt industry instead.

In fact, now that I have all this power over Big Fro-Yo, I might start asking them for donations. That's the other reason lawmakers seek out specific committee assignments: money. If you're on the financial services committee, you can expect huge contributions from banks. If you're handling laws that regulate agriculture, you can expect Monsanto to come knocking. It's an updated version of the symbiotic relationship developed by fundraising king Mark Hanna in the 1890s. In many cases, those relationships are even formalized within the parties. Some committee assignments and chairs come with specific targets—the more lucrative the industry being overseen, the higher the fundraising goal.

Ever since Reed's rules were established, the House has belonged to the party in power. But the modern committees add another bias to the mix: a bias against change. Imagine, for example, that Belle invests in a huge new clean-energy program. She'll create hundreds of thousands of jobs, and billions in profits for American companies. The problem is that those jobs and profits would be spread around the country. Any jobs and profits she threatens, meanwhile, are located in a few specific areas—and representatives from those areas, who take donations from the interests that oppose her, are likely to be on the committee she must survive.

This same dilemma faces new banking regulations in the Financial Services Committee; farm subsidy reforms in the Agriculture Committee; expanded mass transit in the Transportation Committee; and countless others. The more aggressively a bill challenges the status quo, the lower its odds of survival.

Nor is it just the committee as a group that Belle must contend with. She must also win the favor of the individual who chairs it. Even after Gingrich, chairs are like feudal lords and ladies, exercising remarkable control over their fiefdoms. If a bill is a top priority for the national party, the Speaker likely calls the shots. But for the vast majority of issues, the chair's whims—no matter how parochial, esoteric, or politically unsound—must be honored.

This doesn't necessarily mean the committee and its chair will kill Belle. They may choose to alter her appearance instead. During what's known as "markup," committee members can amend Belle in any number of ways: watering her down; larding her up with pork; attaching a "poison pill" amendment so loathsome that she's no longer able to win a vote of the entire House. And even if Belle does make it through the relevant committee or committees mostly intact, and also survives a subcommittee (essentially the same thing but in miniature), her worries aren't over. There are more hurdles she must overcome.

The first is Appropriations, which even among its fellow power committees stands out. Most bills tell the government to do something—provide school lunches to children, say—but they don't necessarily give the government the money to do it. That's where the Appropriations Committee comes in. Every year, appropriators dole out the funds that turn laws into realities. If they can't or don't provide the funding, a law that is technically alive may nonetheless enter a kind of coma, unable to do anything even though it still exists. Appropriators can also defund a part of the government already in existence, kneecapping Belle years, or even decades, after she's passed.

Belle must also win the approval of the Speaker's office. In today's Congress, Speakers don't just throw their considerable weight around when assigning committee seats or selecting chairs. In fact, their greatest power has nothing to do with elevating or demoting members. In a chamber where the doomsday clock is always ticking, the Speaker controls the calendar. With a wave of the hand, Speakers can put a bill onto the schedule for a vote. They can just as abruptly cancel that vote, leaving Belle to die.[*]

In addition to exercising power over the calendar on a bill-by-bill basis, Speakers can also make informal rules regarding entire categories of legislation. A good example is known as the "Hastert Rule," after Republican Speaker Dennis Hastert, who served in the early 2000s. (It says something about the Hill's cloistered mentality that, even after it emerged that Hastert had sexually assaulted at least four children during his pre-Congress career, the rule continues to bear his name.) The Hastert Rule, which tends to be adopted by Republicans

---

[*] Because nothing is simple in Congress, the House "calendar" is actually four different calendars, a mess of overlapping schedules that would give even the most ardent polyamorist a headache.

and dismissed by Democrats, establishes yet another veto point: if a majority of the members of the majority party disapprove of a bill, it can't become a law.

To understand how the Hastert Rule works in practice, look at what happened with immigration reform in 2013. A bipartisan reform bill passed the Senate. The same bill had wide bipartisan support in the House. But in order for it to receive a vote in the lower chamber, yet another condition had to be met. One hundred twenty-one Republicans—half the members of the majority plus one—had to support the bill. When then-Speaker John Boehner realized he couldn't reach that magic number, he refused to bring immigration reform to the floor. Thanks to the Hastert Rule, a bill that met Washington's cup-and-saucer test perfectly, with wide popular support and elite approval, nonetheless failed to become a law.

Of course, by now, a bill's untimely demise shouldn't be surprising. It's a minor miracle that any bills survive at all. When we say Belle needs to "pass the House," what we really mean is that she must, at minimum, accomplish the following:

- Get introduced by a lawmaker.
- Win a majority of the relevant committee.
- Win over the committee chair.
- Win a majority of the relevant subcommittee.
- Win over the subcommittee chair.
- Secure the necessary funding.
- Earn a spot on the calendar from the Speaker of the House.
- Win a majority of the majority party (if the Hastert Rule is in effect).
- Win a majority of the House.

By my count, then, the "popular branch" is not a popularity contest. It is, at minimum, eight separate popularity contests. If Belle loses just one of them, she dies.

No less important, in today's House, nearly every veto point nudges the legislative process in one of three ways: by making it easier to pass bills that preserve the status quo rather than bills that change it; making it easier to pass bills that appeal narrowly to a few powerful individuals rather than bills that appeal to the House as a whole; or making it easier to pass bills on the partisan fringes rather than those in the mainstream.

Unlike, say, our campaign finance system, the House is by no means dysfunctional. Because it's tightly controlled by the majority party, which is in turn tightly controlled by the Speaker, the chamber is capable of getting things done. But the bias against doing big, important things for the country is present regardless of who's in charge. The more a would-be law makes real the promise of America—that we can overcome our greatest challenges together—the harder it becomes to pass.

To put it slightly differently, and in terms Washington and Jefferson would readily understand, the coffee isn't just lukewarm. It tastes funny, too.

☆

At the risk of sounding procedurally smitten, there is one last Thomas Reed epigram I must share. For all his willingness to change the House rule book, Reed loved the chamber in which he served. Although the phrase "wisdom of crowds" was decades from coinage, he believed in it wholeheartedly.

"The House," he used to say, "has more sense than anyone in it."

Let's assume Reed was right. What would a more sensible House look like today?

An improved House of Representatives would hardly guarantee Belle's passage. Our goal should not be to pass enormous volumes of laws for its own sake. Nor, in today's polarized political age, can we return to a pre-Reed era, one where every bill requires both parties' support. That would be a recipe for dysfunction.

Instead, we should keep Thomas Reed's basic framework, while bringing back some of the popular-branch spirit our Founders spoke of. If a majority of the American people likes Belle, she should have a good chance of passing the House. And if an overwhelming majority likes Belle, she should have an overwhelming chance of passing the House.

As we've seen, it's not especially difficult to tweak the lower chamber in pursuit of that goal. For a would-be John Adams, sketching out a perfect government on paper, there's an endless supply of unlikely but fun-to-imagine reforms. (My personal favorites: tripling the number of House seats, and allowing the American people to bring a bill straight to the House floor via a national popular vote.) The most realistic and effective changes, however, fall into just two categories—give bills more time to complete their journey, and rearrange the bridges and trolls they face.

Short of a constitutional amendment, there's no way to extend the House doomsday clock past two years. But within those two years, the Constitution says almost nothing about how lawmakers must spend their time. As part of his 1995 overhaul, Newt Gingrich cut the House's number of "working" days—days when legislation can be considered—from five per week to just three. The House still had roughly the same number bills to get through. But it had 40 percent less time to get through them.

Even after Gingrich was ousted, the amount of working time has never recovered to pre-1995 levels. This isn't because members of Congress are lazy. It's because they want to spend time back home. Meeting with voters (and, unfortunately, raising money) is an important part of a representative's job, particularly when control of the chamber hangs in the balance from election to election.

But if we ever find ourselves in a genuine Skywalker Window— with a rare, real chance to pass bills into law and get them signed by the president—we should squeeze as much working time as we can from those two years. Adding one more working day per week would be the equivalent of extending the doomsday clock by three and a half months over the life of the Congress. Imagine how many more bills could pass during that time.

There's even a way to increase Belle's chances of passage without diminishing a lawmaker's time spent at home. Let representatives vote remotely. Nothing in the Constitution says that yeas and nays must be issued inside the House chamber. In fact, until fairly recently, lawmakers could in some cases vote by proxy. They'd simply hand a colleague a card with their voting instructions, the same way you might text a friend your drink order if you're running late. But proxy voting was outlawed by—you guessed it—Newt Gingrich.

There are some good reasons to be wary of unlimited congressional teleworking. I won't name names, but certain lawmakers would never leave the campaign trail if they didn't have to return to the Capitol for votes. In the twenty-first century, however, there are also some good reasons to bring proxy voting back. When Senator Tammy Duckworth was a member of the House, she once asked permission to use a proxy because she was about to go into labor. This was for an internal vote within the Democratic caucus, not even for a vote on a bill. Even so, under the rules, she was denied. I think that's a little ridiculous, don't you?

The other big change since the Gingrich years, one that makes proxy voting far more viable than it used to be, is the internet. It takes lawmakers the same amount of time to get from their districts to D.C. as it did thirty years ago. But the amount of time it takes large volumes of information to get from D.C. to those districts has shrunk by a factor of infinity. Industry after industry has recognized that in the twenty-first century, allowing at least some teleworking is good for productivity. It might be good for Congress, too. (Even if we decide lawmakers shouldn't be allowed to cast their *final* votes from anywhere, we could bring back proxy voting in committee, or for routine procedural business.)

Along with expanding the amount of working time in the House calendar, we can remove and change its veto points, giving the most popular bills the best possible chances to survive. Let's start by getting rid of the Hastert Rule. We can't stop Republicans from adopting a majority-of-the-majority requirement the next time they control the House, but there's no reason we have to pretend some unwritten, intermittently used measure deserves to be called a "rule" at all. Giving the most extreme faction of your party a veto over our laws is not a requirement. It's a choice. And in our democracy, we should hold leaders accountable for their choices.

When it comes to accountability, We, the People, can also play a larger role in the committee process. Today the two distinguishing features of the congressional committee system are that (a) they're really important, and (b) almost no one outside Washington cares about them. That is nearly always a recipe for disaster.

I'm not suggesting future candidates should base their campaigns around the subcommittee they'd like to chair. But there's a layer between "Washington insiders" and voters who don't even know their congressperson's name. According to a recent poll, 12 percent of Americans made a political donation in 2016. You don't have to give candidates money to be civically engaged, but still, it's a useful proxy for determining the number of Americans especially active in politics, and 12 percent of American adults comes to about 21 million people.

Properly organized, that's a large enough population to change the House without changing the rules. To return to our earlier hypothetical, imagine if hundreds of thousands of Americans demanded the Speaker appoint legislators to the Tasty Treats Committee who would reform Big Fro-Yo rather than do its bidding. Lawmakers would still want to be on the committees that most affected their voters. Speakers would still control assignments. But activists could add a powerful new incentive to the mix, one that would shift the committees' composition toward broad national interests over narrow local ones.

Finally, and by far the most important, we can bring back a time-honored method for getting past bridge-guarding trolls. We can pay them off.

I'm not suggesting we bribe on-the-fence lawmakers. I am, however, suggesting that we fund their pet projects in exchange for allowing Belle safe passage. For decades, this was done using something called "earmarks."

A common misconception is that earmarks increase the total amount of money taxpayers spend. They don't. Instead, earmarks allow lawmakers to designate a tiny bit of the government's predetermined budget to a priority of their choice. (The word itself comes from a fifteenth-century agricultural term. If I wanted to designate a single cow or sheep from the collective herd as my own, I'd carve a notch into its ear.)

Historically, earmarks were used for infrastructure: roads, bridges, schools, and the like. Residents of Gordo, Alabama, have earmarks to thank for their library. Visitors to the Hoover Dam have earmarks to thank for the public toilets.

The problem, however, was that earmarks could be awarded in secret, and secret earmarks were frequently abused. One congressman used an earmark to touch up the beach near his vacation home. Others funded roads that never saw a driver. Duke Cunningham, a California representative until his guilty plea in 2005, traded earmarks to a defense contractor in exchange for cash, the kind of explicit bribery even John Roberts wouldn't abide. A new, transparent earmarking process was created, and the corruption mostly ceased. But it was too late. With earmarks' reputation besmirched, an unlikely combination of Tea Partiers and good-government reformers got rid of them entirely in 2011.

Today, an equally unlikely combination of Donald Trump and good-government reformers wants to bring earmarks back. It turns out that, despite the Tea Party's hopes, eliminating earmarks doesn't shrink government; the funds not allocated by Congress are simply allocated by bureaucrats instead. Meanwhile, the deficit continues to balloon. The most famously wasteful earmark project, a "Bridge to Nowhere" in Ketchikan, Alaska, would have cost taxpayers about $315 million. It sounds like a lot of money. It *is* a lot of money. But the tax bill Republicans passed in 2018 adds that much money to the national debt every fifteen hours. Earmarks are not going to affect our financial health.

They will, however, affect Belle's chances of survival. Plenty of ideas are popular nationwide but contentious within an individual district. Other ideas might help Americans as a population, but antagonize a small but powerful group. When bills like these are introduced, a newly paved highway interchange or refurbished school can be just the kind of deal-sweetener that takes a member of Congress from no to yes. By creating a patchwork quilt of local incentives, we can pass more bills that a majority of Americans support.

None of this will change the fundamental nature of the House. And frankly, that's okay. The doomsday clock will tick. Bad things will sometimes happen to good bills, and vice versa. But if Belle is the kind of bill the popular branch was designed to promote—if she can translate the will of the people into the reality we live each day—then she deserves the best possible chance to rise above the rest, win the approval of the House, and move on to the upper chamber.

At which point her inspiring story will come to a screeching halt. Because for a meaningful, bold, sweeping piece of legislation—the kind of proposal that frequently passed Congress when the original Bill sang his heart out—stepping into today's Senate is like stepping into a woodchipper. If the House is a legislative Hunger Games, the Senate is a straight-up massacre.

How did Washington's "cooling saucer" become the modern version of Judge Smith's graveyard? Mitch McConnell had a hand in it, of course. But before we get to him, our story starts with a pigheaded Roman, a Polish vampire, and an American who tried to sell a large chunk of our country to Spain.

9

THE SPARTAN RETENTION OF THE BODY'S JUICES

The Senate

Approximately 2,100 years ago, had you gone for a stroll in the capital of the world's mightiest republic, you would have noticed a small boy being dangled from a window and vigorously shaken. This was Cato the Younger, and he was among the most stubborn human beings the planet has ever produced.

The adult doing the dangling was a friend of Cato's parents, a politician named Pompaedius Silo. A few minutes earlier, Silo had teasingly asked young Cato for his support. The request was obviously a joke—a tiny child's endorsement is hardly coveted—but even so, the boy wouldn't play along. Cato's glaring refusal so incensed the older man that he grabbed the child, thrust him out the window, and threatened to drop him onto the streets of Rome below unless he changed his mind. Yet Cato refused to yield. Stunned and defeated, Silo ultimately brought the boy back into the house and withdrew his request.

Fast forward several decades. Cato, now a senator in the Roman Republic, remained as politically inflexible as ever. But by this time, he was also a keen observer of parliamentary procedure. The Senate's schedule operated like most businesses, opening each morning, closing each evening, and picking up the next day where it left off. Most of the time, this worked well. But in 60 BC, when a tax bill came up and Cato opposed it, he did something radical: he spoke all day, refusing to yield to his fellow senators. The next morning, when Senate business resumed, the floor was still his. Once again, he wasted every last minute of the Senate's time.

This went on for six straight months. While Cato held the floor, no one else could get a word in. In theory, the tax bill had the votes to clear the Senate, but no vote could be taken. The law couldn't pass. Finally, like Pompaedius Silo before them, the weary senators admitted defeat and withdrew their bill. Later that year, when the Senate seemed certain to pass a land-reform act he detested, Cato once again employed his delaying tactic. Once again, the offending bill was withdrawn. By occupying his legislature's entire calendar, and refusing to yield the floor to his colleagues, Cato had created his own brand-new veto point.

Cato's third marathon speaking session was his noblest: he shut down the Senate to delay Julius Caesar's rise to power. But this time, the stubborn senator had gone too far. Romans were fed up with a legislature that couldn't function, and Caesar, taking advantage of their frustration, bypassed the upper chamber entirely and seized power in a popular vote. Rome descended into tyranny. Even the most tenacious senators were unable to stop the backslide. Fourteen years after his delaying tactics backfired, a thoroughly defeated Cato committed suicide in such grisly fashion that I'll allow you to decide for yourself whether to google it. Let's just say it was a good thing he was a stoic.

As admirers of the Roman Republic, our Founders were almost certainly familiar with Cato the Younger's principled life and gruesome death. But they didn't need to go back thousands of years to find cautionary tales involving legislative veto points. In fact, at around the same time that America was declaring its independence, Poland was wrapping up its own experiment with parliamentary delay.

In the Polish Sejm (pronounced "Same," but with a downcast inflection suggesting harsh and unyielding winter), every legislator possessed what is known as the "free veto." This procedural mechanism, which originated in the 1500s, actually sounds kind of fun. If you were a Sejm deputy, and you objected to a piece of legislation, you could leap from your seat and cry, "Sisto activitatem!" (Latin for "I cease the activity!") Upon utterance of these magic words, any bill under consideration would crumple lifeless to the floor.

The noblemen who made up the Sejm quite liked having the power to kill any proposal they disapproved of, so in the mid-1600s, they expanded the free veto even further. Now your *sisto activitatem* wouldn't merely dispose of a single bill. It would bring the whole legislative session to an immediate end, disbanding the chamber for a year or more.

You don't have to be John Adams to see how such a system of government might cause trouble. Soon after the free veto's expansion, cranky legislators were regularly bringing the entire Polish state to its knees. During a single twenty-four-year period, half of Poland's legislative sessions were cut short by veto. One year, the Sejm was disbanded before it even convened. Meanwhile, Poland's neighbors, notably Russia, exploited this parliamentary vulnerability, bribing Polish noblemen to sabotage their own government. Weakened by corruption and sapped by delay, Poland entered a century-long decline. In 1795, the country was partitioned and annexed by rivals.

Today, Poland looks back on its experiment in unlimited veto power with something less than fondness. According to one Polish folktale, Władysław Siciński, the first nobleman to disband a legislative session via *sisto activitatem*, was immediately struck by lightning as divine punishment. When he died, his body failed to decompose and instead clawed its way out of the ground and haunted his hometown like a vampire.

While Siciński sightings are rare these days, you can still find loathing for the free veto embedded in a variety of European languages. Modern Swedish, Norwegian, Danish, German, Finnish, and (most cruelly) Polish itself all employ the idiom "Polish parliament." It roughly translates to "clusterfuck."

Eager to avoid a Polish parliament of their own, our Framers handed out veto power carefully. According to the Constitution, the president is the only person who can single-handedly veto a bill—and even a presidential veto can be overturned. In the House and Senate, whose bill-killing abilities are irreversible, veto power belongs not to any individual, but to the chamber as a whole.

For the same reason, despite the American Senate's role as a cooling saucer for legislation, our Constitution does not give would-be Catos the right to seize the floor indefinitely in protest. Instead, our Framers fashioned the Senate in a way that encouraged careful deliberation without endless delay. Senators served for six years instead of two, so they didn't have to constantly worry about getting reelected. Senators represented states rather than districts, so they could take less parochial views. Until 1913, senators were also elected by state legislators rather than directly by voters, which further insulated them from populist whim. Finally, a higher age requirement, thirty years instead of twenty-five, made senators theoretically more mature than their colleagues in the House.

The structure of the Senate made the chamber, in the words of James Madison in Federalist No. 62, "in all cases a salutary check on the government." Senator George Frisbie Hoar, whom we last saw defending the Bedford Decree in chapter 6, had an even more poetical term for the upper chamber. The Senate, he said, was created to express "the sober second thought of the people." It's a comforting image: at two in the morning, when you've had a few beers, the Senate is the voice in your head telling you not to send that email. Allowing for this sober second thought on one hand, while avoiding Poland-style paralysis on the other, was one of our Founders' most impressive achievements.

Then Aaron Burr got involved.

Burr's association with the Senate began with the 1800 presidential race, which as you may recall resulted in an Electoral College tie with Thomas Jefferson for first place. You will also recall that since America still had its original version of the Electoral College, when Burr finally lost the White House he became vice president as a consolation prize. It was in 1804, toward the end of his first term, that he shot Alexander Hamilton to death on a New Jersey dueling ground.

After a brief hiatus, Vice President Burr returned to work, where he assigned himself a brand-new project. In his role as presiding officer of the Senate (one of the few responsibilities the Constitution actually grants the vice president), he would tidy up Thomas Jefferson's manual of parliamentary procedure.

You may be wondering what qualified Burr to single-handedly thrust his hands into the guts of the Senate rulebook. The answer, apparently, is nothing. Nor was there any problem with Senate procedure—the chamber was working just fine. But for whatever reason, Burr decided the Senate rule book was overly wordy, and he began suggesting lines and paragraphs to trim.

One reason Burr's act of carelessness gets so little historical notice is that it was sandwiched between two far wilder acts of malice. There was the fatal duel with Hamilton a few months before. Two years later, Burr was arrested and charged with trying to hand large tracts of the Louisiana Purchase to Spain. Acquitted of treason on a technicality, Burr slunk across the Atlantic, where he attempted to convince an increasingly skeptical assortment of Europeans to fund an invasion of Mexico. When that plot failed, Burr returned home. He died in 1836 on Staten Island.

Which means Aaron Burr didn't live to see his greatest contribution to our democracy. Neither did any other Founder or Framer. It wasn't until 1837 that Burr's true legacy, one more significant than his attempted treason or even the shooting of Hamilton, would be noticed. A group of senators began talking and couldn't be forced to stop.

Unlike Cato the Younger, the lawmakers who brought the Senate to its knees were not debating a consequential piece of legislation. Opponents of Andrew Jackson, they hoped to stop a pro-Jackson majority from repealing a censure of the president that an earlier Congress had passed. But the pettiness of their cause notwithstanding, so long as the senators held the floor, the entire chamber was frozen solid. Understandably peeved, pro-Jackson legislators went flipping through the rule book, looking for a way to compel their colleagues to cease making speeches and vote.

In fact, such a debate-ending mechanism existed. When the House of Representatives had faced a similar problem, it turned to *Jefferson's Manual*, where members stumbled across what was called the "previous question motion." While the previous question motion was originally intended for a separate, unrelated purpose, some long-forgotten parliamentary MacGyver realized it could be used to force a vote, thereby cutting off obstructionists. The anti-Jackson lawmakers' stunt never would have worked in the House.

Nor should it have worked in the Senate. After all, the upper chamber used *Jefferson's Manual*, too. But when desperate senators searched for the previous question motion in their rules, it was missing. Thirty-two years earlier, Aaron Burr had deemed it redundant and engineered its removal.

The result wasn't a full-on Polish clusterfuck. Senators couldn't cancel an entire legislative session with a few magic words. Nor could they go home each night, as Cato the Younger had, to rest up and resume the next day. But without a previous question motion, a handful of senators could pass speaking privileges among each other, allowing one to continue talking while the others regained strength. Individual senators still didn't possess a free veto. But for all intents and purposes, any small group of them now did.

Our Founders didn't want a Senate filibuster. They didn't design it. They didn't live to see it. But the Senate filibuster had nonetheless arrived.

Like the House, the Senate has committees, subcommittees, chairs, and a calendar. But there's no need to go through them all again. Instead, this chapter is devoted almost entirely to Aaron Burr's singular contribution. By removing lawmakers' ability to end debate and force a vote on a bill, the filibuster did not just alter our upper chamber. It redefined our upper chamber. The filibuster is to the Senate's legislative body what DNA is to a human one.

Which is why, if you want to understand why Belle is so profoundly doomed in the Senate, the filibuster should be your beginning, middle, and end.

Unlike the House, the Senate is not reborn every two years. In fact, it's not reborn at all. The upper chamber opened more than two centuries ago, and 1,974 Americans have now served there, but technically it has not once closed up shop. As of this writing, we're on our 116th incarnation of the House. We're still on our very first Senate.

The Senate's oak-like consistency has long been a point of pride for its members. "Administrations come and go," wrote Republican Henry Cabot Lodge, "Houses assemble and disperse, Senators change, but the Senate is always there in the Capitol, and always organized, with an existence unbroken since 1789."

As a practical matter, however, the Senate's unbroken existence makes it extremely difficult to change the rules. If the previous motion question had been deleted in the House, the Speaker could simply have reinstated it when the rules were rewritten at the start of the next term. In the Senate, however, the rules are *never* rewritten from scratch. Changes to the rules must be agreed upon using whatever rules already exist. Any attempt to undo the filibuster, in other words, can be filibustered itself.

Legendary Kentucky senator Henry Clay found this out the hard way. Clay was known as the "Great Compromiser," exactly the kind of cooling influence Washington hoped the Senate would provide. But he didn't see the filibuster as a catalyst for compromise. He saw it as a hazard. In 1841, after yet another obstructionist delay, Clay threatened to undo Burr's copy edit and reinstate majority rule. But it brought him up against what historian Robert Caro describes as "perhaps the ultimate legislative Catch-22: any attempt to close the loophole allowed the loophole to be used to keep it from being closed."

Even the word "filibuster" reflects lawmakers' frustration with this new state of affairs. In the nineteenth century, *flibustiers* and *filibusteros* pirated the seas on behalf of the French and Spanish, respectively. To filibuster, then, was to take the lawmaking process hostage rather than accept its result.[*] Yet thanks to the structure of the Senate, legislators couldn't defeat the legislative *flibustier*. They had to learn to live with procedural piracy.

This they did by inventing something called the "unanimous consent agreement," or "UC agreement" for short. In 1846, after a delay over a treaty with Britain lasted more than two months, Ohio's William Allen offered a proposal. Since the treaty was vital, and everyone knew a vote would eventually be taken, why not have everyone get together and agree on a date? Remarkably, it worked. Every senator— even the stubborn *filibusteros*—eventually agreed to allow a vote. The treaty was signed and a precedent established.

The unanimous consent agreement—a touchy-feely declaration of legislative togetherness—provided a counterweight to the filibuster's egotistical extremes. In fact, with the official rules so resistant to change, Senators began turning to UC agreements not just to prevent filibusters, but to accomplish almost anything. Today the Senate has a

---

[*] Nor was the word "filibuster" limiting to any specific legislature or parliamentary trick. As you'll recall from the last chapter, the disappearing quorum that Thomas Reed abolished was known as the filibuster in the House.

formal rule book. But unlike in the House, that rule book is frequently ignored by unanimous consent.

Here's just one example. Every morning, the Senate's formal rules require a complete, out-loud recitation of the previous day's journal. This is the world's most boring diary, a list of bills introduced, votes tallied, and other dry logistics; no senator wants to hear it read aloud. But senators never change the journal rule. Instead, they circumvent it, each day agreeing to skip the reading via unanimous consent.[*] You'll often hear Hill staffers say the Senate "runs by UC." This sort of handshake deal is what they mean.

Balancing the post-Burr yin and yang—the filibuster on one hand and the UC agreement on the other—was a remarkable achievement. Rather than sliding into Poland-style chaos, the American Senate continued to provide the nation's sober second thought. Still, while the Senate that Aaron Burr created was far from dysfunctional, it functioned quite differently than it had before. Individual senators didn't have veto power over legislation, but they did have veto power over the UC agreements by which that legislation was passed.

Just as we saw in the House, rearranging the Senate's veto points made some bills more likely to survive and others less. Where Washington's cooling saucer placed a premium on wisdom and moderation, Aaron Burr's Senate placed a premium on near-total consensus, which is not always the same thing. Second, in Burr's Senate, intensity of opposition was more important than breadth of support. If 90 percent of the chamber liked a bill, but 10 percent absolutely hated it, the bill was doomed.

It was this feature of the Senate that, in 1917, threatened to tear the body apart. A German U-boat had just killed 123 Americans aboard the *Lusitania,* and President Woodrow Wilson sought to arm American

---

[*] For the sake of convenience, UC agreements don't require every senator to come to the floor to signal approval. Instead, senators are given a chance to object to the agreement; if no one does, unanimous consent is assumed.

merchant ships in response. Most lawmakers were happy to oblige, but a handful were adamantly opposed. Like generations of procedural pirates before them, they seized the Senate floor and refused to allow a vote.

This was a dangerous escalation. In the opinion of most Americans, it was also no way for a budding superpower to behave. "The Senate of the United States is the only legislative body in the world which cannot act when its majority is ready for action," Wilson raged. "A little group of willful men, representing no opinion but their own, have rendered the great Government of the United States helpless and contemptible."

With America's national security and global prestige at risk, lawmakers were finally open to filibuster reform. A large group of senators favored eliminating the filibuster altogether; smaller groups felt it should take three-quarters of senators to break a filibuster or that no change should be made at all. In the end, lawmakers compromised and created a new formal rule. If two-thirds of senators came together, a speaker could be cut off and a filibuster broken. A grumpy trio or quartet could no longer slam the brakes on the entire legislative process.

But even after the Wilson-era reforms, a faction of senators—a group larger than a handful but smaller than a majority—could still kill any bill it pleased. One faction in particular was large and well organized enough to make good use of the new filibuster: southern Democrats. And the issue to which they were allergic was civil rights.

Consider what happened in the early 1920s, when Henry Cabot Lodge, deep admirer of the Senate's steadfast consistency, introduced a bill to combat lynching. At the time, most Americans, regardless of party, were not pro-lynching. An antilynching bill passed the House and had majority support in the Senate as well. But to take advantage of that majority support, the bill needed to be voted on. To ensure that never happened, southern senators executed what can best be described as a ballet of obstruction.

You'll recall from just a few pages ago that the Senate's daily journal reading was skipped each morning by UC. Now, however, southern Democrats withdrew their consent. This meant the journal, in all its bureaucratic tedium, had to be read in full. Then, in a pirouette of parliamentary delay, the filibusterers began offering amendments to the journal during the reading. These could be as meaningless as inserting a senator's middle name or changing a single world in a speech. Yet the vote on each amendment could be filibustered as well.

After a week of fruitless exhortation, Lodge realized he had only two options: abandon the rest of the legislative session or scuttle the antilynching bill. He scuttled the bill. Over the next few decades, Congress would consider nearly two hundred antilynching measures. Thanks to the quirks of the Senate, not one became law.

In 2005, the Senate passed a resolution formally apologizing to lynching victims and their descendants for the chamber's inaction. The text was brutally honest about the horrors of what it called "the ultimate expression of racism in the United States following Reconstruction." Yet the apology made no mention of *why* lynching had been allowed to persist. Americans were left to conclude that the Senate had examined half a century's worth of antilynching bills and, upon careful, cooling-saucer consideration, dismissed them as unwise. In fact, this wasn't the case at all. The antilynching bills weren't rejected by a sober, cautious Senate. There was nothing to reject. They never received a vote.

The upper chamber in the early and mid-1900s was hardly dysfunctional. It passed the bulk of the New Deal, the Marshall Plan, the Interstate Highway System, and plenty of other big, ambitious bills worthy of a superpower. Yet during that the same time, for almost half a century, no civil rights bill met the two-thirds threshold necessary to break a filibuster and become law. Americans were murdered, unjustly imprisoned, denied the right to vote, treated by their own democracy as subhuman—all because of the Senate's unique and often venerated veto point. What kind of sober second thought is that?

And on that depressing note, let's talk about middle-aged white men trying not to pee.

☆

In 1939, Senator Jefferson Smith, determined to secure a campsite for his beloved Boy Rangers and expose a corrupt land-grab scheme, refused to yield the Senate floor. After speaking for nearly a full day, the lanky westerner collapsed, but his lonely stand was not in vain. Smith's self-sacrifice spurred his crooked colleague to attempt suicide, saved a parcel of public land for his beloved Rangers, and became the most famous filibuster in American history. Most impressive of all, throughout the day-long affair, the senator did not once feel the urge to urinate.

As you may already be aware, Jefferson Smith's ability to withstand nature's call—a talent *Time* magazine once delicately described as the "Spartan retention of the body's juices"—was due largely to the fact that he was fictional. Played with golly-gee enthusiasm by Jimmy Stewart, the record-setting filibusterer was the titular role in the film *Mr. Smith Goes to Washington.*

Among real people, however, the body's juices proved harder to retain. In 1935, for example, the charming, demagogic populist Huey Long refused to yield the floor. Speaking out against a New Deal provision he felt would hurt him politically, he railed against the Roosevelt administration, conducted a highly idiosyncratic analysis of the Constitution, and read a recipe for fried oysters. He lasted fifteen and a half hours, and would have made it even longer had his bladder not betrayed him around 4 a.m.

When it came to postponing bodily functions, no senator worked harder than South Carolina's Strom Thurmond. In 1957, a civil rights bill was coming dangerously close to passage, and the virulent segregationist was determined to speak out against it for as long as possible. For days before his speech, he subjected himself to dehydrating steam baths. Once on the floor, the senator stationed an aide with a pee bucket nearby, so that he could keep one foot on the Senate floor, maneuver his other foot (along with a few additional parts) into the cloakroom, and take care of business.

Also, Thurmond cheated. At the very end of the proceedings, Arizona conservative Barry Goldwater used a procedural trick to buy his colleague enough time for a trip to the men's room. With Goldwater's help, Thurmond officially lasted twenty-four hours and eighteen minutes, a record that stands today.

Yet the most remarkable thing about Thurmond's filibuster was not the steam baths, the cheating, or even the pee bucket. It was the fact that the entire twenty-four-hour speech—just like Long's fifteen-hour speech a few decades earlier—was purely for show. Long before Thurmond opened his mouth, his southern colleagues had cut a deal: if senators defanged the 1957 Civil Rights Act, its opponents would allow it to pass once Thurmond's tantrum was finished.

Thanks to *Mr. Smith*, we still tend to think of the filibuster as a feat of endurance. Even in a non-senatorial context, someone is "filibustering" if they drone on in an attempt to run out the clock. But thanks to the Wilson-era reforms, the so-called "talking filibuster" has been a ceremonial gesture for more than a century. If you recruited a large enough faction to block a bill, there was no need to give a long speech. If you failed to gather enough allies, the bill was going to pass whether you gave a long speech or not.

In the end, like so much about our upper chamber, the Senate's golden age of delayed urination—a period lasting roughly from 1917 to 1964—raises more questions than it answers. How did Washington's cooling saucer become a place where grown men were willing to urinate into buckets to oppose legislation they already know would pass? On the other hand, how did a legislature with so many avenues for obstruction work as well as it did? To put it in the language of *Time* magazine, how did the political body of the Senate retain its juices?

After spending several weeks examining this question, reviewing research and diving into Senate lore, I finally uncovered the truth: no one knows. The inner workings of the Senate are like the inner workings of someone else's marriage. We can speculate. We can criticize if we're feeling judgey. But we can never truly understand.

"The more I learn, the more confused I've gotten," I confess to Sarah Binder, a professor at George Washington University and an expert on the upper chamber.

"Sounds like the Senate," she replies.

Professor Binder is talking with me on the phone, not in person, but her enthusiasm for Senate procedure is easy to hear. She wrote a book on the filibuster in 1997, and one on gridlock in 2003—when it comes to legislative dysfunction, she's way ahead of the curve.

And she offers some very good explanations for why, until roughly ten years ago, the Senate functioned fairly well. For most of American history, Binder reminds me, senators had a highly practical reason to limit their filibustering: "There was no air-conditioning." Even in D.C.'s more pleasant seasons—the month of April and about two weeks in fall—the Senate floor would have been a rather unpleasant place, especially after dark. "They were burning candles," she explains, adding that those candles were made of beef tallow. "It stank."

Senators who seized the floor were imposing a sweaty, stinky fate not just upon themselves, but upon their colleagues as well. Just as in the House, senators could call for a quorum—if fewer than 50 percent of lawmakers were present, business paused, giving obstructionists a chance to regain strength. In order to beat a filibuster, then, a majority of lawmakers had to cancel plans, drag cots into the disgusting Senate chamber, and remain there until their colleagues gave in. One of the greatest deterrents to the filibuster, especially in its earliest incarnations, was good, old-fashioned social shame.

In the post-Wilson era, there was another reason the filibuster was used sparingly: it was indelibly associated with segregation. There were exceptions, most notably Oregon senator Wayne Morse, who in 1953 spoke for almost a full day to protest offshore drilling. But the more closely procedural tricks became associated with Jim Crow, the less most senators wanted to legitimize them.

In a strange way, then, the 1964 Civil Rights Act was a triumph both for and against the filibuster. On one hand, over the objections of

Thurmond and his southern colleagues, Republicans and Democrats teamed up to force a vote on the landmark bill. On the other hand, once Jim Crow's defenders could no longer use their favorite tactic, that tactic became more acceptable for non-segregationists to employ. The number of filibusters—on all sorts of issues—began to climb.

It was a cruel irony. For the first time in history, the Senate was air-conditioned, sweet-smelling, and capable of protecting civil rights. And yet, for precisely these reasons, the chamber was now in danger of grinding to a halt. The country had clearly outgrown the post-Wilson filibuster. It was time to change the rules once again.

The new filibuster rules, created through a series of tussles and backroom deals in the 1970s, made the following changes. First, the majority of Senators required to force a vote on a measure was lowered from two-thirds to three-fifths. In our 100-member Senate, that meant a filibuster now took just 60 votes to break.

Two additional changes were more subtle, but ultimately no less consequential. In the past, filibustering blocked all Senate business from moving forward. It was like screeching to a halt on a one-lane road. But as part of their new reforms, senators added a second lane. Refusing to yield the floor would now block only the specific bill being filibustered. Other Senate business—legislating, approving nominations, delivering grandiose speeches in the hopes of a future presidential run—could detour around it.

Finally, senators could now filibuster remotely. Gangs of obstructionists no longer had to hold the floor in a round robin of boring speeches. Their colleagues no longer had to drag cots into the Senate chamber to wait them out. Under the new rules, if a lawmaker signaled an intention to filibuster Belle, that would trigger a filibuster in and of itself. If 60 senators could be found to support Belle, she'd be voted on and have a chance to pass. If not, she'd be held up indefinitely.

All three of the Mansfield filibuster's distinguishing characteristics— the sixty-vote threshold, the two-lane Senate, and the ability to block legislation without summoning your colleagues to the floor—were designed to make bills easier to pass. Under the new rules, any group of forty-one senators could still form a veto point. But if and when they used that veto, the rest of the Senate's business would continue around them. There was no danger of the entire chamber grinding to a halt.

In hindsight, however, the Mansfield filibuster was practically custom-tailored for abuse. Because filibusters now held up just one bill, rather than the entire chamber—and because staging a filibuster no longer required your angry colleagues to drag cots onto the Senate floor—the social and political cost of procedural piracy fell dramatically. Senators were now free to filibuster every bill that peeved them.

The only thing holding the upper chamber together was the hope that senators—some of the world's most power-hungry people—would exercise their new power with restraint. And remarkably, for the longest time, that's exactly what they did.

Martin Paone spent several decades helping the most powerful people in America wield their power, but at the start of 1979, he made his living parking cars. A transplant from Boston with the accent to prove it, the most prestigious D.C. job he could find was as an attendant at an aboveground lot. Luckily for him, that lot happened to be reserved for Senate staff.

Through a friend, he heard of an opening in the Senate Democratic cloakroom. At the time, he didn't even know what a cloakroom was,[*] and the job turned out to be little more than an administrative assistant post, but Marty got the gig and fell in love with his new workplace immediately. He also fell for, and eventually married, a young woman from North Carolina named Ruby Smith. She worked in the Senate, too. Marty and the institution he served became inseparable.

---

[*] It's a small office, just off the Senate floor, that acts as a clearinghouse for information and a kind of remote workspace for lawmakers during lengthy debates. Each party has one.

His specialty was procedure. As we've seen, the Senate rules are less of a formal code than a palimpsest of precedent, tradition, and handshake agreements, and Marty understood them all. John Dingell Jr., the longest-serving member of the House, once described the legislative process this way: "You write the substance, let me write the procedure, and I'll do you in every time." For twenty-nine years, under four different Democratic Senate leaders, if you wanted to do someone in (or avoid being done in yourself) Marty was your guy.

I myself met Marty in the White House, where, starting in 2015, he used his parliamentary savvy on behalf of President Obama. In the 9 a.m. Senior Staff meetings in the Roosevelt Room, Marty could always be found standing in a corner—never sitting at the big table in the center. Hiding behind his glasses, he looked like someone's kindly father who had wandered in. Even when he was answering a question, he somehow managed to be behind the scenes.

Yet when he spoke, with the remnants of that Boston accent, it was as though the Senate itself were speaking. For some political staffers, authority flows from sheer self-confidence or powerful connections or impressive hair. But Marty was different. He had the calm, straightforward command of someone who is quite obviously among the world's foremost experts on the subject about which he is talking. Marty was not just an institutionalist. He was an institution.

He still is. When I meet him in his new office, a private-sector palace compared to his cramped White House confines, he is wearing a tie decorated with different styles of ancient columns. He can still thump a thick book of Senate precedent onto his desk at a moment's notice. To you or me, those pages are incomprehensible. But to Marty, they tell a story.

It's one specific chapter of that story I've come to Marty's office to ask about. The bulk of his time in the Senate, beginning in 1979 and lasting until 2008, coincided with a modern golden age. The chamber was quite capable of passing bills—and unlike in the mid-twenty-first century, it wasn't the nation's signature impediment to civil rights.

Meanwhile, despite the rules changes from the 1970s—including the one giving any group of forty-one senators the ability to veto legislation—the filibuster was used relatively sparingly. Lawmakers had the power to kill any bill they disapproved of, yet they frequently chose let bills live.

Why?

One common answer is that the secret to the Senate's success was the filibuster itself. Senators lived in a state of mutually assured destruction: torpedo my bill, and I'll torpedo yours. Members of the minority had veto power, so the majority had to respect their views. At the same time, senators knew that too much obstruction might trigger a backlash, a rewriting of the rules like the ones that occurred in 1917 and 1975. According to the filibuster's most passionate defenders, these competing pressures and threats encouraged compromise and consultation, rather than flat-out partisan war.

Yet when Marty Paone tells me why he thinks the filibuster was rarely employed, he points to a different element of Senate procedure, one known as "open amendments." In the majority-rules House, no amendment can be voted on without the approval of the House Rules Committee. But in the upper chamber, everything is fair game: any senator can offer an amendment on any subject at almost any time. Open amendments gave minority parties and lawmakers a way to influence our laws *without* resorting to the filibuster.

A second reason filibusters were relatively rare forty years ago is that Senate control tended to be more lopsided than it is today. During the 1970s, when the rules on ending debate were last rewritten, the majority party held an average of fifty-eight seats—just two shy of the number needed to break a filibuster. Over the last decade, on the other hand, the majority party has held just fifty-two seats, making a partisan filibuster far harder to break.

Third, and finally, obstruction used to be less common because the parties were fractured. On social and racial issues, southern Democrats could not have been more different from their northern or western colleagues, yet they belonged to the same partisan team. When Republicans controlled the chamber, their liberal New England members played a similar black-sheep role.

The same regional differences that created unruly alliances within the parties created strange bedfellows between them. Measuring a lawmaker's ideology is an inexact science. Still, regardless of which metric you use, the Senate once contained much more common ground.* In 1964, the year the Civil Rights Act passed, the most economically conservative Democrat, pee bucket–wielding Strom Thurmond, was to the right of about half of his Republican colleagues. The most liberal Republicans, New York's Jacob Javits and Vermont's George Aiken, were further left than thirteen Democrats. That's a lot of ideological overlap, and with it, a lot of potential for bipartisan compromise.

These pillars—unrestricted amendments, uneven majorities, and unlikely friends—propped up the Senate's golden age. By 2008, all three pillars had crumbled.

The trouble began when the battle for control of the Senate got competitive. It's hard to picture today, but a half century ago it seemed preordained that that Democrats would run the chamber. For twenty-six straight years, from 1955 to 1981, they did not once relinquish their majority. For half that time, Democrats held sixty seats or more. To put this streak in context: punk rock legend Sid Vicious was born, grew up, joined the Sex Pistols, embarked on an ill-advised solo career, was arrested for his girlfriend's murder, and died of a heroin overdose—all without ever seeing a Republican Senate majority. I'm sure it was his greatest regret.

Compare Sid Vicious's Senate to that of pop star/actor/heartthrob Justin Timberlake, who was born in 1981. In JT's lifetime, Republicans

---

* For our purposes, we'll use a widely accepted scoring system called DW-NOMINATE. The math behind it is complicated, but the basic idea is simple: using vote histories, we can measure the ideological closeness between any pair of Senators, giving us a relationship map of the Senate as a whole.

have held the majority for twenty-two of thirty-nine years, or 56 percent. There's nothing wrong with the Senate being up for grabs. In fact, it's probably healthy. But that same competitiveness makes compromise less appealing. If you can beat your opponents tomorrow, there's no need to join them today.

In strange, zigzaggy fashion, competitive elections also brought about the end of open amendments. Senators in the minority, hoping to create fodder for campaign ads, began offering proposals whose sole purpose was to force colleagues to cast a controversial vote. In response, majority leader Trent Lott—a Republican who won his post in 1996 by promising to be more combative than his predecessors— began to "fill the amendment tree."

Here's how filling the tree works. When amendments are submitted on the Senate floor, they take a spot on line, a little bit like customers at a bakery. The line is called the amendment tree, and for reasons we won't get into, the number of available spots is limited. If you're a majority leader who wants complete control over the debate, you simply occupy each spot with a meaningless proposal. (You might introduce an amendment to change a bill's text from "June 1" to "June First," or to replace the words "Justice Department" with "Department of Justice.") By keeping the line full at all times, you keep the minority party from introducing any amendments of its own.

Trent Lott didn't invent tree-filling, but he reinvigorated the practice for a new and more partisan age. When Democrats regained control of the Senate, they frequently filled the tree as well. At key moments, with crucial legislation on the line, the minority party found their seat at the table had vanished.* Senators in the minority were left with only two choices: accept a bill as offered, or try to kill it with a filibuster. Frequently, they filibustered.

---

* I think an objective look at the record makes it clear that, in the escalating parliamentary war that consumed the Senate, Republicans have been the more aggressive party. But it's more important to know what happened than who started it.

When Marty's career began, lawmakers from both parties might have been able to come together and halt the procedural arms race. But during his time in the Senate, the bipartisan common ground shrank and then disappeared. In 1987, for the first time in seventy-four years, there was no ideological overlap in the Senate. Every single Democrat was to the left of every single Republican. In 1995, it happened again. By 2007, it was happening every year. As ideological differences within each party faded, senators began voluntarily ceding their influence over procedural matters to the party caucus as a whole. The majority leader in the Senate can't rule with the iron first of a House Speaker. But the two roles have never been more alike.

The gradual extinction of conservative Democrats and liberal Republicans also torpedoed the chances for compromise. Imagine the ideological spectrum of American politics as a one-hundred-yard football field, with a left-wing end zone, a right-wing end zone, and a moderate fifty-yard line in the middle. In 1979, when Marty got his first job in the Senate cloakroom, the average Democrat stood on the left-wing nineteen-yard line, while the average Republican stood on the right-wing twenty-two, for fifty-nine yards of distance between them. That's a lot.

But it's nothing compared to what we have today. Political reporters frequently refer to the Senate as "polarized," implying both parties sprinted from the middle toward their respective extremes. In fact, that's not the case. In 2008, when Marty left the upper chamber, Democrats were standing on their twenty, one yard *closer* to the center than they had been three decades prior. Republican senators, however, had barreled toward their own end zone: they had moved from the twenty-two-yard line to the eleven.* The divide between Democrats and Republicans was greater than ever, all because of one party's rightward lurch.

---

* This trend has only accelerated. In the last Congress, Democrats stood on the sixteen-yard line. Republicans were just one yard away from their end zone.

In other words, by the time Barack Obama took office, the minority's ability to change bills via amendment was limited, the parties were completely distinct ideological groups, and room for compromise had vanished. Also, just two years earlier, Senate Republicans had chosen a brand-new leader.

Mitch McConnell is as procedurally knowledgeable a lawmaker as America has yet produced—in a different life, he could have been the Republican Marty Paone. But his most successful parliamentary maneuver was alarmingly simple. Where McConnell's predecessors had filibustered some things, McConnell and his party filibustered everything. The new Republican Party was allergic not to a bill or to an issue, but to an entire presidency.

There are many ways to measure the extent of McConnell's obstruction. The average number of filibusters per legislative session nearly doubled between George W. Bush's two terms and Obama's. Previously straightforward UC agreements became impossible to reach. Senator Ted Cruz put a "blanket hold" on Obama's nominations to the State Department—every single one—to protest the Iran nuclear deal. "Of all the cloture motions ever filed or reconsidered on district court nominations," writes former Senate staffer Bill Dauster, "97 percent were on President Obama's nominees."

Yet the Senate, as we've seen, runs on tradition, and far more meaningful than any number or anecdote is the precedent Mitch McConnell set. He didn't formally rewrite the rules the way his predecessors had in the 1970s. He didn't put his new blueprint for the Senate to a vote; if he had, he would have lost. Instead, by gathering the support of less than half his colleagues, he changed the very nature of the chamber in which he served.

Before 2009, in almost all cases, it took 51 votes to pass a bill in the U.S. Senate. Now it takes 60 votes instead. That's true regardless of which party is in charge. At first glance, McConnell's new filibuster might seem like a tiny change. In fact, no one has done this much damage to the Senate since Aaron Burr.

☆

Let's get something out of the way: the difference between 60 and 51 Senate votes may not appear that big, but it's enormous. To use just one example, if senators themselves required 60 percent of the vote to get elected, nearly two-thirds of their seats would currently be vacant. For Belle, the odds of overcoming Mitch McConnell's filibuster are in nearly all cases zero. In an era where Republican and Democratic lawmakers genuinely disagree on nearly everything, asking the Senate to find 60 votes is not much different from asking them to find 100.

The only types of proposals that pass the new Senate are those that fit into a handful of exceptions—and every one of those exceptions benefits Mitch McConnell's party over its opponents.

First, Belle could have the good fortune to be introduced by a party that controls sixty seats in the Senate. This isn't impossible. But it's quite unlikely. In my thirty-three years on the planet, the total amount of time either party has held a sixty-seat Senate majority is less than seven months.

Thanks to Gunning Bedford Jr., if a party ever does reach sixty seats, it will almost certainly be the Republicans. As we discussed in chapter 6, the average state is much more Republican than the average voter. In fact, according to the Partisan Voting Index, Republicans could win sixty Senate seats without winning even one from a blue-leaning state. The simplest filibuster-proof path for Democrats, on the other hand, requires winning every seat from every state bluer than South Carolina. Even if Democrats could pull together such a majority, the deciding, 60th vote would belong to someone conservative enough to win a deep-red seat.

The second way for Belle to pass the Senate is for her to earn the support of more than 60 senators of both parties. Even now, such bipartisan bills are not entirely unheard of. Perhaps Belle expedites loans for veterans, or creates a commemorative coin, addresses a truly urgent crisis, or can be shoehorned into the annual funding bill that keeps the government's lights on. Those kinds of proposals still survive, particularly when Republicans control the Senate and have at least some interest in showing voters they can get things done. But while passing a small amount of unambitious bipartisan legislation is better than passing no legislation at all, nothing about these few survivors screams "superpower." If Belle is built to do something big—whether it's repealing Obamacare or fighting climate change—she'll never reach 60 votes.

Both parties are frustrated when the Senate can't pass ambitious legislation. But one party is far more frustrated than the other. That's because of something political scientists Jacob Hacker and Paul Pierson call "drift." Like smartphones and hairdos, regulations inevitably become obsolete. Hacker and Pierson use the federal minimum wage as an example: since 2009, it's been stuck at $7.25 an hour, while inflation continues to grow. In real terms, that $7.25 is now worth 18 percent *less* than it was thirteen years ago.

In other words, raising the minimum wage, a progressive priority, requires the Senate to pass legislation. But cutting the minimum wage, a conservative priority, requires the Senate to do nothing at all. And thanks to Mitch McConnell, doing nothing has never been easier. By stalling the legislative process indefinitely, conservatives can weaken popular government programs without ever having to vote against them.

Belle's best hope for avoiding the McConnell filibuster, then, is not to win friends across the aisle, but to avoid the filibuster entirely via "budget reconciliation." Budget reconciliation (or just "reconciliation" for short) began as a narrow administrative procedure in the 1970s, one of the efficiency-minded reforms of the Mansfield era, but by the 1980s it had expanded into a kind of senatorial hall pass. Once per year, the Senate can ignore the filibuster and pass a bill by simple majority vote.

This magic bill must follow a strict set of rules. It must deal directly with taxes, spending, or the debt ceiling. It can't touch Social Security.

It can add to the deficit for a few years, but not indefinitely. But if Belle meets these rules, and is chosen for this honor, the filibuster will not apply to her.

Short of one party winning a 60-seat majority, reconciliation is now the only way to pass a big new law. But it's an unwieldy instrument, one clearly not designed for the purpose it serves. Picture one of those reality show challenges where contestants must complete a ropes course wearing wedding dresses or cook an entire Thanksgiving dinner over an open flame. Reconciliation is that, but for legislation. Except, instead of embarrassed bachelorettes and underdone turkey, we get laws that completely upend our lives.

Such an ill-fitting process is a particularly bad fit for progressive priorities, because solving big, complex problems is complicated and often expensive. For conservatives, on the other hand, reconciliation has been invaluable. Republican senators used it to slash spending under Reagan and lower top-bracket tax rates under George W. Bush. In the Trump era, Republican senators came within a single vote of using reconciliation to repeal Obamacare; when that failed, they used it to pass Trump's $2 trillion tax cut instead. Both parties are free to use the hall pass—but it's much more useful for one than the other.

There's one final instance in which a Senate filibuster can be avoided, although technically it doesn't apply to bills at all. Whereas legislation requires 60 votes, a president's judicial nominees can now be confirmed by a simple majority.

What makes this loophole possible is something called "the nuclear option," and it's a perfect example of the fictions within fictions that make up the Senate rules. In 2013, after President Obama's would-be judges had been held up for years, the then-Majority Leader, Democrat Harry Reid, changed the Senate's procedure. He did this not by offering a proposal but by making an assertion: for all nominees other than those for Supreme Court, he claimed, the filibuster did not apply. This claim was obviously false, so Reid was overruled by the senator presiding over the debate. Ordinarily, that would have ended things.

This time, however, Reid appealed the ruling. Bear in mind that, technically, he wasn't saying that the filibuster *shouldn't* apply. He was saying that the filibuster *didn't* apply, which was simply and untrue. Yet according to the Senate rules, an appeal of a parliamentary ruling is one of the few things that can be decided by majority vote. Fifty-two Democrats joined Reid's position, and the nuclear option was triggered. In its strange, roundabout way, the filibuster for most judicial nominees disappeared.

In 2017, McConnell expanded the nuclear option to cover all nominees, including those for the nation's highest court. President Trump's first Supreme Court pick, Neil Gorsuch, was confirmed with 54 votes. A year later, Brett Kavanaugh won confirmation by a vote of just 50 to 48, the smallest margin of any Supreme Court justice since 1881.

The nuclear option is not limited to judicial nominations. McConnell could have deployed it to end the filibuster for all legislation, and, in fact, he faced great pressure to do just that. In 2017 and 2018, Republicans controlled the House of Representatives by a large margin; a majority-rules Senate could have passed nearly all the party's priorities into law. Even President Trump urged the abolition of the filibuster, via one of his typically thoughtful tweets. "Can't get votes, END NOW!" he wrote.

But I hope that by this point you can see why McConnell resisted the president's all-caps demand. Most current Republican priorities, from bringing back preexisting conditions on health insurance to cutting taxes on the rich to reducing restrictions on polluters, aren't popular. Team Mitch's goal is to enact an agenda that voters don't approve of without paying an electoral price.

The current Senate rules make such a goal achievable. They maximize power while minimizing accountability. Legislative drift reduces regulations and rewards McConnell's corporate allies. Conservative judges, confirmed by simple majority vote, can overturn well-liked laws without facing voters' backlash. On the rare occasions when a bill is deemed worth voting on, such as tax cuts and Obamacare repeal,

Republican senators can use reconciliation to make sure the filibuster does not apply.

Today's Senate isn't anything close to the cooling saucer Washington spoke of, or the sober second thought that George Frisbie Hoar extolled. Instead, the Senate is a place where it's nearly impossible to pass the simplest legislation, yet it's easy to slash taxes for the rich, strip health care from millions, or appoint a new Supreme Court justice for life. Our current Senate rules simply don't make sense.

It's become a cliché to say the Senate "doesn't work." Yet in this case, that cliché is entirely untrue. For Mitch McConnell and his party, our dysfunctional legislature is working just fine.

How do we solve a problem like the Senate? Every generation of Americans has confronted this question, with varying degrees of success. Now, it's our turn.

The first option is to do nothing. After all, McConnell's sixty-vote threshold prevents senators from passing wise, popular bills, but it also prevents them from passing unwise, unpopular ones. Shredding public education; slashing Medicare and Social Security; defunding Planned Parenthood nationwide; implementing Hans von Spakovsky's wish list of restrictive voting rules—if Democrats hadn't been able obstruct Trump's agenda in much the same way Republicans obstructed Obama's, all these ideas and more might have become law. The McConnell filibuster is less than ideal, but maybe it's the best we can do.

Alternatively, we could weaken the filibuster slightly, preserving some of but not all its bill-killing power. We could reduce McConnell's 60-vote threshold for legislation to 55, or 54, or 53. We could make filibustering more difficult, forcing procedural pirates to once again take the floor and talk for hours if they hope to block a bill. Or we could expand reconciliation, increasing the odds that Belle will make it through the Senate with a simple majority vote.

When I first began looking into the Senate's rules and history, I liked these partway fixes. After all, the Senate has had some form of filibuster for nearly two centuries. Surely it would be better to uphold that tradition in some form. But the more I learned, the more I came to a very different conclusion: when Democrats retake the Senate, they will find themselves in the same position that Thomas Reed and the Republicans once did in the House. Unless they do something bold, their entire agenda will be dead on arrival. Senator McConnell has created a new kind of tyranny, forcing us to make a choice. We can have the filibuster. We can have democracy. We can't have both.

Not all the experts I spoke to agree that the filibuster threatens our very republic. But most of them did. They weren't excited about the prospect of a majority-rules Senate. They're well aware big rules changes are always messy. They know that when a majority can pass legislation unimpeded, the ruling party can do a lot of damage quickly. And those who study the Senate really do admire its principled stand for minority-party rights.

But there's another, higher principle at stake, one that Sarah Binder, the GW professor, put quite simply. "Legislatures should legislate." She doesn't care if the Senate passes or kills lots of bills. But she does think the Senate should be *voting* on lots of bills. And the McConnell filibuster is custom-made for not voting—especially when Team Mitch is in charge.

Marty, at his desk in an office filled with heavyweight books of procedure, takes a similar view. He'd like to restore the open amendment system, so that all senators have a seat at the table once again. But when it comes to the filibuster, he's seen firsthand the way the Senate's defining feature has become the its Achilles' heel. He's well aware that his party—the party that believes government can work effectively and improve Americans' lives—needs a Congress that can vote on laws.

Most important, Marty has spent time around Kentucky's senior senator. He battled Team Mitch in the Senate, and then again in the

Obama White House. And he's completely convinced—as are most McConnell watchers I've met—that whenever the 60-vote threshold no longer benefits the Republican Party, the Republican Party will immediately scrap it. The real question is not whether the Senate should remove the filibuster. The question is when. And the answer matters a lot. If the filibuster's demise opens the floodgates to an unchecked authoritarian agenda, the United States will be well on its way to becoming a one-party state.

But what if instead, we paired a majority-vote Senate with steps to strengthen our democracy, rebuild accountability, and reestablish the consent of the governed? Imagine the filibuster's demise followed immediately by statehood for D.C. and Puerto Rico, automatic voter registration throughout America, tougher disclosure laws for political donors, a public campaign finance system, and more.

The dawn of majority rule would still be a jarring change for our country. If Republicans earned the support of the American people, they'd be able to actually pass their agenda; ditto Democrats when they took charge. We would not have a perfect country, or a perfect Senate. But Belle would at least stand a fighting chance of passage. There's a very real possibility that if the American people wanted something to happen, it would get done.

Yet there would also, without question, be unintended consequences to ending the Senate as we know it. That's why, as I exit Marty's office, I can't help but end our conversation on a cautious note. We know the rewards to our democracy if we allow the majority to rule. But what can we do about the risks?

Marty sighs. It's a sober sigh, a quiet, behind-the-scenes sigh. Then the ultimate institutionalist purses his lips and looks at me through round-rimmed glasses.

"Strike first," he says.

10

POSSUM KINGDOM

The Lobbyists

We've now covered two-thirds of the *Schoolhouse Rock!* journey. But even if Belle beats the long odds and passes the House and Senate, her trip to the White House is one we'll skip. While the president remains an important veto point, the process hasn't really changed since 1973: if the president signs Belle, she becomes a law.

Instead of dealing with the Oval Office, the remainder of this book will examine two veto points that were completely absent from Bill's musical number. The *Schoolhouse Rock!* creators didn't ignore these veto points because they were lazy or disinterested. They ignored them because when *Schoolhouse Rock!* was written, these veto points didn't exist. To an extent that Bill could not have imagined, and to an extent unmatched in your lifetime, Belle's fate will be decided by leaders who do not work for us, men and women whom we did not and cannot elect.

But I'm getting ahead of myself. About 130 years ago, in a rough-and-tumble New Mexico mining town, one prospector shot another in the leg. Let's start there.

The shooter's name was Edward Doheny. Born in 1856 in Fond du Lac, a Wisconsin logging town, he headed west to seek his fortune at just fifteen. By his early twenties he could be found in Kingston, the thriving, lawless center of a New Mexico silver-mining boom. One evening, for unknown reasons, an angry drunk chased Doheny from a saloon and pursued him down the street. Doheny whipped out his pistol and could easily have killed his pursuer, but instead merely maimed him. In 1880s New Mexico this was considered extremely gracious, and one of Doheny's fellow prospectors made a point of congratulating him on his restraint. That man's name was Albert Fall.

Skip ahead three decades. Doheny, having relocated even farther west, was now the oil king of Southern California, with wells pumping vigorously throughout the state and all the way into Mexico. Long before Hollywood was Hollywood, Doheny was leaving his stamp on Los Angeles. (Even today, when you travel from Beverly Hills toward the Sunset Strip, you sit in traffic on Doheny Drive.)

Albert Fall's career was less lucrative than that of his sharpshooting acquaintance, but no less colorful. Staying put in New Mexico, Fall rose simultaneously through the ranks of New Mexico's Democrats, legal establishment, and organized crime. In fairness, these groups were sometimes hard to tell apart. In 1896, for example, Fall's chief political rival, an anticorruption Republican named Albert Fountain, vanished under mysterious circumstances. Fall served as the defense attorney for the accused assassins, who were found not guilty. Pat Garrett, a famed sheriff whose posse joined the search for Fountain's killers, was himself murdered a few years later. Once again Fall defended the accused in court. That man was found not guilty, too.

Then the political winds shifted, and Fall happily went from dispatching Republicans like Fountain to joining them. In 1912 he became one of his state's first senators as a member of the GOP. In 1921, after President Warren Harding's first choice for interior secretary was shot to death by a jilted mistress, the cabinet post went to Fall. Suddenly a chance encounter outside a territorial saloon mattered a great deal. Ed Doheny wanted all the oil he could get his hands on. Albert Fall had access to every drop sitting beneath America's public lands.

The result was a deal that, apart from its secrecy, was handled much like any other business transaction. Fall took control of vast oil reserves set aside for the U.S. Navy, divvied them up, and handed them to Doheny and his fellow oil baron Harry Sinclair. In exchange, Doheny and Sinclair gave Fall a combination of cash, no-interest loans, and cattle worth about $404,000, or $5.6 million today.

Earlier in this book, we looked at the many ways money influences our elections. But what Doheny and Sinclair did was different. They used their wealth to influence our *government*. Rather than buy votes on behalf of a candidate, they bought favors from a public official. Their quid pro quo with Albert Fall, and the outcry that followed, became known as the Teapot Dome Scandal.

The aftermath of Teapot Dome shapes our laws even today. (Among other things, it's the reason lawmakers can examine Americans' tax returns and issue subpoenas—in the wake of the scandal, Congress realized it needed new tools to investigate the executive branch.) The bribery scheme also remains an archetype of government corruption. Nearly a century after Harding's death, high school history textbooks breeze past nearly all of his administration. But they still cover Teapot Dome.

The reason I bring up Teapot Dome here, however, is not because it's so educational, but because it's so misleading. Most government corruption looks nothing like the grubby deal reached between Doheny and Fall. Outright bribery does occasionally happen. (There's certainly reason to believe it's happened more often under President Trump.) But in American politics, the explicit exchange of money for favors is exceedingly rare. Even when the definition of "quid" in quid pro quo is expanded to include campaign contributions, not just personal gifts, this kind of blatant corruption is quite uncommon.

That doesn't mean money has no influence over our government. But it does means money influences our government in complicated ways. If we concern ourselves only with outright bribery, we'll overlook a far greater threat. In recent decades, there's been an influence-peddling boom in Washington to rival the silver rush that brought Edward Doheny and Albert Fall to New Mexico all those years ago.

Much like those roughnecked miners, the people turning private money into public policy operate below the surface. But this chapter is about bringing their work to light. Because if we want Belle to become a law, we need to understand what influence peddling really looks like, how much of it there really is, and how it really works.

☆

There is nothing more fundamentally American than lobbying. I'm serious. Right there in the First Amendment, after free speech, freedom of religion, a free press, and freedom to assemble, you'll find the freedom to "petition the government for a redress of grievances." The language is fusty. "Petition" these days is more often a noun than verb, and "redress of grievances" sounds like a cocktail in a bar where every employee wears an obnoxious hat. But regardless of word choice, this simple clause protects our right to lobby. We don't have to wait until the next election to tell our leaders what to do. We can bother them seven days a week, 365 days a year.

Not only is lobbying enshrined in the Constitution, it is as old as America itself. There's a common story told that in the 1870s, President Ulysses Grant was pestered by favor-seekers on the ground floor of the Willard Hotel, and the term "to lobby" was born. But that's not true. As *Merriam-Webster* helpfully points out, English had the verb "lobby" long before the Willard Hotel had the noun. Ordinary people lobbied their legislators. Local governments lobbied Washington. Senators lobbied representatives, and vice versa. From the very beginning, we had lobbying.

What we didn't have were lobby*ists*. For the first few decades after our country's founding, lobbying was the province of amateurs. It wasn't until 1840 that professionals appeared on the scene, and even then, there weren't many of them. As late as 1950, Washington was home to just 312 registered lobbying organizations, which reported $10.3 million in spending each year. That's not nothing—if you took that money on an airplane, you'd have to check a bag. But even adjusted for inflation, and with the understanding that reporting laws were much less strict back then, $10.3 million is approximately one-thirtieth of what America spends on lobbying today.

What explains the runaway increase? How did influencing the government go from constitutional right to big business?

One reason that companies spent so little on lobbying in the 1950s is simple: they didn't need to spend much. As the economy boomed in the post–World War II years, big corporations were not just popular but a source of national pride. American icons like U.S. Steel and AT&T had no reason to throw their weight around in Washington— the people and politicians were already in their camp.

That changed in the 1960s. *Silent Spring*, published by Rachel Carson in 1962, launched the environmental movement. Three years later, Ralph Nader released *Unsafe at Any Speed*, his exposé of the auto industry, and modern consumer protection was born. New government regulations soon followed. Americans began to distrust big business and as a result, big business began to distrust Washington.

In 1971, several years into a bipartisan regulation boom, a corporate attorney named Lewis Powell wrote a now-famous letter to his colleagues at the U.S. Chamber of Commerce. It's known today as "The Powell Memo," but "Powell Manifesto" would be just as accurate. Despite its author's blue-blooded bona fides (one of his distant relatives, Nathaniel Powell, was a non-voting colonist at Jamestown), his apocalyptic tone would fit in easily today on talk radio or Fox News. "No thoughtful person can question that the American economic system is under broad attack," read one typical passage. "It must be recognized that businessmen have not been trained or equipped to conduct guerrilla warfare with those who propagandize against the system," read another.

Powell suggested plenty of specific ways to fight back against environmentalists and Naderites. But more than that, he called for a change in attitude. "The day is long past when the chief executive officer of a major corporation discharges his responsibility by maintaining a satisfactory growth of profits, with due regard to the corporation's public and social responsibilities. If our system is to survive, top management must be equally concerned with protecting and preserving the system itself."

Powell's thesis, put simply, was that American business could no longer survive on its own. It needed to merge with government. The Powell Memo is a bit of a chicken-and-egg situation. Did corporations flock to Washington because he wrote it? Or did he write it because corporations wanted a reason to flock? Regardless, a migration took place.

In *Winner-Take-All Politics* (the same book that coined the term "legislative drift"), Jacob Hacker and Paul Pierson chronicle the corporate colonization of our nation's capital. In 1972, the National Association of Manufacturers, one of the nation's largest corporate interest groups, announced it would move its headquarters from New York to D.C. "The thing that affects business most today is government," said its chairman, Burt Raynes. That same year marked the founding of the Business Roundtable, a Jedi Council composed entirely of major CEOs. The Chamber of Commerce, Hacker and Pierson write, "doubled in membership between 1974 and 1980. Its budget tripled."

Fill-in-the-blank-industrial complexes sprouted all over the place. "In 1971," write Hacker and Pierson, "only 175 firms had registered lobbyists in Washington, but by 1982, nearly 2,500 did." That's a 1,400 percent increase in a decade. Like the Bee Gees, Quaaludes, and Pet Rock, organized corporate power is a product of the 1970s.

To get a sense of precisely how that power was organized, it's helpful to look at three lobbying legends whose careers began around that time.

Bryce Harlow spent half a century striding—proudly, and by all accounts with integrity—through the revolving door between government and business. A World War II vet, he wrote speeches for President Eisenhower, left to work for Procter & Gamble, joined the Nixon White House, left to work for Procter & Gamble, rejoined Nixon White House, and left to work for Procter & Gamble yet again.

Despite spending much of his career in the private sector, Harlow thought of himself as a lifelong public servant, or as he once described it, a "little 'go-fer' for Uncle Sam." Like his close associate Lewis Powell, he didn't believe bringing big business into Washington would corrupt America. He believed it would save America. This idea—the lobbyist as pure patriot—is quite attractive to lobbyists. That's one reason the annual Oscars of government relations are still called "The Bryce Harlow Awards."

Thomas H. Boggs Jr., on the other hand, was loudly and proudly self-interested. He grew up around politics—Boggs's father was a powerful Louisiana congressman, and when he died, Boggs's mother took his seat. When Boggs Jr. grew up and started lobbying, he sounded not unlike a hardhearted film noir PI. "We pick our clients by taking the first one who comes in the door," he once quipped, only half in jest. Where Harlow saw corporate interests as an extension of his beliefs, Boggs saw them as an expansion of his pocketbook.

Along with his proudly mercenary nature, Boggs's great innovation was to combine the lobbyist—previously a sole practitioner—with the long-standing institution of the law partnership. Patton Boggs opened its doors in the sixties, but it was in the seventies that the firm really took off. To maximize potential profits, it hired, and was hired by, Republicans and Democrats alike.

Then there was Charls Walker. And no, that's not a typo. Walker's mother removed the "e" from his name to make sure no one would ever call him Charlie. Naturally, he was known as "Charly" throughout his life.

Walker, born in the hamlet of Graham, Texas, was living proof that beauty and charisma are not synonymous. A photo from 1971, when he served as Nixon's undersecretary of the Treasury, reveals a fortress of a nose, a whiteboard of a forehead, and a complex integration of jowls and chins. Yet the man was irresistible. Despite holding a degree in finance from Wharton, and cutting his teeth as a top executive for the American Bankers Association, Walker radiated down-home charm. He described GM, Gulf Oil, and the steel giant Alcoa as "a few mom-and-pop clients," and got away with it, too.

Where Harlow worked for a single corporation, and Boggs worked for whoever could pay, Charly Walker split the difference. On behalf of a broad coalition of like-minded businesses, he nudged (and sometimes hip-checked) the tax code for decades. When Reagan cut corporate rates in 1981, Walker helped direct the effort. When lawmakers tried to end the tax-deductible three-martini lunch, Walker was there to save it. Yet despite his clear lack of interest in the little guy, Democrats loved Walker just as much as Republicans did. How could you not? In stuffy, suit-and-tie D.C., who else could burst into a conference room and introduce himself by announcing, in a deep country accent, "Hi! I'm from Possum Kingdom."

Walker was referring to Possum Kingdom, Texas, the small town where he owned a lake house. But in my view, his phrase works just as well for the entire sprawling influence industry in which he spent the bulk of his life. Possum Kingdom is a kind of shadow government inside Washington, D.C.

To be absolutely clear, I don't mean to imply that lobbyists themselves are rodential in any physical respect. Plenty of terrific people are employed as lobbyists, and many of them, as we'll see, make America a better place. Still, there's something nocturnal about the entire enterprise. You know influence-peddlers are out there, but you don't see them unless you know where to look. They may not play dead in a truly possum-like manner, but they'll happily feign powerlessness when it suits them.

Also, they proliferate. Once the Powell Memo kicked things off, lobbying begat more lobbying with stunning speed.

Partly it was a matter of familiarity. The more that CEOs understood how government worked, the more they invested in making it work to their advantage. Meanwhile, Reagan's rhetoric aside, government kept growing, not just through the 1970s, but in the following decades as well. As federal programs became more expansive, spending higher, and regulations more complex, there were more things to lobby about. A government as sprawling as ours is what the scholar and writer Jonathan Rauch calls an "open game." Imagine a poker table with no real limit to the number of players, the number of bets, or the size of each player's bankroll. The logical strategy is to raise, in a circle, ad infinitum. That's what happened with lobbying.

Finally, there's a protection-racket aspect. If I hire a lobbyist to attack your favorite legislative carve-out, you need a lobbyist of your own to play defense. Once the dust settles, both our lobbyists have strong incentives to come up with scenarios that require even more lobbying in the future.

To figure out just how dramatically the lobbying industry has grown, I seek out Lee Drutman, a political reform expert at New America, a nonprofit in D.C. We meet at Pret, the sandwich-slash-coffee shop, where I order a peppermint tea.

"I'll try something new," Lee announces, with a kind of devil-may-care enthusiasm. He's wearing a sweater that doubles as a blazer, a skinny tie from the more fashionable section of J.Crew, and glasses that bridge the gap between young hotshot and distinguished academic. We sit at a table in the window, where he takes a tentative sip of his cayenne-and-ginger juice shot and grimaces.

"Ugh, that's really spicy."

"In a good way or a bad way?" I ask. Lee thinks for just a moment, a kind of thoughtful drumroll.

"A good way!" he announces.

It's fortunate that Lee gets a kick out of distasteful combinations, because he's been studying big money and government for years. (His book *The Business of America Is Lobbying* is one of the best, and best titled, works of political science on the market.) Over our respective drinks, Lee explains that measuring the size of Possum Kingdom is harder than you might think. Lobbying disclosure requirements have been around since 1946, but back then they were easy to dodge. It was only in the 1990s, when Congress passed a new set of disclosure requirements, that we started to get a clear picture of the growing influence industry.

Here's what we learned. From the relative pittance spent before Powell's 1971 manifesto, the amount of money spent on lobbying Congress leapt to $1.45 billion per year by 1998. But the open game was just getting started. During George W. Bush's eight years in office, lobbying spending more than doubled, reaching a new high of $3.31 billion. When Obama took office, Possum Kingdom broke its own record, reaching $3.5 billion in a single year, before plateauing during Trump's first years in office.

And these official lobbying numbers tell only a small part of the story. There are many ways to spend money on influence without having to disclose that spending on a form. To offer one example, a few years ago I was invited to Google's D.C. holiday party. It was held in the Anthem theater, on a floor about the size of a football field, in the center of which sat a massive, pastel-colored cube about two stories high. Emanating from the cube were Plexiglas pipes. At the base of each pipe was a touchscreen. Push a button, and individually wrapped candies of your choosing shot down the tube and into your possession.

All night long, Google's guests—including many of the same congressional and executive branch staff in charge of regulating Google— stood around the cube dispensing candy into plastic bags or open palms. There's no doubt goodwill was being purchased with every Snickers or Laffy Taffy. But technically, no lobbying took place.

This sort of thing happens all the time in Washington. CEOs might donate to a senator's favorite charity or generously sponsor a bipartisan congressional event. Well-heeled organizations spend millions on "grassroots" advocacy campaigns. Meanwhile, on a given night you can find at least a dozen free-food events on Capitol Hill, all sponsored by various businesses and trade groups, plying congressional staff with snacks or beer.

The huge amount of money spent on what Drutman calls "shadow lobbying" makes it impossible to tell just how large the influence industry has grown. All we know is that it's grown enormously and quickly. Lobbying may be as old as America. Professional lobbying may go back centuries, and corporate lobbying decades. But over the last thirty years, and during the twenty-first century in particular, lobbying has morphed into an entirely new beast.

Perhaps most striking is this: since the early 2000s, the amount of money spent lobbying Congress has been larger than the budget for Congress itself. When Bill sang his way through Capitol Hill, the influence industry was a tiny corner of Washington. When Belle attempts to become a law, the influence industry will be bigger than the House and Senate combined.

You may be comfortable with this fact. You may not. But in our current system of government, regardless of how you feel about the place, Possum Kingdom holds Belle's future in its hands.

In 1938, on a winding road between Chicago and Minneapolis, Bob LeFevre did something rather impressive: he drove for more than twenty miles while sound asleep.

In fairness, LeFevre (pronounced "Le-FAVE") had help. The Great Host of Ascended Masters was looking out for him. Equally supportive were, in no particular order, the Mighty I AM Presence, Saint Germain, the Beloved Lady Master Nada, and "The Messengers," a pair of gaunt midwesterners whose given names were Guy and Edna Ballard, but who went by the pseudonyms "Godfre Ray King" and "Lotus" and whom LeFevre referred to as "Daddy" and "Mama."

If all this sounds a bit bananas, you should try reading the rest of LeFevre's book. Called *"I AM" America's Destiny*, it's a testimonial for a new spiritual movement founded by Mr. Ballard, aka Godfre, aka Daddy, in the early 1930s. At its height, I AM had as many as a million followers, but to certain skeptics it appeared to a religion than a scam. These skeptics included federal authorities, and a few months after *America's Destiny* was published, the Ballards were arrested for fraud. LeFevre was indicted but never formally charged.

You may wonder why Robert LeFevre's story belongs in these pages. It's not because of the sect he joined as a young man, but because of the sect he helped found as an older one. "Libertarian Philosopher Robert LeFevre Dies," wrote the *Los Angeles Times*, in a 1986 obituary that made no mention of the I AM movement. "LeFevre had been a leading exponent of libertarianism—which stresses the value of personal freedom and the free-enterprise system while advocating an end to government regulations."

If people like Lewis Powell viewed influencing the government as an investment, people like Bob LeFevre viewed influencing the government as a religion. And as Daddy and Mama Ballard could tell you, a successful new religion, like a successful new investment, can bring in lots and lots of money.

By 1960, Bob LeFevre and a few of his former I AM cultists could be found on a remote campus in the pine forests of Colorado, which they named "The Freedom School." While it boasted a "fine libertarian library" and promised instruction in "the Principles of Human Liberty," the Freedom School was not what most of us would call distinguished. The chair of the history department, Dr. James J. Martin, went on to become a leading American Holocaust denier. Many of the required readings were written by LeFevre himself. Several of the school's neighbors, alarmed by what they believed to be an anarchist collective in their midst, filed reports with the FBI.

Yet for a small set of followers, the Freedom School was a sanctuary. And unlike LeFevre's neighbors, LeFevre's followers were often fantastically rich. Roger Milliken, a textile heir who ran his family's South Carolina business, made Freedom School mandatory for all new executives. Milwaukee Steel baron William J. Grede joined the board. So did a Kansas industrialist named Charles Koch, who shared a passion for small-government fundamentalism with his younger brother David.

The Freedom School was perhaps the most colorful organization of its type, but by no means was it alone or even exceptional. In the decades following the New Deal, as corporate profits soared and the specter of communism loomed, spiritualism for rich people flourished. Ayn Rand published *Atlas Shrugged* in 1957. A year later, candy baron Robert Welch (he invented Junior Mints) stepped back from his business to run the John Birch Society, which alleged that the United Nations was attempting to take over America, Communists were putting fluoride in our tap water, and President Eisenhower was a Russian stooge. These theories were ridiculous. But they were certainly no more ridiculous than Bob LeFevre's behind-the-wheel snooze.

Like influence-as-investment, influence-as-religion was a new force in the United States. As late as 1953, eminent historian Daniel Boorstin could write the following about American ideology: "The tendency to abstract the principles of political life may sharpen issues for the political philosopher. It becomes idolatry when it provides statesmen or a people with a blueprint for their society. . . . One of the good fortunes of American civilization has been the happy coincidence of circumstances which has led us away from such idolatry."

Within a decade, Boorstin's happy pronouncement was becoming obsolete. So-called "movement conservatism"—small-government as moral philosophy, rather than as a means to an economic or social end—was on the rise. Where Lewis Powell saw lobbying as a business decision, movement conservatives thought of themselves not as investors, but as crusaders, spending their millions to protect America from the vague but threatening "Left."

The upshot of all this is that the total amount of money spent on influencing government soared. It was a bit like cardiologists and

Orthodox Jews teaming up to form a League Against Bacon. Each group arrived at its position for different reasons, and there was of course some overlap between the two. But together, the business leaders and movement conservatives had more power—and deeper pockets—than they would have on their own.

If the preferred tool of corporate America was the well-paid professional lobbyist, the preferred tool of the idol worshippers was the private family foundation. That's because gifts to these foundations are entirely tax-deductible. As Jane Mayer puts it in *Dark Money*, her sweeping history of the American right wing, "This arrangement enables the wealthy to simultaneously receive generous tax subsidies and use their foundations to impact society as they please."

The family foundations could, in turn, donate money to politically minded nonprofits. This explains another shift that took place in the 1970s: the rise of the partisan think tank. Before that crucial decade, think tanks considered themselves scholarly research centers, eschewing partisanship in favor of academic merit. But as funders shifted their priorities, a new type of institution emerged. Founded in 1973, the Heritage Foundation was explicitly built to provide intellectual firepower for the conservative movement. The Cato Institute, a similar organization but specifically geared toward libertarians, arrived a year later.[*]

Many nonprofits, while not technically think tanks, still use donors' money to influence how government behaves. The American Legislative Exchange Council, or ALEC, copies and pastes conservative bills from one state legislature to another. Judicial Watch launches investigations of Democrats and promotes right-wing conspiracy theories. The Family Research Council is a clearinghouse for anti-abortion and anti-gay talking points. Today the list of these groups is endless—and remarkably, almost none of them existed fifty years ago.

---

[*] The organization is indeed named after Roman senator Cato the Younger, the one who gruesomely killed himself by . . . actually, if you haven't googled it yet, maybe just don't.

Exactly how much has the world of partisan nonprofits grown? It's hard to say. These are private organizations, and as President Trump demonstrated for decades with his own crooked family foundation, they operate with little scrutiny. But we can make a few estimates. As of 2018, U.S. foundations had assets worth $890 billion, and each year, they're legally required to spend at least 5 percent of their holdings. If just 5 percent of these foundations were politically minded, and they spent the bare minimum required by law, that would come out to $2.2 billion per year. None of this spending would be official lobbying. It wouldn't even be shadow lobbying. But it would be part of the broader influence industry nonetheless.

A final sector of the influence industry isn't new, but it's new to us: the partisan media. Two hundred years ago it was easy to find a Fox News equivalent. When Abraham Lincoln launched his campaign in 1859, for example, one of the very first things he did was purchase a newspaper to support him. But starting in the early 1900s, with the growth of department stores and other major advertisers, the media stopped relying on partisans for financial support. Objectivity became journalism's new goal.

Objectivity is still the goal for many reporters, who do their jobs bravely even as they find themselves increasingly under attack. But more and more news outlets are now proudly ideological in nature. A smattering of these (my former Obama colleagues' Crooked Media among them) are geared toward liberals. But for most part, the creators of partisan mass media are movement conservatives. Rush Limbaugh entered national syndication in 1988. Fox News launched in 1996. Small-government spiritualists bought new channels, built new programs, took over existing newspapers and stations—and found they could make lots of money in the process.

The combined effect of movement conservatism—both the partisan nonprofits and the partisan mass media—make the typical survey of the influence industry inadequate. Lobbying, both the official and shadow varieties, makes up just a part of the whole. Like the impact of organized corporate power, the impact of what Daniel Boorstin would have called "idolatry" is impossible to precisely quantify. But we know it's very large and that, until recently, it was very small.

In the last three decades, America hasn't technically added a branch of government. It's not like the Constitution requires Belle to get through the House, the Senate, and the Influence Industry to make it to the president's desk. But practically speaking, that's exactly what she must do. In our current system of government, the emissaries of Possum Kingdom are always watching. They can smooth Belle's path, or they can seal her fate.

These unelected lawmakers, men and women who played a trivial role when Bill was singing his heart out to an earnest little child, play a crucial role today. So it seems important that We, the People, know exactly what they do.

Whether you like it or not, the federal government is much bigger than it used to be. Compared to a half century ago, we spend around eighteen times more money. Government has grown in war and peace, bull markets and bear markets, Democratic and Republic administrations.

So here's a question. Given that we've vastly expanded our government's responsibilities over the last fifty years, how many people have we added to the federal workforce to keep up?

The answer is zero. In fact, it's less than zero. In 1970, there were 2.2 million full-time federal employees. There are just 2.1 million today. During that time, the country kept adding people, so as a percentage of the population, the government workforce has been cut by about two-thirds.[*]

---

[*] The total size of the federal workforce is larger when you count private contractors, but it's hard to get data going back fifty years. Regardless, the size of this "blended" workforce has grown by just 5 percent since 1984—about eight times *slower* than the population.

In Congress, where so much of our policymaking takes place, the decline in employment has been even more severe. In the Brookings Institution's "Vital Statistics on Congress," the scholars Norm Ornstein and Thomas Mann looked at all non-administrative congressional jobs—office staff, personal aides, committee staff, research support—between 1979 and 2015. They found that the number of people who work for Congress has dropped by 25 percent. Imagine what it would mean for, say, Baskin Robbins if their number of customers went up by half but they laid off one in four employees.

Most Americans don't know about these massive job cuts. In a recent survey, for each respondent who said the number of congressional staffers had shrunk over the last two decades, thirty-seven said it had grown. To put it another way, for every person who was right, thirty-seven people were wrong.

In fairness, the number of "personal staff," aides employed directly by members of Congress, hasn't declined. In 1975, the House decided each member of Congress could employ a maximum of eighteen people, and that limit remains in place today. But while congressional office sizes have stayed constant, the size of the population has grown. The number of Americans per district has gone up by 50 percent, even as the number of people hired to serve those Americans hasn't budged.

Meanwhile, outside of representatives' personal offices, staff counts haven't just flatlined. They've fallen off a cliff. When Newt Gingrich took over after the 1994 elections, he slashed the number of committee staff—who tend to be older and have more institutional expertise than staff in members' personal offices—by one-third. He also took the Government Accountability Office and the Congressional Research Service, nonpartisan organizations that function much like internal think tanks, and cut those by a third as well.

Today, those who can find jobs as congressional staffers aren't just extremely overworked. They're extremely underpaid. The average House staff assistant, an entry-level role, makes $30,000 per year. According to an MIT calculator, that's nearly 20 percent below D.C.'s living wage, for a job that can easily require sixty or seventy hours of work per week. (In the Senate, the pay is better, but not by much.) The most senior of senior staff can expect salaries in the low six figures, but that's still only a fraction of what they would earn if they went to the private sector.

Low wages wreak havoc on the economic diversity of the people who write our laws. Those with parents who can help support them and with no student loans to pay off have a much easier time forging Hill careers. Underpaying employees relative to what they're worth also leads to high turnover. According to one recent survey, a large majority of Washington's legislative staffers like their work, yet 63 percent of them hope to find a new job within a year. Among those who did leave, low salaries were "the top reason cited in their decision to leave employment."

In Congress, the impact of these staff cuts and turnover are even more severe than they'd be in most organizations, because the bosses, the legislators themselves, usually arrive on the Hill with no experience. Tom Harkin, an Iowan who served five terms in the upper chamber, once defined a senator as "a constitutional impediment to the smooth functioning of staff." But today, thanks to slashed budgets, outdated limits on hiring, and low pay, that staff is stretched thinner than ever before.

So who picks up the slack? The answer, as you might have guessed, is Possum Kingdom. Thanks to the shrinking of congressional staff and the expansion of the influence industry, huge chunks of public service have been outsourced to the private sector. The overwhelming majority of people who go to work each morning hoping to shape our laws do have constituents: lobbying firms, clients, corporate partners, wealthy donors. But in a very literal sense, most of our professional policymakers no longer work for us.

Unfortunately, the influence industry's true role in our legislative process is poorly understood, even by many of those who crusade against it. That's not a knock on the crusaders. I understand how easy it is to oversimplify the role of lobbyists, because I've succumbed to the temptation myself. In 2016, a friend of mine was writing remarks for Katy Perry at the Democratic National Convention and asked if I could chip in last-minute. "On November eighth, you'll be just as powerful as any NRA lobbyist," Ms. Perry wound up declaring. The line got a big round of applause, and I felt very good about myself, ignoring the fact that this is not at all how power in Washington works.

While it's politically useful to claim an opponent is "bought and paid for" by the gun lobby, or Big Oil, or Big Labor, or Big Abortion, or Big Tech, it's a woefully unsophisticated explanation. Also, the logic quickly breaks down. Senator Bill Cassidy, Republican of Louisiana, has taken $2.9 million from the NRA. Do we really think that if a gun-safety group gave him $3 million, they could buy back his support?

Of course not. When it comes to the relationship between money and our elected officials, we tend to swap cause for effect. Generally speaking, lawmakers don't take policy positions because lobbyists give them money. Lobbyists give lawmakers money because of the policy positions those lawmakers already hold. Lee Drutman, quoting a professional influencer he once interviewed, passed along an excellent analogy: "Bringing a check to a fundraiser is like bringing a bottle of wine to a party." You're not bribing your way onto the guest list. You're saying thank you for the invite.

Perhaps unsurprisingly, the best explanation of the real exchange between lawmakers and lobbyists came from the Trump administration. Before he was President Trump's acting chief of staff, Mick Mulvaney was a Tea Party congressman from South Carolina. Describing his former life to a group of bankers, he said this: "If you were a lobbyist who never gave us money, I didn't talk to you. If you were a lobbyist who gave us money, I might talk to you. If you came from back home and sat in my lobby, I talked to you without exception."

People were understandably appalled to hear Mulvaney's frank description. But it's worth putting aside our distaste for a moment and paying careful attention to the system of government he described.

For a politician, the voters are like family. You have to deal with them no matter what. The outside groups, on the other hand, are more like friends. You spend time with the people you get along with and can count on. If some ungrateful jerk consistently refuses to bring wine to the party, or checks to the fundraiser, that person may find himself outside the friend group. To a politician, lobbyists—whether official or shadow, working for nonprofits or for corporations—are the family you choose.

The idea of lobbyists as lawmakers' friends sounds unpleasant. It *is* unpleasant. But in a world where the number of employees available to public servants is smaller than ever, elected officials frequently have no choice. The most valuable service outside groups perform isn't providing money. It's providing staff.

Political scientists call this the "legislative subsidy theory." In plain English, it means that lawmakers rely on lobbyists for far more than you might think. Need talking points for your speech? A think tank can send some over. Need a small-business leader for a photo op? A trade group can have that arranged. Want to grill a witness with a particularly hard-hitting question? A lobbying firm can write one up for you.

Most important, the influence industry helps write legislation. Let's say you're a lawmaker who wants to protect our drinking water. Your personal staff probably isn't big enough to have a clean-water specialist, and committee staff have hundreds of priorities competing for their time. But if you reach out to a large environmental group, they'll happily help you fine-tune a bill, sign up co-sponsors, develop your messaging, plot your procedural strategy, and advise you on which amendments to accept or reject.

When your bill passes, and millions of Americans are drinking cleaner water, the new law will have your name on it. You and your staff will rightly deserve credit. But the full story will be more complicated—your bill got by with a lot of help from its friends.

This system is arguably less corrupt than the straight-up sale of laws for campaign cash. But it is also far more insidious. If politicians could be bought and sold, a few bighearted billionaires could simply purchase them and give them back to the people. Alternatively, you could crack down on campaign contributions, and Possum Kingdom would shrivel up.

But in the real world, that won't happen. So long as the official government relies on the invisible government, the symbiotic relationship between them will endure. And like the structure of our official government, the structure of our shadow government has a lot to do with whether Belle lives or dies.

The siren songs of special interests are heard in every legislative hall.
—Ronald Reagan

I believe we are a nation of special individuals, not special interests.
—George H. W. Bush

We have to do everything we can to show the American people that their Government works for them and not the special interests.
—Bill Clinton

I don't need a book this thick of bureaucratic rules written by special interests in Washington.—George W. Bush

We can't have special interests sitting shotgun.—Barack Obama

I don't want lobbyists, I don't want special interests.—Donald Trump

You get the picture. As of this writing, presidents have said "special interests" on 1,012 separate occasions during my lifetime. In nearly every case, the phrase was synonymous with "interests I don't like." To say that Possum Kingdom benefits special interests is both true and meaningless. Not to get all Barney the Dinosaur, but every interest is special.

Far better is to look at which types of interests our invisible government currently favors. Thanks to its massive growth over the last few decades, Possum Kingdom has become its own veto point—so which legislation is it most or least likely to veto?

The first answer is simple: the influence industry favors corporate priorities over noncorporate ones. Private businesses are not the only organizations that hire lobbyists. Unions have lobbyists. The ACLU has lobbyists. Catholic Charities has lobbyists. The grassroots campaign to impeach President Trump had lobbyists, and as Katy Perry will tell you, so does the NRA. Lots of people spend money on influence.

It's just that business spends lots more money on influence than everyone else. "For every dollar spent on lobbying by labor unions and public-interest groups together," writes Lee Drutman, "large corporations and their associations now spend $34." Corporate groups outspend all noncorporate groups, combined, by a factor of four to one. And that doesn't even count other types of spending, like receptions thrown for congressional staff or ads at Reagan National Airport that target lawmakers waiting for flights home. Thanks to the First Amendment, we can all demand a seat at the table. But thanks to the influence industry, business gets far more seats than we do.

This may be one reason that actual staff think the American people are more conservative than they really are. A 2018 study asked high-ranking legislative aides to guess the percentage of people in their district who took the liberal or conservative position on five different issues: the minimum wage, guns, infrastructure, climate change, and health care. On four out of the five (health care being the lone exception), staffers underestimated the progressive position's popularity in their district, and by large margins. Seventy-eight percent of staffers guessed too low when it came to support for limits on carbon emissions. For gun background checks, it was 91 percent.

Reporters found that long-serving staffers were no more likely than newcomers to guess their constituents' views correctly. It likewise didn't matter whether the districts were represented by Democrats or Republicans, or whether they were considered electorally competitive or safe. What did matter, the researchers found, was the number of meetings staffers took with corporate-backed groups.

"We hypothesize," the authors concluded, "that greater relative staffer contact with business-based groups will result in less accurate perceptions of public opinion because business-based groups are less likely to represent the preferences of the general public." To put that concisely, by making Possum Kingdom part of the legislative process, we've given corporations a big advantage.

This is particularly true when it comes to what political scientists called "low salience issues," and the rest of us call "things we don't think that much about." If you're a relatively informed American, you likely have an opinion about expanding health insurance, or reforming the immigration system, or taxing the rich. But when it comes to the details, your preferences are probably less well developed. Should oil and gas partnerships be treated for tax purposes like law firms or corporations? Exactly how much money should the federal government spend studying postpartum depression? How many jobs must a foreigner create in order to be guaranteed a visa?

The reason you've probably ignored these questions is not apathy. It's that laws are complicated and you have a life. Even lawmakers don't have the time to understand every detail of every bill. That's why, in addition to advancing corporate priorities, Possum Kingdom favors small groups with strong preferences over large groups with weak ones. Let's say you had two competing bills. One would give fifty dollars to a million people, while the other would give a million dollars to just fifty people. In a democracy, you might expect the first bill to have an edge. But thanks to the influence industry, the second bill is actually far more likely to pass.

You may not realize it, but you participate in exactly this type of struggle every Tax Day. There's no reason the IRS can't file most Americans' taxes automatically, and for free. That's how lots of other countries operate, and if we passed a bill joining them, millions of Americans would save a little money on tax-preparing software.

Unless, of course, you're an American who *sells* tax-preparing software. In that case, free tax prep for most Americans would mean millions in losses for you. That's why Intuit, the maker of TurboTax, has successfully lobbied both Congress and the IRS to block automatic tax filing. (They've also had help from movement-conservative allies, who want Tax Day to be maximally unpleasant.) In essence, millions of Americans pay a small tax to Intuit each year. That's the cost of living in a country with a privatized legislative process.

Finally, Possum Kingdom amplifies the government's existing status quo bias: doing nothing is always far easier than doing something. At every point in Belle's journey through the legislative process, the influence industry can take advantage of existing veto points to attack her. It's as though every bridge were now guarded by twice as many trolls.

In fact, influence peddlers can even kill Belle after she's been signed into law via something called the rule-making process. In part because Congress employs so few people, and in part because it wouldn't make sense for lawmakers to micromanage, details of laws are often delegated to the executive branch. For example, Obamacare required fast-food chains to post calorie counts on their menus. But the specifics of those requirements (What font size should restaurants use? Is 7-Eleven a fast-food chain? Does ketchup need its own calorie count?) were left to the Food and Drug Administration to decide.

In other words, long after Belle is approved by Congress and the White House—and thus long after the media and public have moved on to other issues—officials will still be figuring out exactly what she looks like. If you can lobby those officials, you can give Belle a surprise makeover—or stab her in the back. This didn't happen in our calorie-count example, but it's easy to see how it could have; just imagine if all nutritional information had to be printed in size-six font. The rule-making process is full of these sneaky opportunities. The influence industry can't pass a bill that's already been killed, but it can kill a bill that's already been passed.

Adding Possum Kingdom to the legislative process, as we've done over the past several decades, hasn't exactly put our government up for sale. But it has biased our government in clear and profound ways. Belle's chances of passage now improve if she favors corporations over workers and consumers, and favors narrow interests over broad ones. Also, her chances of passing (and of remaining intact afterward) are lower than they were before.

Put it all together, and power within Washington—just like power at the ballot box—is shifting toward a smaller and smaller group of people, almost all of whom already had lots of power to begin with.

☆

Under the current administration, the blurry line between official and invisible governments has basically disappeared. President Trump has appointed the following people to the following positions:

A coal-mining lobbyist to run the Environmental Protection Agency; an oil-and-gas lobbyist to run the Interior Department; a banking lobbyist to run the Labor Department; a steel-industry lobbyist to run the U.S. Trade Representative's Office; a defense-contracting lobbyist to run the Pentagon; and another defense-contracting lobbyist to oversee the U.S. intelligence community. That's to say nothing of the 275 additional former lobbyists President Trump has appointed to senior positions in cabinet agencies and the White House.

It's possible you believe, as 1970s super-lobbyist Bryce Harlow once did, that this is not just acceptable but terrific. If what's good for coal mines, Wall Street banks, and munitions suppliers is good for America, you want the government run by people who can give those industries a hand. But if you believe our government should represent the entire American people, rather than a few of its largest industries, it's impossible not to conclude that Possum Kingdom is out of control. That's not going to change while Donald Trump is president.

But then again, and thank goodness, Donald Trump won't be president forever. When the official government is once again run by people who represent the entire country, and not just its most privileged slice, what should they do to curb the influence industry's power?

The easy answer is a lobbying ban. That's what President Obama tried, and briefly won some praise for. After George W. Bush packed the government full of former and future influence peddlers, Obama promised to bar from his administration anyone who had been a registered lobbyist in the past two years.

The main issue with the lobbying ban was that it didn't really work. It was designed to solve the problem Americans think we have (a government bought and paid for) rather than the problem we actually have (a government that relies on private interests to do the work of staff). Lobbyists for the Children's Defense Fund were treated no differently than a partner at a mercenary firm-for-hire, despite their wildly different priorities and salaries. In many cases, people with exactly the kind of expertise and experience the administration needed—people who had been waiting out the Bush years in the hope of reentering government service—had registered as lobbyists before the ban was announced.

On eighty-three occasions, former lobbyists were deemed so essential to the administration that they were granted "ethics waivers" to skirt the ban. This was highly practical. Some of these former lobbyists were my White House colleagues, and I can promise their commitment to public service was undiminished by their previous work. But that only goes to show that the lobbying ban wasn't all that necessary in the first place. In most cases, the reason Democrats don't hire industry lobbyists to regulate industry is not that some arbitrary rule prohibits them from doing so. The reason Democrats don't hire industry lobbyists is that they don't think it's a good idea.

The same is true of President Trump, but in reverse. He let corporate lobbyists run the government not because his ethics pledge wasn't strict enough, but because those lobbyists shared his political and policy goals. In a rather perfect coda, under Trump, the government even arranged to sell off the same Teapot Dome oilfield that Albert Fall had tried and failed to hand to captains of industry nearly a century ago. And this time, oil companies didn't even have to bother with bribery. Under our current system of government, when one of our two parties is in charge, the wheels come pre-greased.

De-greasing those wheels will not be simple. We can't rely on waivable ethics pledges and temporary lobbying bans. And we have to confront the real way money influences our government, not just try to prevent another Teapot Dome.

We can start by making official lobbying slightly more difficult. During the Democratic primaries, Elizabeth Warren put forward a plan that would ban former federal lawmakers, judges, and top administration officials from lobbying for life, and ban legislative staff from lobbying for between two and six years. Warren's plan would also bar lobbyists from engaging in fundraising entirely—in essence, they could still show up to the party, but they couldn't bring wine. Perhaps most important, Warren's proposal would be enacted by passing a law that applies to everyone, rather than by one party setting a good example and hoping the other follows along.

Still, I suspect that in practice, such a law would have a smaller impact than you might think. For one thing, former lawmakers who want to sell their influence can easily do so without becoming official lobbyists. (Newt Gingrich famously made $1.6 million as "historian" for the mortgage giant Freddie Mac.) Also, even if lobbyists can't technically fundraise, it wouldn't be difficult to hire one person to push bills on lawmakers and another to cut checks. In fact, banning lobbyists from fundraising might expand the corporate advantage, because big companies can afford to hire separate sets of staff, while small public-interest organizations cannot.

Which brings me to my greatest concern with lobbying bans, whether enacted by pledge or administrator: they treat all lobbyists the same. If you're a lobbyist for Planned Parenthood, I'd love to see you join a Democratic administration. Conversely, if you're a top executive at Exxon Mobil, I personally don't believe you should be running the Environmental Protection Agency, regardless of whether you checked the "lobbyist" box on a form. I have no doubt many Republicans share these opinions, only in reverse.

The real way to manage Possum Kingdom is not just through ever-stricter lobbying bans. It's to shrink the influence industry's influence, while simultaneously restoring some of the power the rest of us have lost.

That starts with measuring, far more accurately, exactly how much money is spent trying to change our leaders' behavior. Right now, companies have to disclose the amount they spend on registered lobbyists. But as we've seen, that ignores the enormous amounts of spending they do in secret. I'll leave the details to the experts, but I think our democracy would be better off if we knew how much money corporations spent on free candy for legislative staffers, or donations to political nonprofits. It's time to bring shadow lobbying out of the shadows. We can't shrink Possum Kingdom until we know how large it really is.

We should also allow members of Congress to incorporate that knowledge as they debate new laws. Right now, a congressional "rule of decorum" bars lawmakers from discussing the influence industry on the floor. I can say Big Oil is bad. I can say that my colleague's vote against a climate bill is bad. I can't, however, say that my colleague met with Big Oil lobbyists right before announcing his vote. In fact, I likely wouldn't even know such an encounter took place. The White House, regulators, and lawmakers don't need to publicly disclose whom they meet with, or what's discussed in those meetings. It's simply assumed that everyone is acting in good faith.

At one time, these rules made sense. We didn't want people carelessly accusing their colleagues of corruption. But when the influence industry is larger than Congress itself, Congress should be able to talk without restriction about its influence. What was once a useful protection of civility today feels more like a modern-day gag rule.

Lawmakers—and constituents—have a right to know which interest groups a lawmaker has chosen to ally with. And We, the People, should be given more insight into which lobbyists meet with whom, and about what. After all, you learn a lot about someone by knowing who their friends are.

Just as we can make buying votes more expensive in our elections, we can also make buying influence more expensive in our government. I'll again leave the details to the experts, but there are a few ways to do it. The most direct would be some kind of sliding-scale tax—after a certain amount, an ever-increasing percentage of each dollar you spend on lobbying is diverted to Uncle Sam. What's nice about this approach is that it doesn't try to pick good interests from bad ones. Instead, it takes on concentrated power regardless of the source.

Another way to make influence buying more difficult involves the structure of corporate political action committees, or PACs. Most people don't know it, but corporate PAC money—money that is then turned into campaign contributions—doesn't come from corporations themselves. It comes from employee donations. According to the Public Affairs Council, a kind of adult education resource for those in the government business, "the average contribution by an individual employee to a corporate PAC is $316." Yet while all employees can give to a PAC, almost none of them has a say in how the money is spent. If leadership of corporate PACs were required to include workers, and not just senior management, there's little doubt the PACs' priorities would change.

One final way to increase the cost of influence is rather simple: end the tax deductibility of political nonprofits and family foundations. If you want to spend your billions promoting a fringe political agenda, you have that right. But you don't have the right to do it tax-free.

Tracking lobbying, bringing it out the shadows, and making it more difficult to trade money for influence will help restore some of the balance that has tipped so decisively toward corporate and conservative interests in recent years. But you can't get rid of the invisible government entirely. To give Belle the best possible chance of becoming a law, we can't simply reduce the power of Possum Kingdom. We also must employ something similar to Rick Hasen's "level-up" strategy for campaign finance, expanding the public's power to advocate for bills we like.

Lee Drutman has a few novel ideas for how to do this. Among the most striking is an "Office of Public Lobbying" to support groups that are well represented in America but underrepresented on Capitol Hill. The program would be modeled on the public defender's office. Public lobbyists (perhaps paid for by the new sliding-scale tax on private ones) would be required to advocate for any point of view that has sizable public support but that lacks the financial power to hire professional influencers of its own.

Wealthy donors can help restore the balance of power as well. In both media and nonprofits, conservatives are enjoying a several-decade-long head start. The problem is not that rich progressives don't exist, or that they don't spend money. It's that the progressive movement has tended to focus on electoral politics to the exclusion of everything else. The next election is important—but so is building the institutions, from the think tanks to advocacy networks to broadcasting platforms, that can help make future elections easier to win.

Last, and quite likely most important of all, we need to stop outsourcing the policymaking process to business—which means policymakers need more staff who work directly for us. We can start by vastly increasing the budgets for the in-house congressional think tanks, like the Government Accountability Office, the Congressional Research Service, and the Congressional Budget Office. There's no guarantee that these offices will provide perfect information. But when taxpayers fund the analysis of a bill or issue, we at least know it won't be biased in favor of whichever interest foots the bill.

Legislative staff should be expanded as well. In the congressional committees, more staff would mean more in-house subject matter experts who can handle a wider range of issues, and more institutional knowledge handed down even as individual lawmakers come and go.

Members' offices should grow as well. Many lawmakers, maybe even most lawmakers, really do want to deliver for their constituents. But they're hamstrung by the fact that their staff must by law be less than half the size of the average Taco Bell. By increasing the number of people each member of Congress can hire, we'll reduce the reliance on lobbyists to make our laws.

Finally, congressional staff should be paid more. At an absolute minimum, if you work for a member of Congress, you should be able to afford to live in the city in which you work. Meanwhile, when it comes to salaries for more senior staff, no one expects public-sector workers to make *more* than their private-sector counterparts. But it's ridiculous that they make so much less. In Singapore, for example, salaries for public officials are set at 60 percent of what they could earn outside government, meaning top ministers often make about $800,000 per year. That's nothing compared to the largest corporate paychecks, but it's enough to ensure that Singapore has one of the lowest corruption rates of any nation on earth.

If we give the American people more influence—supporting ourselves through public-interest lobbying, donor-backed institutions, and well-paid legislative staff—we can make sure Belle has powerful allies by her side. We won't end the influence industry entirely. But we can make sure that the bills most likely to pass are those backed by broad coalitions of Americans, not tiny pockets of concentrated power and wealth.

Unraveling Possum Kingdom is complicated business. But ultimately, the goal is simple: to return the policymaking process to the people. In our democracy, laws that affect us should be made by people who work on our behalf. And if those people don't do their jobs adequately, we should be able to fire them and hire new ones.

Which brings us, at last, to Belle's final hurdle. Because, after all this journeying—a scramble through the House, a miraculous escape from the deep freeze of the Senate, a nervous tiptoe through Possum Kingdom—Belle's fate will ultimately be decided by a group of government employees it is literally impossible to fire.

11

SLAPPING STEPHEN FIELD

The Judges

Most drummers aren't allowed to name the band after themselves. Then again, Jay Sekulow isn't most drummers.

What distinguishes the leader of the Jay Sekulow Band (or "JSB" to superfans) isn't his musical pedigree. While the group's guitarist and singer are professional musicians, the band's namesake is an amateur, a sixty-four-year-old attorney who shows up to gigs sporting a blazer and what looks very much like either a hairpiece or plugs. Nor is Sekulow a hidden talent. I recently ran some JSB samples by my friend Brent Katz, an indie rock drummer and journalist. He told me Sekulow is "sticking to his basic high-hat snare beat the way a kid learning to swim sticks to the shallow end." Among percussionists, this is apparently quite a withering insult.

No matter how uninspiring Jay Sekulow may be as a drummer, I can confidently say that as a lyricist he is much, much worse. A few of

JSB's dad rock covers are actually kind of catchy. But the band's catalog of originals is—and I say this as someone who respects the creative process, and who appreciates how hard it is to make something new and put it into the world for public judgment—bad. Their biggest original hit, "Undemocratic," sounds like something from a Guns N' Roses tribute band whose members are simultaneously on mushrooms and in dire need of a nap.

> *Strummin' on my Gibson*
> *singin' my song now,*
> *Hopin' that the Feds*
> *won't take it away now*

Later in the song, Sekulow's band rhymes "become problematic" with "smell of melodramatic." Like I said, not good.

And yet here's the remarkable thing about JSB: they're popular! They book talk shows, rocking out in front of adoring studio audiences. They do massive livestreamed concerts on Facebook, where their page has 135,000 fans and counting. They're not world-famous. But somehow, despite a glaring lack of quality, they're for real.

Fall deep enough down the JSB rabbit hole, and you start questioning everything you thought you knew. After all, in pop music, there's no truly objective way to judge good from bad, so who's to say those Sekulow superfans aren't right? Perhaps fifty years from now, Beyoncé will be forgotten. "Undemocratic," grating lyrics and all, will be remembered as the defining anthem of the 2010s.

While such a transformation in taste may seems unlikely to you, the drummer leading JSB has every reason to believe it's possible. Because when he's not jamming on *Huckabee*, or holding a benefit concert for the right-wing nonprofit run by his family, Jay Sekulow is one of the most influential conservative lawyers in America. These days, he's probably best known for defending Donald Trump during the president's impeachment trial, but his real specialty is constitutional

law. Over his nearly five-decade career, Sekulow has seen firsthand
that the way we interpret our nation's bedrock document is largely a
matter of taste. And with his help, the judicial branch of our govern-
ment has been transformed into a far-right hit parade.

Today, judges who would have been laughed at just a few decades
ago—the JSB of the judiciary—have soared to the top of the charts.
Their unprecedented rise means that Belle faces a final brand-new veto
point, yet another hurdle that did not exist for Bill. How did that new
veto point get here? What does it mean for Belle, and for us? Those are
the questions we'll seek to answer as her journey, and ours, near their
respective ends.

Nothing in the Supreme Court's origin hints at the mighty institution
it would become. On February 1, 1790, the very first day of the Court's
inaugural term, half the judges were missing. Thus, the first official act
of America's first chief justice was to glumly postpone a meeting and
go home.

The original justices themselves did not inspire much confidence
either. There were six of them, handpicked by George Washington, all
duds. Illness forced two to resign, one after five years and the other af-
ter just a week. Chief Justice John Jay spent his entire tenure obsessed
with his political career; in 1795 he got the opportunity to run for gov-
ernor of New York and quit the bench. Washington tried to promote
another member of the founding six, John Rutledge, to the chief justice
role, but the Senate refused to confirm him. Rutledge, who'd been bat-
tling depression long before the Senate's decision, attempted suicide.
While he lived, he promptly resigned from the Court.

That left just two of the original half dozen, James Wilson and Wil-
liam Cushing. You may remember Wilson from chapter 6, where he
compared the Great Compromise to a poison. He was a brilliant jurist.
But he was terrible with money. On two occasions, Wilson found him-
self simultaneously a sitting judge on the nation's highest court and an

inmate in debtors' prison. He died ducking creditors in 1798. Cushing, meanwhile, lasted twenty-one years on the court but accomplished almost nothing. He wrote only nineteen opinions, most of little consequence. Apparently, he just didn't like working hard.

It was an unimpressive start for America's judiciary. Then again, the judiciary itself was an unimpressive branch of government. After devoting about 2,000 words to the role of lawmakers and more than 1,000 to that of the president, the Constitution gave judges just 375. If you visit the National Archives and examine the original copy of the document the Framers produced, you'll even notice that the S in "Supreme Court" isn't capitalized. All three branches of government were coequal. But among these equals, the judiciary came last.

What changed? Here's the story as I learned it in high school. Chief Justice John Marshall, appointed by President Adams in 1801, swooped in and gave his fellow judges vast new powers. In *Marbury v. Madison*, he declared a federal law unconstitutional, single-handedly inventing the concept of "judicial review." Ever since, the Court has been the ultimate interpreter of the Constitution, on equal footing with the other branches.

Kind of. Not really. For one thing, while judicial review wasn't specifically mentioned in the Constitution, the idea that the Court could rule laws unconstitutional was at least a decade old by the time *Marbury* was decided. Alexander Hamilton wrote about judicial review in the Federalist Papers. Justice James Wilson believed in judicial review as well, and probably would have brought it to the Court himself had he stayed in good health and out of debt. John Marshall didn't create the Court's most important power. He just made it official.

He also used his power sparingly. What most American students never learn is that, after overturning an act of Congress in *Marbury v. Madison*, the Marshall Court never overturned an act of Congress again. In fact, justices wouldn't strike down another federal statute until the 1850s. They did, however, often strike down state laws. In other words, judicial review was not a tool for judges to assert their power over other branches. It was a tool for the federal government to assert its power over the states.

Marshall's care not to encroach on the other two branches' territory was in part a matter of principle. As *America's Constitution* author Akhil Amar points out, the Founders never expected or intended that judges would possess a veto power to rival the president's. But there were other, more practical reasons for the judiciary to tread carefully around Congress and the White House. The Constitution gave presidents and lawmakers enormous power to punish courts it didn't like.

For one thing, unless and until the executive branch administers judges' opinions, those opinions are no more compelling than yours or mine. After one ruling against him, in *Worcester v. Georgia*, Andrew Jackson is said to have exclaimed, "John Marshall has made his decision. Now let him enforce it!" In fact, the real sign of the Court's weakness was that Jackson never said those words and never had to. Wary of an unwinnable showdown with the White House, Marshall issued a theoretical judgment against the president in *Worcester* but never even tried to have it enforced.

In struggles with Congress, the danger for the judiciary was not being ignored but being downsized. The Constitution requires that we have a judicial branch, that it contain a Supreme Court, and that, once appointed, federal judges can serve until they retire or die. But that's it. The number of Supreme Court justices, the number of lower courts, and the number of judges on those courts are all up to lawmakers to decide. Congress can expand and shrink those courts at will. With a two-thirds majority in the Senate, it can even impeach and remove a sitting judge.

Finally, Congress controls "appellate jurisdiction," the rules that decide which cases go to which courts. Today, our court system is a single pyramid, with the nine Supreme Court justices at the very top. But for the first hundred years of American history, our court system contained multiple pyramids. In many cases, second-tier courts had final, unappealable say, with the Supreme Court cut out of the process entirely.

Yet from these inauspicious beginnings, the judiciary, and the Supreme Court in particular, slowly gathered power. As America became riven by fault lines—regional, partisan, or both—the courts became seen as a refuge from politics and a steward of the public trust. While other branches loudly bickered, judges quietly accumulated strength. In 1891, Congress willingly surrendered its authority over appellate jurisdiction, granting the Court the right to review any federal case it pleased. In 1925, justices were also given the right to *refuse* to hear any case they didn't want to.

These changes make a big difference for Belle, just as they did for Bill before her. Assuming she becomes a law, the Supreme Court will automatically have to power to judge her. And if they judge harshly, Belle, despite everything she's been through, is toast.

Along with judicial review and the gradual expansion of its jurisdiction, there's one final reason the Supreme Court became so powerful: for a very long time, John Marshall didn't die. During an era when the average white, thirty-year-old male wasn't expected to reach sixty-five, Marshall made it to seventy-nine. Also, and no less important, he never retired. His thirty-four-years on the court set a precedent. Justices remain justices for the rest of their careers, and often for the rest of their lives.

The average tenure for a Supreme Court justice is now 16.9 years. Lawmakers flow in and out with political tides. Presidents serve a term or two and write their memoirs. But judges can last for generations. There's a lot of power in that.

From the very beginning of partisan politics, politicians have hoped to capture some of that judicial power for themselves. In particular, presidents have hoped to shape the Supreme Court. The relative importance of the Court has only increased in the modern era. That's because the number of lower-court seats has ballooned—it's currently 861—while the number of Supreme Court justices has for over a century been fixed at nine. The difference between appointing a regular judge and a justice is the difference between scoring two points in basketball and scoring two goals in soccer. The first is nice but hardly earthshattering. The second completely changes the game.

Picking a Supreme Court justice ought to be the most consequential action a president can take that doesn't involve blowing someone up. In practice, however, judges are like twenty-two-year-old quarterbacks on draft day—it's hard to know how they'll behave once picked. "I could carve out of a banana a judge with more backbone than that," fumed Teddy Roosevelt after one of his choices, Oliver Wendell Holmes, ruled against him. "It isn't so much that he's a bad man," Harry Truman said of a similar disappointment, Justice Tom C. Clark. "It's just that he's such a dumb son of a bitch."*

There's a good reason American history is littered with cussing, flabbergasted presidents: the public likes the Court's independence from politics, and the Court itself goes to great lengths to protect it. Unlike Congress (which controls trillions of dollars) and the White House (which controls the armed forces, among quite a lot else), the justices draw their power almost entirely from their reputation for integrity. Where presidents tend to see adverse rulings as a betrayal, judges see them as proof, both to themselves and to the public, that they belong to no political party or faction.

Judicial independence was further bolstered by the very nature of judicial review. Over the centuries, constitutional law has developed into a philosopher kingdom, with its own abstract language, jargon, and debates. Consider the long-running conflict over "textualism." A textualist believes that when interpreting a document, you should look only at the words in the document, while an "intentionalist" believes (as you might expect) that it's better to examine authors' intentions. This is the kind of debate you might imagine taking place between

---

* If you're paying very close attention, you may remember Justice Clark as the judge whose last-minute change of heart proved decisive in *Baker v. Carr* and established One Person, One Vote. On that occasion at least, the dumb son of a bitch came through.

two stoned English majors, not judges who hold the fates of millions in their hands.

But precisely because these arguments are so airily removed from the political realm, "conservative judges" and "liberal judges" haven't always mapped neatly onto the Republican and Democratic parties. Back when Roosevelt and Truman were picking judges, to guess how someone would rule on a future case based on their legal philosophy was like guessing someone's favorite song based on their favorite genre. And by long-standing convention, presidents weren't supposed to directly ask would-be judges how they planned to rule on specific cases, because that would undermine their independence.

As Abraham Lincoln rather bluntly put it, "We cannot ask a man what he will do, and if we should, and he should answer us, we should despise him for it."

Another unwritten rule of the Court, one that similarly protected judicial independence, is called *stare decisis*. Dressing up the concept in Latin makes it sound like you had to go to law school to understand it, but it's really quite simple: current judges shouldn't undo what past judges have already done. Times change, of course. Sometimes justices find an old Court ruling so reprehensible they simply have to overturn it. But they're expected to recognize that the Court's power—its authority and integrity—would collapse if the Constitution's meaning flopped about depending on who was in charge. Each ruling therefore sets a precedent that future rulings are meant to follow.

The final barrier to a president nominating lackeys to the bench has been the nominating process itself. On paper, it's a simple two-step procedure. The president picks a judge. A majority of senators confirms that judge. The end. But over time, a series of hurdles emerged to make extremists and cronies more difficult to appoint. To begin with there was the filibuster. For all its flaws, the filibuster necessitated a trade-off. The president had to be willing to pick judges who would win at least some support from both parties. In exchange, senators from both parties had to be at least somewhat willing to vote for the president's picks.

A second Senate tradition reduced the president's control of the nomination process even further. If you were a senator, and someone from your state was nominated to be a judge, you could withhold a "blue slip," signaling your disapproval, and that person would not be confirmed. This meant the White House had to secure the agreement of a nominee's home-state senators, regardless of which party they belonged to, before that nomination was announced.

The judiciary, then, was the little branch of government that could. From its false-start first meeting, the one postponed for lack of attendance, the Court grew into a sturdy and unyielding institution, independent from politicians and immune from voters. John Marshall had trod carefully around the other branches. Yet his successors would soon challenge them, at times overruling not just individual laws, but entire agendas that our leaders were elected to pursue.

No blood was shed in these clashes, at least not directly. But they became some of American history's great power struggles—and our country would be very different today if the winners hadn't won.

☆

Around 7 a.m. on August 14, 1889, Supreme Court justice Stephen J. Field was riding on a train from Los Angeles to San Francisco when an acquaintance named David Terry approached him and, in the words of historian J. Edward Johnson, "slapped his face several times."

This was typical behavior for David Terry. Once the chief justice of the California Supreme Court, Terry had seen his judicial career cut short after he shot and killed a sitting U.S. senator in a duel. Terry then entered private practice, met a young divorcee named Sarah Hill, took her on as a client, and married her. Hill's divorce from her first husband got ugly, and a few months before their fateful train encounter, Justice Field ruled against Terry and his client-slash-bride in an important proceeding. Hence the slapping.

That said, if you were going to pick someone to hit repeatedly in the face, Stephen Field was probably not the best choice. As a younger man, lured to California by the gold rush, he had an overcoat specially made with two extra-large pockets so that he could shoot people without the inconvenience of drawing a gun. Now older and more distinguished, he delegated matters to his bodyguard, who politely asked Terry to cool it with the slapping. When Terry ignored this warning, the bodyguard shot him through the heart.

That's how Stephen J. Field became the first and only Supreme Court justice ever arrested for murder. Soon after, he became the first and only Supreme Court justice acquitted on murder charges. And yet, remarkably, that's not even the most interesting thing about him. What really makes Stephen Field special—the reason he's worth our attention here—is that he is also the first and only person to become the tenth justice on the Supreme Court.

The man responsible for adding Field's seat was none other than Abraham Lincoln. We rarely include it in history books today, but the Civil War was not just fought at Bull Run and Gettysburg, but in the courtroom. In 1862, opponents of the war argued that it was unconstitutional. If the Supreme Court agreed with them, the war effort would be thrown into complete and possibly permanent disarray. And given that the Court's chief justice was Roger Taney, who in 1857 had issued the infamous *Dred Scott* decision expanding slaveholders' power, it was far from certain the Union would win.

But picking a fight with President Lincoln was as foolish as slapping Stephen J. Field in the face. With the Court threatening the very existence of the United States, Honest Abe fired back. As you'll recall, Lincoln's Republican allies in Congress were already busy carving up new states and territories to expand their power in the Senate. Now, with the justices debating the merits of the Civil War case, they also passed a law expanding the Supreme Court from nine seats to ten.

The purpose of this expansion was twofold. First, for all future rulings, Lincoln would have an extra pro-Union justice to help tip the balance in his favor. Second, and perhaps even more important, Congress was sending the Court a message: rule the wrong way on the Civil War case, and a tenth justice is only the beginning. The Taney Court took the hint. In 1863, the justices found the war constitutional by a vote of 5–4. Soon after, the violent but undeniably brainy Stephen Field joined the Court as an insurance policy. The judiciary never seriously hampered the war effort again.

Lincoln's successor, Andrew Johnson, was also responsible for changing the Court's size, albeit in an entirely different way. Republican senators, worried their new president was too sympathetic toward the South, refused to let him fill new Supreme Court seats when they became vacant. Instead, they gradually shrank the Court to seven members before allowing it to creep back up to nine in later presidencies.

In this turbulent era for the judiciary, there remained one cantankerous constant: Stephen J. Field. Just forty-three years old at the time of his confirmation, he ultimately outlasted the great John Marshall, setting a new record for length of tenure on the Court. Ironically, while Field's appointment helped settle the first great clash between the judiciary and the White House, his 12,614 days as a justice set up the next great showdown. A strong believer in individual liberty, with an attitude toward property rights forged in the gold rush of his youth, Field helped establish a genre of pro-business legal thought known as "laissez-faire constitutionalism."

This is where the musical-taste aspect of constitutional interpretation comes in. For several decades between the end of the Civil War and the Great Depression, as states created regulations to stave off a looming Gilded Age, the laissez-faire Court struck them down. The arguments in favor of the Court's decisions were sound. But so were the arguments against them. Asking why the Constitution forbade economic regulations during the 1890s is like asking why doo-wop peaked in the 1950s. When a trend sweeps the nation, it's impossible perfectly identify the cause.

The problem came when the public grew tired of laissez-faire and the Supreme Court did not. In 1932, Franklin Roosevelt was swept into office, promising to reshape the relationship between Americans and government with his New Deal. The Court's nine justices—seven of whom had been appointed by Republicans—were equally determined to make sure he did not succeed.

As it happens, the person who wrote the book on the clash that followed was one of my first bosses. Jeff Shesol is a former Bill Clinton speechwriter, syndicated cartoonist, and Rhodes scholar. He's also a current appreciator of peaty scotch and a writer of popular history. *Supreme Power*, which he published in 2010, is his detailed and dramatic account of what became known as "the court-packing fight."

It's possible you already know the basics: Roosevelt tried to get Congress to expand the Supreme Court and fill new seats with loyal judges; he failed; such a scheme hasn't been tried since. But that's like saying the story *Lord of the Rings* is that two friends visit a volcano. It's not wrong, but it's also not exactly right.

For one thing, the Court that FDR faced was not just conservative. It was blatantly anti-Roosevelt, lurching rightward in direct and partisan response to his election. The Court also expanded its scope. Where Stephen Field had overturned state regulation of economic activity, the 1930s Court began striking down federal laws as well. "Between 1933 and 1936," writes Shesol, "the Court overturned acts of Congress at ten times the traditional rate. To accomplish this, justices disinterred long-neglected doctrines and breathed new life into obscure clauses of the constitution."

Roosevelt, in other words, found himself in a position even more infuriating than Lincoln's seventy-five years earlier. American voters had given him a clear mandate. Now the Supreme Court, a supposedly apolitical body, was going out of its way to make sure his mandate went unfilled. Still, FDR's proposed counterattack—to add as many as six Court seats if justices over the age of seventy didn't retire—was far more aggressive than anything his predecessors had attempted.

He came far closer to pulling it off than most Americans realize. In fact, FDR's failure could be largely blamed on sheer bad luck; at a pivotal moment in the fight, one of his chief allies, Senate Majority Leader Joe Robinson, dropped dead.

At the same time, the Roosevelt White House made more than its fair share of mistakes. Rather than being honest about his motivations, FDR insisted he was reforming the Court for purely logistical reasons, something nobody believed. Offered compromises as his position weakened, the president foolishly refused to budge. The general postmortem conclusion was not that the Court bill was a terrible idea, but that, as one White House aide put it, "We have played a good hand badly."

And even this badly played hand quite possibly saved the New Deal. By putting the judiciary's fate in the hands of elected politicians, Roosevelt forced the Court to respond to public opinion. Under threat from reformers, justices bent over backward to show that they didn't need to be reformed. Within weeks of FDR's unveiling his proposal, the Court began shifting conspicuously toward the center, as judges who had once overturned minimum wage laws changed their opinions overnight. In the year following his reform push, Roosevelt's administration went 12–0 in major New Deal cases.

The conventional moral of FDR's crusade is that taking on the Supreme Court never works. But we ought to learn the opposite lesson: taking on the Supreme Court sometimes works quite well. Unlike with Lincoln, Roosevelt's plan to *expand* the Court didn't succeed. But like Lincoln, he was able to ensure more favorable rulings, thus saving the agenda he was elected to pursue.

If we define "court-packing" as appointing friendly judges, rather than simply increasing the total number of Supreme Court seats, then FDR eventually succeeded there as well. Between retirements and resignations, by the time Roosevelt died in office, he had picked eight of the Court's nine justices. I don't know about you, but I'd consider that pretty well packed. Thanks to a single dogged president, our collective taste in constitutional law had changed.

In fact, the justices' role in American life had done a 180-degree turn. For most of the post–Civil War era, the Court had been staunchly conservative: enabling Jim Crow; siding with corporations over workers; refusing to intervene when democracy was being undermined. Now the Court went from impeding social and political trends to accelerating them. This was especially true during the period from 1953 to 1969, when the chief justice was a former California governor named Earl Warren.

We saw the Warren Court's impact earlier in this book—it was responsible for *Baker v. Carr* and the slew of other cases that established One Person, One Vote. But that was just the tip of the iceberg. Thanks to the Warren Court, schools can't be segregated, cops have to read you your rights when you're arrested, you're entitled to a lawyer even if you can't afford one, President Trump can't frivolously sue the *New York Times* for defamation, states can't ban the sale of birth control, and Black people and white people are allowed to marry each other.

To many Americans, myself very much included, the Warren Court is a model for what the judiciary should be. The justices used their independence to stand up for those on the margins, defending those powerless who were powerless defend themselves through traditional political means. Also, call me crazy, but I think segregation was bad and birth control is good.

To a certain set of conservatives, however, the new Court was positively terrifying. In their view, the justices were engaged in a liberal power grab to rival the conservative power grab that infuriated FDR. Small-government spiritualists, those we encountered in the previous chapter attending meetings of the John Birch Society and studying at Bob Lefevre's Freedom School, found the Warren Court particularly menacing. Their criticisms of the Court's opinions were frequently not just impassioned but unhinged. Fred Koch, father of Charles and David, once wrote, "If many of the opinions of the Warren Supreme Court had been written in the Kremlin they could not have served the Communist better."

Say what you will about Earl Warren; he wasn't even close to a communist sympathizer. And that's not the only place where facts failed to support the movement conservatives' views. As we've seen, the justices FDR confronted were striking down acts of Congress, an aggressive overreach that had little in common with John Marshall's understanding of judicial review. But Earl Warren mostly overturned state laws, far more in keeping with the Founders' expectations.

Also, and importantly, the showdowns under Lincoln and Roosevelt were between elected public servants and unelected judges. The Civil War and the New Deal were not tangential to their political moments. They *defined* their political moments. By taking on the Court, presidents were prioritizing the majority of all Americans above the majority of a very specific nine. The showdown over the Warren Court was different. The Court's staunchest opponents were not elected leaders with a nationwide mandate, but partisan ideologues with lots of money. And the positions they wanted the Court to take—on race, on economics, on social issues—had little to do with popular opinion.

If these considerations ever occurred to Fred Koch, his sons, or their fellow travelers, however, they proved unconvincing.

And so, in their understated way, a low-key group of warriors—one that would eventually include the drummer of the Jay Sekulow Band—plotted a legal revolution to accompany their political one. They wouldn't be as dramatic as Roosevelt. They wouldn't try to change the judiciary overnight. They wouldn't try to expand the number of justices. But they would nonetheless succeed where FDR had failed.

They were going to pack the Court.

☆

It's a strange historical irony that without the help of a right-wing oligarch, Elizabeth Warren would not be married to her husband today.

The meet-cute took place in the lobby of a Key Biscayne hotel, on a summer Sunday in 1979, when a legal historian named Bruce Mann glanced over from the reception desk and spotted a gaggle of fellow lawyers. This was hardly surprising, as he was attending a law professors' conference. What was surprising, to Mann anyway, was one particular brunette. To hear him tell it, it was love at first sight from twenty-five yards away.

To hear Senator Warren tell it, it was more complicated—but only a little. "That was a Sunday, late afternoon, when we met," she recalled to CNN's M. J. Lee. "I wasn't completely in love with him until sometime mid-morning on Monday."

"Mmmph," said Lee, with the sudden, panicked expression all young people adopt when forced to contemplate old people having sex.

"He was in the row ahead of me," Warren quickly explained.

Warren and Mann were in South Florida for seminars on "Law and Economics," a subject that sounds vague and timeless but in fact was specific and new. Like laissez-faire capitalism, Law and Economics, (also known as "L&E"), is a genre of constitutional interpretation, and it arrived on the legal scene in the 1970s.

Like most legal theory, L&E is both complicated and less complicated than it claims to be. Basically it says that when making a legal decision, we should consider its economic impact. Here's an example: Jean Valjean is caught stealing a loaf of bread to feed his starving family and sentenced to five years in jail. Given the enduring popularity of Les Misérables, that's probably not most people's idea of justice.

But an L&E adherent might see the situation differently. If a wildly harsh punishment deters would-be bread thieves at a lower cost than hiring more police, then Jean Valjean's sentence is a money-saving way of reducing crime, and is therefore justified. For many years, in part because its conclusions were so strikingly amoral, Law and Economics was like Bob LeFevre's Freedom School, relegated to the backwoods of American legal thought. Then L&E's founder, Henry Manne, caught the eye of John M. Olin.

Olin was a fabulously rich manufacturer of arms and chemicals who, in 1973, devoted his family foundation to the conservative cause.[*] Overnight, Manne became one of the best-funded legal theorists in America, and L&E began appearing at America's most prestigious law schools. Today, there are John M. Olin programs and fellowships at Harvard, Yale, NYU, Stanford, Virginia, Georgetown, Berkeley, Michigan, and more. Olin also funded all-expenses-paid L&E junkets to sunny Florida, including the one where Warren met Mann. "By one count," writes Jane Mayer of these trips, "forty percent of the federal judiciary participated, including the future Supreme Court justices Ruth Bader Ginsburg and Clarence Thomas."

Olin and his team referred to their programs as "beachheads," and as it happened, America's law schools were especially vulnerable to intellectual assault. Even by elite standards, the American legal elite is elitist. Of all the current and former clerks employed by the nine sitting Supreme Court justices, three-quarters come from just 3 percent of America's law schools. Two hundred ninety-five of them—49 percent of the total—attended either Harvard or Yale. The same handful of institutions churns out future judges, senators, law professors, and high-profile attorneys. Breach this one small corner of the ivory tower, and the ripple effects will be felt nationwide.

Which bring us to the real reason Olin spent a total of $68 million promoting L&E: partisan politics. Not everyone who studied Law and Economics became a Republican. But Olin understood that because of its natural inclination to favor the profits of corporations over the rights of workers and consumers, judges fluent in L&E were more likely to rule in ways that favored the Republican cause. Henry Manne, the L&E guru, fancied himself a philosopher king. But in a very real way, he was a pawn. For Olin, investing in a professor was no different

---

* We've actually encountered Olin once already. Remember when Nixon's reelection campaign was hoovering up secret campaign cash, and donors brought their checks to a private game reserve? The reserve belonged to John Olin.

than donating to a politician or a think tank. Possum Kingdom had arrived in American law.

Olin's investment, and many more like it, did not just nudge the judiciary rightward. They were essential prerequisites for court-packing. The more independent the judges, the less likely they are to do what you want once on the bench—and as you'll recall, one of the guardrails of judicial independence was that the fact that constitutional theories and political parties didn't neatly align. Olin and his fellow wealthy donors changed that. Today, conservative jurisprudence and the Republican Party's political positions are a near-perfect match.

But funding new legal theories was only one way the conservative movement began aligning judges and partisan politics. They also began building loyalties between the judiciary and other branches of government. To that end, in 1982, the Olin Foundation helped launch a new kind of campus organization: The Federalist Society.

The best way to think about the FedSoc (pronounced "Fed Sock") is as a nationwide Elks Club for conservative lawyers. From its humble beginnings with just four founding members, the Society has grown into an association with 70,000 attorneys and an annual budget of $20 million. They organize campus chapters, host dinners and networking events for law students and alumni, and offer continuing legal education to practicing attorneys. It all sounds fairly innocuous.

In fact, the Federalist Society is revolutionary, an attempt to impose rigid ideological dogma on a profession once known for intellectual freedom. It's common knowledge that if you're an ambitious law student—and is there any other kind?—you have to become part of the Federalist Society if you want access to the best conservative legal jobs. And to remain a member in good standing, you have to believe certain things to be true, regardless of whether or not they actually are. I suppose it's a bit like working for Philip Morris in the nineties. The more certain you were that smoking didn't cause cancer, the more likely you were to rise through the ranks.

The result is that judges who are Federalist Society members rule differently—and more predictably—than judges who are not. This is true even when compared to fellow Republican appointees. In 2009, a pair of political scientists looked at a specific type of case, one involving police power, that traditionally divides liberal and conservative jurists. They found that among judges appointed by the first President Bush, those considered "most conservative" by a traditional metric took the conservative position 72 percent of a time. But if they were *also* Federalist Society members, their odds of casting a conservative vote shot up to 94 percent. Remarkably, even the "least conservative" FedSoc judges voted more conservatively than the most conservative nonmembers.

I must once again stress that I'm no constitutional scholar. Were I to debate a Society member (or, for that matter, any law school graduate), they would surely throw around terms and cite cases I don't understand. But I've been around politics for a while, and I understand this: with uncanny accuracy, the Federalist Society's interpretation of our laws tracks the goals of the conservative political movement at any given time. To put it slightly differently, Federalist Society members—including those now on the Supreme Court—are the pro bono defense team of the Republican Party.

This is hardly compatible with judicial independence. And that's precisely the point. In the same way that Lewis Powell and the Chamber of Commerce merged government with business, John Olin and his fellow donors merged the judiciary with the broader conservative movement. Ted Cruz is a senator. Clarence Thomas is a Supreme Court justice. As of the writing, Pat Cipollone is the White House counsel for President Trump. Three men; three different branches of government. Yet as FedSoc members, they have each pledged their loyalty to the exact same set of goals.

There is one final way in which the modern conservative legal movement, as exemplified by the Federalist Society, has undermined judicial independence. To understand it, consider the video found on the FedSoc "About Us" page. In the very first clip, a former law clerk of Justice Samuel Alito's named Barbara Smith, now a law professor at Washington University in St. Louis, describes the organization in rapturous terms. "The Federalist Society is a beacon of hope for conservative and libertarian lawyers that believe in a Constitutionally based federal government and a judiciary that says what the law *is* as opposed to what it should be."

At first glance these words sound bland, almost corporate. In fact, they are radical. I'm not even talking about the implication that non-conservatives don't believe in a constitutionally based government, which is both condescending and untrue. Instead, let's focus on Smith's final half-sentence: "What the law *is* as opposed to what it should be."

I emailed Professor Smith to ask her more about her experience with the Federalist Society, and, in a spirit of intellectual inquiry and open debate, she declined to email me back. But what she's saying in this video is quite simple. The Constitution is not open to interpretation. Our bedrock document says one thing and one thing only. Adherents of this judicial philosophy frequently refer to it as "originalism," but "fundamentalism" would be more accurate.

Whatever you call it, this approach flies in the face of centuries of American jurisprudence. If the Court's job is to interpret the Constitution, then by definition, it must be open to interpretation. In the FedSoc view, the Constitution is fixed and knowable. Every Court case has a right and wrong answer, and the justices' job is to pick the correct side. This is not just a rigid approach to judgment, but an attack on the very idea of judicial review. After all, if the Constitution has only one valid meaning, how can justices claim to interpret it?

This question is not theoretical. Under guidance issued by the Reagan Department of Justice, federal lawyers were expected to follow the vision of the Constitution set forward by the administration, even if it conflicted with the one set forth by the courts. In essence, the Reagan White House said that when it disagreed with the Court, that was because the Court was wrong—and if the Court was wrong, there was no reason to take its opinions seriously.

A fundamentalist approach to law similarly weakens judicial restraint. In a world where the Constitution has One True Meaning, *stare decisis*, the doctrine that current judges should follow prior precedent, makes no sense. If every case has a right and wrong answer, and a previous ruling was wrong, then judges have not just the ability but the obligation to overturn it ASAP. At the moment, the only conservative jurist willing to take this idea to its logical conclusion is Clarence Thomas. "When faced with a demonstrably erroneous precedent, my rule is simple," he's written. "We should not follow it." But while other FedSoc judges still pay lip service to *stare decisis*, they also believe in a version of the Constitution that does not allow for it.

It has now been forty years since two young law professors locked eyes in the courtyard of a Miami hotel. A lot has changed in that time. For one thing, Elizabeth Warren is no longer a Republican. But a far more sweeping change has come in the law itself. Conservative legal theory is much more likely to match up with a partisan political agenda. Conservative judges are more likely to see themselves as cogs in a larger ideological machine. And when those judges issue rulings, they are less likely to feel bound by *stare decisis* and judicial restraint.

In other words, after centuries of unsuccessful assault by politicians, the wealthy donors of Possum Kingdom were finally able to deal judicial independence a mortal blow. They had filled the country with lawyers who could turn the courts into a wing of the Republican Party. All the Republican Party had to do was get those lawyers onto the bench.

On a fall day in late 1987, Judge Roger Miner, a genial man with a high forehead and a trim, small-*c* conservative mustache, picked up his phone and heard the voice of a prominent Republican on the Senate Judiciary Committee. The judge had been expecting this. President Reagan's Supreme Court nominee, the far-right Robert Bork, was flailing. The well-regarded Miner was assumed to be next in line.

What Miner didn't expect, however, was the question the senator asked him: What was Miner's view on *Roe v. Wade?*

As you may recall from the start of this chapter, such direct questions had for centuries been off-limits. You may further recall Lincoln saying that "We cannot ask a man what he will do, and if we should, and he should answer us, we should despise him for it." Lincoln was clearly comfortable pressuring the courts, but even he understood that if you crossed this line—if you demanded policy outcomes in exchange for nominations—the judiciary as we knew it would be finished.

Roger Miner's wife, Jacqueline, who was active in Republican politics, later told the *New York Times* that she urged her stubborn spouse to play along. To the judge's credit, he passed Lincoln's test. A Supreme Court seat is literally the job of a lifetime, but rather than promise to overturn *Roe*, Miner said he would decide each case on the merits.

"My reputation was too high a price to pay for a seat on the Supreme Court of the United States," Jacqueline Miner later remembered her husband saying. We'd be lucky to have a justice with that kind of integrity, don't you think?

Apparently the Republican senator on the phone didn't think so. Neither did President Reagan, who chose the anti-abortion Anthony Kennedy instead. Nor was Miner's snub an isolated incident. Where Truman could be found swearing at disappointing judges, and Teddy Roosevelt was left lamely whittling bananas, the McConnell–era Republican Party has engineered judicial loyalty more aggressively and strategically than ever before. Today, those efforts have paid off. Just as Reagan hoped—and as Lincoln feared—today's judiciary is a completely different, less independent branch of government than it was when Roger Miner took that call.

The first president to seize full control of the judicial nominating process—not just for the Supreme Court, but for the circuit courts below it—was actually Jimmy Carter. Before then, most judicial nominations were what *Time* magazine called "political plums," rewards bestowed on loyal friends of senators, local officials, and party machines.

But rather than pack the courts with liberal true believers, Carter used his leverage to increase diversity on the bench. As Mark Joseph Stern detailed for *Slate*, Carter appointed five times more women than all thirty-eight prior presidents combined. He appointed fifty-seven non-white judges, nearly tripling the nation's total.

"The first time I ever thought of being a judge was when Jimmy Carter announced to the world that he wanted to change the complexion of the U.S. judiciary," said Ruth Bader Ginsburg in 2015. We don't give Carter credit for his impact, partly because he never got to pick a Supreme Court justice and partly because we tend not to give Carter credit for anything he did as president. But if he'd won a second term, the courts would be vastly different today.

Instead, Ronald Reagan took over. Under his administration, the White House retained control of the judicial nominating process. But where his predecessor prioritized diversity, Reagan prioritized ideology. He saw the courts as a tool for shifting American policy to the right.

Fashioning that tool became the job of the Justice Department's Office of Legal Policy. I know that sounds like the kind of bureaucratic backwater where staff wear green visors and speak in nerdy Jerry Lewis voices, but the Reagan presidency the OLP was a judicial war room. This was especially true after 1985, when Stephen Markman, one of the earliest FedSoc members, took charge.

If you wanted to become a judge in the Reagan years, here's how the process worked. First, Markman and his OLP team would scrutinize everything you'd ever written, hunting for deviations from conservative orthodoxy. If you made it through the initial screening, you'd fly to Washington, where a team of lawyers would grill you for four to five hours. These interviews included questions like the one posed to Miner. "Of course we discussed particular cases, real as well as hypothetical," said Grover Reese, a top Justice Department advisor at the time. "Otherwise, you're settling for somebody's slogans."

Even after you passed this interview, promising to decide certain cases in certain ways, the vetting process was not finished. It simply moved to the White House, where a presidential committee double-checked your conservative bona fides. Only after that committee approved you did your name go to President Reagan for his consideration. And this was merely for lower court judges. For prospective Supreme Court justices, the process was far more thorough. At the end of Reagan's two terms, the courts didn't just have more Republican-appointed judges than before—those judges were far more reliably conservative than previous Republican appointees.

Reagan's successor, George H. W. Bush, tried to continue the court-packing scheme, with mixed results. On one hand, before the first President Bush, the American Bar Association would give a "not qualified" rating to judges it thought were insufficiently independent. Under pressure from the White House, the ABA changed course, agreeing to rate nominees as qualified even if they were likely to issue partisan decisions once on the bench. Bush also appointed Clarence Thomas, who was and remains the Supreme Court's most conservative justice.

At the same time, the first President Bush also appointed Justice David Souter, whose thin judicial record made him easily confirmable, but who tacked sharply to the left once on the bench. To conservatives, for whom "Soutered" to this day remains an adjective meaning "hoodwinked," this botched nomination was unforgivable, and when George W. Bush took office, he was determined not to repeat his father's mistakes.

Like Reagan, the second President Bush used both the Department of Justice and a presidential committee to screen prospective judges. But he made some updates. For one thing, the full membership of Bush's committee was kept secret. He further diminished the non-partisan role of the American Bar Association, and brought top young FedSoc lawyers into the White House to advise on judges. The most notable of these was Brett Kavanaugh, a Yale Law graduate and leading authority on malt beverages consumed at scale.

Bush's greatest contribution to the court-packing process, however, was to bring in the influence industry. These leading ambassadors from Possum Kingdom became known as "the Four Horsemen" and each served a specific purpose. Jay Sekulow, the conservative movement's favorite drummer, connected Kavanaugh and the White House to the evangelical community. C. Boyden Gray and Ed Meese, who had handled nominations for the first President Bush and Reagan, respectively, provided institutional knowledge.

The final horseman, Leonard Leo, was the Federalist Society's executive vice president. Under Leo, the FedSoc, which had been officially nonpartisan, began to change. As Leo himself later put it, "Judicial confirmations these days are more like political campaigns." The Society spun off a sister organization, the Judicial Confirmation Network, which along with other conservative groups ran commercials backing Bush's nominees. These ads were virtually indistinguishable from Republican campaigns for senator or president—a typical spot warned listeners that if Sam Alito were not confirmed to the Supreme Court, the war on Christmas would be lost forever. (Alito was confirmed, and Christmas was saved.) Supreme Court nominations had always been fundamentally political. But political donors and operatives had never been so directly involved in the nominating process.

Since the end of the Bush administration, America has been home to the following contradiction. On one hand, a small group of extraordinarily wealthy people fund the campaigns of presidents who nominate the judges; the campaigns of senators who confirm the judges; the law schools and seminars that educate the judges; the Federalist Society that reeducates the judges; the nonprofits who write friend-of-the-court briefs that persuade the judges; the lawyers who argue cases in front of the judges; and sometimes, as you may remember from Antonin Scalia's hunting trips, the travel expenses of the judges themselves.

On the other hand, we have a theoretically independent judiciary.

What is perhaps most remarkable about the Republican judge-picking machine is that, for better or worse, Democrats have nothing like it. When Obama took office, there was no liberal equivalent to the Federalist Society. No judicial philosophy mapped neatly onto Democratic Party goals. The deep institutional knowledge—the kind of long-game approach that could elevate a judge up the ranks over decades—simply didn't exist among progressives.

Nor was Obama eager to fill the bench with ideologues. He wanted judges who broadly agreed with him, but like presidents of both parties prior to Reagan, he also wanted judges who thought for themselves. Besides, after George W. Bush's highly controversial nominees, he didn't want to see the courts further politicized. "We went out of our way to find candidates who couldn't be called liberal activists, who wouldn't be controversial at all," said Greg Craig, the White House counsel at the time. Obama's first judicial pick, a midwestern moderate named David Hamilton, even received a begrudging thumbs-up from the president of the Indiana Federalist Society.

Mitch McConnell's Republicans filibustered him anyway. To movement conservatives, any judge who did not fit the Bush and Reagan mold might as well have been the second coming of Earl Warren. Any seat filled by a Democratic president was one that couldn't be packed by a Republican down the road.

For the next six years, nearly every judicial confirmation was a battle. Then, in 2015, Republicans took control of the Senate and judicial confirmations virtually ceased. In 2016, Antonin Scalia passed away while on a hunting junket, Obama nominated Merrick Garland—as close to a true middle-of-the-road judge as you can imagine—and McConnell nonetheless refused to confirm him. In fact, back when it seemed certain that Hillary Clinton would be the forty-fifth president of the United States, Ted Cruz proposed a new court-*shrinking* scheme to deny her the chance to fill any Court vacancies. "There is certainly long historical precedent for a Supreme Court with fewer justices," he said.

Of course, Cruz never had to put his reverse court-packing plan into action. Donald Trump became president, and, thanks to McConnell's obstruction, he had lots of open spots to fill. When Obama took office, twelve federal Courts were considered "understaffed." When Trump took office, it was twenty-nine. "In my first day," President Trump recalled, "I said to one of our assistants, 'How many judges do I have to pick? How many are there?' And I figured I'd hear none or one, maybe two. They said, 'Sir, you have 142.'"

For Senator McConnell, who had spent his entire career trying to amass power without needing popular support, this was a once-in-a-lifetime opportunity. And to seize it, Brother Mitch rewrote the rules yet again.

One important change was covered in a previous chapter: Republicans made Supreme Court nominations impossible to filibuster. But to fill the 142 positions he'd kept open during the Obama years, McConnell went further. He slashed the amount of debate time required for nominees from thirty hours to just two. Now that Republicans were in charge, no stalling would be allowed. For nominations to appeals courts, the tier of the judiciary just below the Supremes, Team Mitch also did away with blue slips, the old tradition that gave senators of either party a veto over nominees from their state. This meant President Trump (or really, at this point, the Federalist Society) could pick whomever they wanted without worrying about whether that pick was unqualified or too extreme.

To say the FedSoc took advantage of this new flexibility would be a bit of an understatement. The American Bar Association found that Republican Senate aide Jonathan Kobes was "unable to produce sufficient writing samples of the caliber required" to demonstrate that he was qualified. He's now a judge on the Eighth Circuit. John Bush wrote a right-wing blog that compared abortion to slavery. He was roughly as undistinguished a lawyer as he was a blogger, but he chaired the Louisville chapter of the Federalist Society. Today, he's a Sixth Circuit judge.

Other Trump nominees, while not incompetent, seem to have trouble following the law. While serving as general counsel for President Trump's Education Department, Steven Menashi devised a plan to access students' Social Security data in order to deny them student loan forgiveness. In a harshly worded reprimand, a judge found the scheme illegal. Just eighteen months later, Menashi became a federal judge himself, on a court far more powerful than the one that over-ruled him.

In fact, by elevating extremist judges, President Trump and the Federalist Society encourage *all* right-of-center judges to become more extreme. To use just one recent example, Judge Neil Gorsuch spent years as an unflashy but highly conservative judge. But during the 2016 campaign, when Trump put forward a shortlist of FedSoc-approved Supreme Court picks, Gorsuch's name wasn't on it. In the months that followed, Gorsuch began issuing sweeping rulings and violating procedural norms, a kind of audition to prove that he could be the firebrand his party wanted. It worked. Today, Justice Gorsuch is on the Supreme Court, and other judges are busy with their own extremist auditions as they hope to catch the president's eye.

Thanks to Mitch McConnell's blockade of Obama's judges, there have been plenty of open spots to audition for. President Trump ap-pointed as many Supreme Court and Circuit Court judges in less than four years as President Obama appointed in eight. When we zoom out to look at all the judges appointed in my lifetime, the numbers are even starker. Sixty-two percent of the active federal judiciary has been appointed by either Reagan, George H. W. Bush, George W. Bush, or Trump. A supermajority of judges has now been chosen through an ideological screening process that did not exist as recently as forty years ago.

If these judges are supposed to be nonpartisan, President Trump seems not to have received the memo. According to the White House website, among the president's accomplishments is "flipping the United States Court of Appeals for the Third Circuit from a Democrat-appointed majority to a Republican-appointed majority . . . The Sec-ond and Eleventh Circuits are likely to flip by the end of this year." For a president to brag about winning a circuit court as though it's a swing state is not just rare. It is unheard of.

Like runners who lose their form in the final few yards before a victory, even Republicans famous for their self-control have begun to celebrate the big win. "We have flipped the Second Circuit, the Third circuit, and we will flip the Eleventh Circuit!" McConnell declared to applause at the Federalist Society's annual black-tie dinner. Brett Kavanaugh's 2018 confirmation hearings—the ones where he blamed sexual assault allegations against him on the Clintons and vowed that "what goes around comes around" even as he promised to be independent—were even more stunning than McConnell's speech. It's no longer just the other two branches who claim the judiciary has been politicized. So does the Court's newest judge.

Frankly, I think we can at least appreciate the honesty. With Kavanaugh's confirmation, three justices are current or former Federalist Society members. Two more (Gorsuch and Alito) are described as "closely associated" with the Society, speaking frequently at its events. All five of these judges are to the right of Anthony Kennedy, the justice Reagan picked when Roger Miner proved too neutral and who, until 2018, was the court's swing vote. Even before Kennedy left, the Supreme Court had tacked for to the right. The Kavanaugh Court will be the most conservative since FDR's first term.

Even this undersells just how different the role of the federal judiciary has become. I'm not saying Republicans will win every single case, but the Court—by the admission of members of all three branches—is now more political than at any time in American history. The next Democratic president will not just confront judges who oppose his or her priorities. He or she will face a judiciary that has been packed by, for, and full of political operatives.

What does this mean for Belle? Well, if she's supported by Republicans, our refashioned judicial branch won't bother her at all. If Belle is a priority for Democrats, however—if she makes drinking water cleaner, reduces gun violence, expands health insurance, protects workers, addresses climate change, or defends a woman's right to choose—then she will face a veto point unlike any in American history. After passing the House, passing the Senate, and being signed by the president, she will inevitably wind up before a brand-new kind of Court.

The people who will render final judgment on Belle were not elected. Nor are they politically independent, by any reasonable definition of the term. Instead, after completing her journey, Belle will have to win the approval of the conservative movement, and by extension the party it controls. If these judges, groomed over decades and handpicked for ideological purity, reject her, then the entire political process will be rendered irrelevant. Belle will die.

I can't promise we can save Belle from a partisan Court, at least not immediately. But regardless of what happens to her, we should be at least as honest as Mitch McConnell about *why* it's happening. For hundreds of years, politicians have tried to break down the judiciary's independence and seize its power. At long last, they've succeeded. The question we face now is what to do about it.

How do you unpack a court?

Historically, the way to fix a lopsided judiciary is simple: you win the White House. Choose a president, and that president gets to choose the judges nominated to the bench. It's not a perfect system, but it's self-correcting. In a very roundabout way, We, the People shape the judicial branch.

Thanks to Mitch McConnell's blockade of judges in 2014, that system is gone. One of the new unwritten rules of American politics is as follows: a Senate majority will never confirm a judge nominated by a president of the opposite party. If we want to appoint new judges, the American people no longer have to elect a new president. We have to elect fifty senators as well. And because the Senate is deliberately built to withstand swings in popular opinion, that's a far more difficult task.

Thanks largely to random chance, the twenty-first-century judiciary is especially removed from people's will. President Bush was declared the winner of the 2000 election in a 5–4 Court decision. He, in turn, nominated two new justices to the Supreme Court. President Trump was legitimately elected thanks to the Electoral College, but as we've noted, a clear majority of voters chose his opponent. Had the people gotten what they wanted, the Court would likely have a liberal majority today. Instead, we have a Court that opposes voting rights, making it even more likely that the people's choice will fail to become president the next time round.

I say this not to complain (okay, maybe a little to complain) but to warn that we are approaching a vicious circle. An unbalanced democracy leads to an unbalanced Court, which tips our democracy further out of balance, and on and on. In such a situation, we can't just hope the problem solves itself. But neither should we give up hope entirely.

And where better to look for inspiration than the bridge of Jay Sekulow's hard rock classic "Undemocratic," which, for completely inexplicable reasons, features a white guy rap in what appears to be an ill-conceived tribute to the Beastie Boys.

> We've got to resist just throwing hands in the air
> We need to reform the pieces already there.
> A chance to restore what's great without any fear
> Where common sense is common here.

The lines may not scan well, but truer words have never been spoken. Today's judiciary is reaching far beyond its historical mandate. Indeed, the moment Democrats regain power in an election, the Court is almost certain to stand in the way of the entire agenda that the American people just chose. But we've been here before. Lincoln faced the threat of an overreaching Court during the Civil War. Roosevelt faced such a Court at the start of the New Deal. Our elected branches of government have taken on the judiciary before. We should do it again.

We should start not with the Supreme Court's questionable rulings, legal theories, or even judges, but with its questionable ethics. One of the most telling examples of the Court's accumulation of power is that it's exempt from even the most basic transparency and conflict-of-interest requirements. The late Justice Scalia is an excellent example. He passed away during a hunting trip Cibolo Creek Ranch, in what *Washington Post* reporters Mark Berman and Christopher Ingraham described as "a 1,100 square foot, $700-a-night room overlooking a lake." Who was paying? Not Scalia. It turned out that John Poindexter, a billionaire who was involved in at least one recent Supreme Court case via his companies, had footed the bill.

The only reason we know any of this is that Justice Scalia died in his hotel room. Judges on the Court are required to report who pays for their travel—but remarkably, they don't have disclose how much those trips cost. We have no idea whether organizations are buying them a coach ticket on Spirit Airlines or flying them by private jet. For gifts of "hospitality," defined broadly as food, lodging, or entertainment, justices don't have report anything at all. Are Supreme Court justices ruling in favor of people who comp them hotel suites or loan them the Gulfstream for a weekend? We just don't know.

Even more stunning, Supreme Court justices are exempt from the same ethics rules that apply to every other federal judge. In 2007 and 2008, for example, Justices Thomas and Scalia attended what the *Post* described as "private political meetings" run by conservative billionaires Charles and David Koch. Lower-court judges would be reprimanded for such blatantly partisan behavior, and required to recuse themselves if future cases presented conflicts of interest. But for some reason, the highest Court in the land has the lowest ethical standards. (That's also why Brett Kavanaugh was never disciplined for his embarrassing confirmation-hearing outburst; had he not been confirmed, and remained an appeals court judge, he would have been in deep trouble.)

For the branch of government that most relies on its reputation for integrity, higher ethical requirements are a must. Yet given the partisan packing of today's judiciary, standards alone are not enough. The courts are meant to be a check on unrestrained power. But like Lincoln and Roosevelt, the next progressive president will have to check the unrestrained power of the courts.

Whoever that president is, he or she should follow Lincoln's rather than Roosevelt's lead. Our goal should not be to replace Republican rubber stamps with Democratic ones, or create enormous numbers of new Court seats just to fill them with cronies. Instead, we should try to restore the Court's necessary role in our democracy—as a neutral interpreter of the Constitution, a center of nonpartisan integrity, and a formidable yet restrained watchdog against abuses of power, especially by the states.

Our goal, in other words, should not be to pack the courts for either party. Our goal should be to protect the republic we love.

To begin with, we can reduce the influence of wealthy partisan donors and the groups they fund. Right now, ads for or against judicial nominees are treated like issue advocacy, as though they're public service announcements. Instead, we ought to treat these efforts as the political campaigns the Federalist Society's Leonard Leo admits they are. Money given to support a judge's confirmation shouldn't be tax-deductible, and it should be fully disclosed.

The same is true of the organizations that pay for "amicus briefs." These are the supplementary materials and arguments that go to the justices before they make their decisions. Today, I can fund a brief in a Supreme Court case without disclosing my identity to the public. In other words, not only are justices being influenced by wealthy donors—we don't even know who those influencers are. Tougher disclosure rules would help the American people understand how politicized our Court has become, and decide for ourselves whether judges are acting independently.

A final way to depoliticize the Supreme Court would be to end lifetime tenure for its members. One of the reasons picking a justice carries so much political weight is that someone like Brett Kavanaugh, who was fifty-three when appointed, could easily serve another thirty-five years. As American life spans grow longer (at least among the kinds of people who serve on the Court), the political value of each pick will only grow.

It's commonly believed that you can't impose term limits for justices without changing the Constitution. But that might not be the case. Gabe Roth, founder of the nonpartisan group Fix the Court, points out that while Article III requires that judges remain on the federal bench "during good behavior," it doesn't say *where* they have to serve. Gabe thinks Congress could pass a law declaring that one Supreme Court justice will be nominated every two years; at the end of an eighteen-year term, he or she would remain on the federal bench, but be rotated down to a lower court, making way for a replacement. (Current justices would be grandfathered out of the new system.)

Finally, if and when we must confront an overreaching judiciary, we should do what Lincoln did with the Union at stake: reassert the power of the government's elected branches.

In a showdown with the Court, Congress and the president have plenty of tools at their disposal. For one thing, there's control over appellate jurisdiction. The reason we've granted the Court so much power, allowing it to examine or ignore any case it pleases, is that we trust it to behave in a nonpartisan manner. If the Court no longer holds up its end of the bargain, lawmakers should take some of its responsibility away.

We should also reestablish the principle that John Marshall, Stephen Field, and Earl Warren all held to. The Court should wield its power primarily as a check on states. As we've seen with recent court fights over everything from Obamacare to the Consumer Financial Protection Bureau, the Republican Party has refashioned the Court into a tool to undo the work of Congress and the executive branch, while leaving conservative state laws (and President Trump's executive orders) intact. It may therefore be time to consider a rather harsh, but entirely constitutional, option: Congress could require a 6–3 or even a 7–2 majority to overturn a federal law.

Given the transformation of the courts over the past three decades, it's also no surprise that politicians have begun talking about an option not seriously considered since FDR's humiliation eighty-three years ago—adding seats to the bench. It is, however, a surprise that the politician most vocally in favor of expanding the judiciary is President Donald Trump.

"Would you like to add a few judges?" he asked a group of Republican senators, Mitch McConnell included, at a recent White House event. "How about adding another hundred or so?" The transcript of the president's remarks noted several other instances of audience laughter. But this time no one laughed. The president's proposal was no joke.

Nor is it just Donald Trump the only conservative who takes the idea of growing the courts quite seriously. In 2017, Steven G. Calabresi, a founding member of the Federalist Society, argued that Republicans should increase the total number of seats by a third.[*] Like FDR, Calabresi pitched his idea as rooted in logistics rather than partisanship. "As it happens," he wrote in *The National Review*, "the judiciary desperately needs more federal judges." As it also happened, Calabresi's plan called for President Trump to fill all the new seats himself.

In fairness, Calabresi wasn't wrong when he said the courts must add seats in order to function properly. Since the last major expansion of the judiciary, in 1978, America's population has grown by nearly half. America's caseload had grown with it. We need more judges to handle all that extra work.

But appointing these judges should be done carefully, with an eye toward restoring balance rather than seizing power. If Democrats are in charge when the Court is expanded, it would be fair to start by filling a number of seats to equal the number McConnell left open during Obama's final two years. But after that, seats should be created, and

---

[*] Calabresi's uncle, Guido Calabresi, was a pioneer of law and economics. Constitutional law is a seriously cloistered world.

filled, in a staggered and scheduled way that lasts beyond a single presidency. The American people should get to decide for themselves what kinds of judges Belle must face.

Finally, Democrats should follow Lincoln's lead and expand the Supreme Court as well. As with the lower courts, there are practical reasons the Supreme Court is overdue for an expansion. We're a more diverse country than ever, and Americans, especially young Americans, want their institutions to look like them. There simply aren't enough Court seats to make that possible.

But the real reason for expanding the Court is not logistical. The way the nine current seats have been filled has devastated the Court's integrity. Democrats shouldn't try to add five seats, or ten seats, or twenty. But they should make sure that when a majority on the highest court issues a ruling, the justices who make up that majority were appointed in a consistent and ethical manner. Put simply, that means adding at least one seat to the Court, to make up for the seat Mitch McConnell held vacant.

Because of the specific cases of President Trump's conduct, I believe we ought to go even further. The president is "Individual #1" in a criminal investigation related to his election. He both asked for and received Russian help during the campaign. Yet his two Supreme Court justices can serve for life despite the deeply questionable circumstances that led to their appointments. That's a dangerous precedent. Whether or not Justices Gorsuch and Kavanaugh serve "under good behavior," the bad behavior of the president who picked them colors every opinion they reach.

The least we can do is establish a new norm in America: if a judge is chosen by a president who committed crimes to win his office, and that judge chooses not to resign, we'll add a new seat to counterbalance that judge's impact on American life.

As both Lincoln and Roosevelt demonstrated, the sooner you confront judicial overreach, the less likely you are to have to confront it in the future. If the conservatives on the Roberts Court know that partisan behavior will cost them their majority, they'll be more inclined to settle for restrained, nonpartisan (but still small-c conservative) rulings instead. Similarly, if future Mitch McConnells understand that packing the courts won't work, they'll be less inclined to try it in the first place.

I don't want to understate the risks here. Any plan to unpack the courts and restore their independence is not guaranteed to succeed. But the situation we find ourselves in today—a selective veto point that nullifies Democratic mandates while enabling Republican ones— looks very similar to the worst-case scenario. We simply don't have much to lose.

And Belle has an awful lot to gain. When we met her, she was sitting on the Capitol steps, presumably singing to a child, or practicing her own unique take on "Oh *yay*-us!" But we now know the truth. In our democracy today, it doesn't matter if Belle would make life better for millions. It doesn't matter if the American people love her. Her odds of navigating a minefield of newly added veto points are stunningly low. And the more ambitious Belle is—the more good she would do—the lower her odds have become.

We can change her path, and ours. Imagine if Belle started her journey in a House designed to give expression to the people's will. Imagine if she then went to a Senate that genuinely deliberated her merits, ensuring that she was not only popular but wise. The influence industry would still affect her, but Possum Kingdom would no longer be shrouded in shadow, and Belle's ultimate success or failure would be decided by people who work for us. Finally, if necessary, Belle would be reviewed by judges who defends the rights of all Americans, not just one party or ideological cause.

Exchanging our current path for a better one will take time and tremendous effort. But that effort is worth it. Back when I was a kid, which wasn't that long ago, our legislative process was inspiring. It was something a child could sing about. Despite all that's been broken in the last few decades, the way we make our laws is—like the way we elect our lawmakers—still up to us to decide. Can we reestablish a legislative process worthy of the greatest country on earth? Can we reassert the consent of the governed, passing laws meant to tackle our most urgent challenges and help all Americans build the kind of future we deserve?

To borrow a pair of phrases: Oh *yay*-us! We can.

EPILOGUE
UNITY PLACE

Eighteen months after I first tried to crash a party at the Phi Tau house in Louisville, I'm once again waiting for a flight out of D.C. It's day two of public impeachment hearings in Congress, the latest reminder that living through the Trump presidency is like watching a train wreck from inside the train. My fellow passengers are glued to the TV at the gate. So am I. That's why I don't notice him.

I only realize something is amiss when the woman sitting next to me simultaneously scowls and recoils. It's an instinctual reaction, both physical and moral, as though she's caught a whiff of rotten fish and in the exact same moment spotted someone reading *Mein Kampf*. Recovering from the shock, she leans over to her two teenage sons, glances toward the check-in desk, and then addresses them in something slightly more than a stage whisper. "Well, I think he's single-handedly destroying our democracy."

Even before my head begins to swivel, I know who she's talking about. I sit up straight, turn left, and there he is.

Brother Mitch.

Later, after our plane lands in Louisville, my Uber driver will tell me she believes in positive visualization, and that the reason Mitch McConnell was on my plane is that I willed the universe to put him there. I suppose in a certain way this is true. Over the last three years, I've thought more about Kentucky's senior senator than about any living creature except my wife, Donald Trump, and my two cats. Sitting in the airport back in Washington, I know McConnell is simply flying home, just like he does every weekend. Still, it feels like fate.

I've been this close to Brother Mitch only once before. It was in 2015, well before I started researching this book, when I attended President Obama's second-to-last State of the Union address. Writing later about the experience, I described the senator as "actually much handsomer in person."

Now, however, the senator looks awful. I've spent an uncountable number of hours reading about his triumph, examining the way he's rewired our system of government so that it favors him and his party. But Mitch McConnell doesn't look like a winner to me. Sallow skin, sunken eyes—despite the snappy blue blazer and pink checked shirt, there's something gray and hollow about the old man shuffling toward the front of the first-class boarding line. He doesn't just seem exhausted, the way so many of us do these days. His steps are clipped and cautious. Despite being flanked by staff and surrounded by bodyguards, his eyes are wary.

That's when I realize something. Mitch McConnell is scared.

Here I wish I could tell you I'm good at confrontation. I'm really not. I saw our old friend Rick Scott once, in this very same airport, and I thought about trying to shame him for disenfranchising so many of his fellow citizens. I even took a halfhearted step in his direction before completely chickening out.

But this moment is different. The senator and I are on the same flight to Louisville. He's already boarded, which means I have no choice but to walk right past him. As I wheel my carry-on suitcase toward the plane's open door, I try to boost my courage with thoughts of the people this man has hurt, all the ways he's diminished the country I love. I'm inside the jetway. I'm through the door. I'm standing next to him.

"Excuse me, sir?" I squeak. From his comfy seat, Brother Mitch ignores me, pretending to read an email on his phone.

"Excuse me, Senator?" He finally looks up. This is my shot. After the countless hours I've spent pondering this person, I get just one question. Options ricochet through my mind. *What was the exact moment you abandoned democracy? How can you support a president you so clearly know is dangerous? Really, and I mean really, how do you sleep at night?*

"So I was talking to a student at the University of Louisville," I hear myself say. "Is it true you own the land beneath the Phi Tau house?"

Suddenly Brother Mitch smiles, and not just because he won't have to talk about Trump. Like many people his age, his eyes, which have gone a bit milky, brighten as he travels back in time.

"No, no way," he says. He sounds amused rather than offended, with an accent much thicker than the one I've heard on TV. The fear has vanished. He chuckles and shakes his head. "I wonder where they got that."

"Oh yeah, he owns the land." About twelve hours have passed since our plane touched down in Louisville, and I'm in Triangle, a frat house on Greek Row's north end. The brother I'm talking to nods, sure of himself, then wavers a tiny bit. "Well, maybe not the mineral rights."

"He sponsored the building," a Lambda Alpha brother informs me that same evening.

"I don't know that he owns it, but he definitely paid to build it," says a brunette in a Delta Zeta sweatshirt.

"Maybe he owns the whole house?" suggests a young man on Beta's front porch.

358 DEMOCRACY IN ONE BOOK OR LESS

Like Senator McConnell, I, too, wonder where they got their information, although I suspect there must be a kernel of truth in there somewhere. Several students told me he helped fund his fraternity's building, which seems quite plausible. Another said that Alpha Omega Pi, a sorority, was supposed to get the choice corner lot, but then Brother Mitch swooped in and claimed the land for Phi Tau instead.

Like many pieces of undergraduate lore, the details vary from person to person, but the overall picture is the same. Greek Row's official name was once "Confederate Place," but it's been changed to Unity Place, and today, every student there can agree on at least one thing: on their campus, within their generation, power is already divided unevenly and unfairly.

Of course, there's a group that could answer my questions better than any other. The Phi Taus themselves. "You should go over there," says one of the Beta brothers, in the hopeful tone of one young soldier talking another into being first over the top of the trench. Then he frowns a bit. "They won't be that welcoming," he warns.

It turns out he's right. In fact, despite what I was promised earlier, I don't even find eighteen Phi Taus lounging on the roof. It's November, and an unseasonable cold snap has pushed temperatures into the low teens, once again leaving me with no parties to crash. "Any idea why no one's out tonight?" I ask a bundled-up kid as he shuffles between dorms.

"I don't know, it's fucking freezing?"

Fair point. I shiver my way around the Phi Tau fortress, noting the beat-up sofa still on the front porch and the Team Mitch sticker still on the back door. But it's hard to summon enthusiasm. I ring the doorbell. No response. As much as I genuinely hoped to talk with the Phi Taus, to get their side of the story and see if they could shed a final ray of light on their most famous alumnus, it's not happening. Defeated, I slump away.

And then, just as I'm about to call a Lyft to take me from Unity Place, a light goes on in the Phi Tau hallway. The door opens. I put away my phone and bound up the steps.

The brother standing in the entryway looks young, even for a college student, with a dopey grin and toothpick legs poking out from baggy basketball shorts. If he's surprised to see a grown man approaching him, he doesn't show it. With the confidence of popular kids everywhere, he introduces himself as Trevor.

"Hi, I'm David. Is it true Mitch McConnell used to be a Phi Tau?"

In an instant his demeanor changes. He's not angry at me, but he's suddenly on high alert, almost twitchy, like a gunslinger who doesn't like his odds. It's an expression I recognize but can't quite place.

"Yeah," he replies cautiously. "But I'm really just waiting for some food to show up."

"That's great!" I say. "Do you all ever talk about Senator McConnell?"

"I really don't know."

"Are there pictures of him inside?"

"Look, I really can't help you." His eyes have become tiny bouncers, but before he can throw me out, I lean into the hallway.

"What about memorabilia?" I ask, just a bit frantic. "Maybe I could poke around?"

And that's when I realize exactly where I've seen the look on Trevor's face. The mix of power and insecurity, haughtiness and neediness, the impunity that comes with knowing the world is carefully arranged in your favor and the terror that comes with knowing your position could crumble at any time. Trevor's eyes are clear and his steps sprightly, but his expression perfectly matches Mitch McConnell's from just a few hours before.

"I don't know about any of that stuff," Trevor says. "It was all so long ago."

Then he shuts the door in my face.

☆

As it happens, about two weeks before my return trip to Louisville, I was sitting in Dr. Fillmore's chair for a six-month dental cleaning when he took hold of my tongue, yanked it to the right, and said, "Mrrm." Somehow, I immediately knew that "Mrrm" was dentist for "maybe cancer."

"It's probably nothing," he said, whipping out a mirror and pointing to a dime-size white circle near the back of my mouth. "You should just keep an eye on it."

"But it's definitely not cancer?" I asked.

And he said, "Probably."

I'm not going to hold you in suspense here. I had extremely minor surgery, a doctor removed a small precancerous patch that was in the very early stages of trying to kill me, and now I'm fine. But for several weeks—weeks that happened to coincide with my finishing this book—I was probably fine, which it turns out is a very different thing. As I revised paragraphs and caught typos and wrote the words you're reading right now, life was feeling very unfair.

There were two types of unfairness in particular that upset me. First, I consider myself a strategic hypochondriac: if I worry obsessively about various untimely demises, the universe will decide I'm already suffering enough and spare me. So when the patch on my tongue was less than benign, I felt the universe wasn't holding up its end of the deal.

Second, and more important, I had just managed to write an entire book about our democracy's decline without once invoking cancer as a metaphor. (The only cancer analogy you've read is, oddly enough, from Mitch McConnell's 1973 op-ed supporting campaign finance reform.)

Unlike my hypochondria, my word choice was less an attempt to ward off evil than cliché. Still, at the exact moment I was applauding myself for my creativity, here was the obvious comparison staring me in the face. At the same time that I was trying to make sense of everything I had learned—the books read, the experts pestered, the Vegas casinos and Taco Cabanas and Disney World lines endured—I was also being forced to fully confront, for the very first time in my life, a rather unsettling fact. My body won't last forever. No body does.

What's true for human beings is no less true for the governments they create. Not to be a downer, but at some point in the future, America really will cease to exist. Hopefully that will be a few billion years from now, when the sun supernovas. Odds are it will happen sooner. Either way, our democracy comes with an expiration date.

I guess I always knew that, but at the same time, did I really? When I joined the Obama campaign at twenty-one years old, there was a part of me that believed my generation would be the one to solve all the problems. I wouldn't have said it out loud, but deep down, I was certain we wouldn't just improve our country. We would fix our country, so that it never needed fixing again.

Donald Trump is president, so clearly things didn't work out that way. But also, things *never* work out that way. Forced to pondered our collective mortality, I thought about all the Americans who built and expanded and defended our system of government—grouchy but brilliant John Adams, overachieving James Madison, wise Justice Brennan, combative Speaker Reed.

Over the past few years, I felt like I had gotten to know these people. But now I saw their efforts in a new light. They had done their best, fought hard to save our democracy, and yet delivered our democracy to the next generation still unsaved. Most of them died convinced America was one false move from tyranny. And most of them were right. To inherit a republic in peril, and pass on a republic in peril, is no failure. It's quite literally the best we can do.

Yet for some reason, even as I unwisely googled symptoms and read political news, I didn't find the unwinnable nature of our fight depressing in the slightest. It's a cliché, but in my case a true one, that during a health scare you feel gratitude more acutely. In the same strange way, as horrified as I am by the assault on our republic that we're enduring, I've never felt more thankful for the democracy in which we live.

After all, at the very same time I was cornering my country's most powerful lawmaker on an airplane and pestering him about a rumored shady land deal, mass pro-democracy demonstrations entered their ninth month in Hong Kong. In Chile, Lebanon, and Iran, hundreds of thousands took the streets to demand just a small piece of the power hoarded by their rulers. Those protestors would give their lives to belong to a republic as flawed as ours. Some of them did.

Today, despite the shaky ground upon which we stand, our democracy is more resilient than a Trump or Putin might have predicted. That's why I have so little patience for despair. Despite the dangers of this moment, the vast majority of us still possess an extraordinary privilege. We don't have to sit by helplessly as our democracy is rendered unrecognizable. We don't have to risk our lives to protect the republic we love.

Consider what's already happened. The Trump administration began with the Women's March, the biggest mass protest in American history. In 2018, despite the votes lost to disenfranchisement and the seats lost to political geography and gerrymandering, the majority of the House of Representatives went to the party that won a majority of votes. In 2019, with the help of the anticorruption laws passed in the wake of Teapot Dome, that majority slowly began holding the Trump administration accountable.

The authoritarians have had plenty of victories as well—there's certainly no guarantee our democracy will survive a second Trump term. But thus far, Team Mitch's efforts to create a one-party state remain unsuccessful.

And Americans of both parties don't want those efforts to succeed. On issue after issue, in poll after poll, we agree about the kind of republic we want to live in even when our politicians don't. We want a country where our rights are respected and our voices can be heard. We don't expect to get everything we want. But we expect to matter.

Which is why, while we haven't been able to stop President Trump from hammering at the foundations of our republic, a clear majority of Americans opposes him. Strongmen elected in other countries have proven quite popular. Given the growing economy, the relative dearth of international crises, an unprecedented campaign war chest, and a right-wing media empire at his disposal (not to mention a bit of help from Vladimir Putin), President Trump should be quite popular as well. He's not.

In fact, President Trump is wildly, historically *un*popular. According to FiveThirtyEight, his approval rating among Americans has never—not once—been higher than 50 percent. On a typical day during Trump's first term, by a margin larger than the population of Texas, we think he's doing a bad job. Back in the Obama White House, when our approval ratings dropped to the low 40s, it was a calamity. When President Trump's approvals drop to the low 40s, it's a Tuesday.

Of course, it is quite conceivable that none of this will matter. We've seen all the ways one party is increasingly content to govern a country without the support of the people who live there, and increasingly confident it can hold power without popular support. I won't sugarcoat it: there's always the possibility that we're living in the new normal, caught inescapably in tyranny's gravitational pull.

But I don't think so.

This book is about all the ways our politics have changed for the worse, in my lifetime and yours. But one thing hasn't changed: *we* get to decide what our democracy will look like. You and I have the chance to be part of this fight.

Over the last few years, I've met countless people who don't have the money of a Sheldon Adelson or the influence of a John Roberts, but who stubbornly refused to yield their country to a handful of its most powerful men. Tracy and Leah are registering voters in Houston. Shelly Simonds now serves her constituents in Richmond. Marc Elias is filing suit after suit to give everyone the right to vote.

Meanwhile, the rest of us—not just activists, but all Americans—are taking notice. The reason Mitch McConnell triumphed, at least in the short term, was that he redesigned our political process while we weren't pay attention. We're paying attention now. When I began writing this book, plenty of people told me it was foolish to write about something as esoteric as our democratic process. But over the last three years, I've felt less and less alone. Across the country, we're arriving at our own Unity Place, and we're reaching a shared conclusion. The only way to solve the challenges confronting our country is to repair our system of government itself.

Remember what John Adams told the people of North Carolina: "The blessings of society depend entirely on the constitutions of government . . . there can be no employment more agreeable to a benevolent mind than a research after the best."

What makes America special is not just that our Founders created a system of government. It's that they understood that every generation would, in its own way, re-form that system. To question and tinker with the inner workings of our republic, expanding society's blessings while protecting our fundamental rights, is the most American cause imaginable. We're ready to take on that cause today.

All we need is the opportunity. I believe we'll get it. I hope we get it quickly: we should do everything possible to make sure our Skywalker Window opens sooner rather than later. But the eternal truth of politics is that nothing lasts forever. Trumpism may be different. But probably not.

And as you now know, whenever our opportunity does arise, we have everything we need to make the most of it. If we move swiftly and decisively, breaking up the concentration of power and returning government to the governed, we can renew our country's promise and beat back authoritarianism in America, not just for an election but for a generation.

I'll never know for sure, but I like to think that that's why Mitch McConnell looked so nervous when I saw him. Yes, he found a way to amass power without earning it. But he knows better than anyone that in America, even under President Trump, that kind of unearned power remains fragile. Give the American people just the tiniest opening, and we can build a democracy where everyone who calls this country home can vote, where every vote matters, and where our representatives fight for us all.

Mitch McConnell has been rewriting the rules for nearly half a century. And yet one small misstep on his part, and the new system of government he's a spent lifetime creating vanish. True, no body lasts forever. But I'm confident I'll see that day. Even better, I'm confident Brother Mitch will, too.

☆

One final story. On July 4, 1858, America's eighty-second Independence Day, a midwestern lawyer named William Herndon was traveling through Massachusetts. There were good reasons for Herndon and his fellow Americans to be gloomy about their young nation's fate. Slavery had not faded away, as many of our Founders anticipated it would, but instead had expanded and now threatened to tear the United States apart. A brittle consensus, built in the wake of revolution and kept alive over the following decades, was on the verge of cracking for good.

Seeking solace, entertainment, or both, Herndon secured a seat in Boston's Music Hall. There the speaker, an abolitionist and Unitarian minister named Theodore Parker, delivered a July Fourth sermon titled, "The Effect of Slavery on the America People."

Given the subject, and the divisions fracturing the country, Parker had every right to be pessimistic. But he refused. Instead, despite a clear-eyed understanding of his nation's moral failings, he believed we could be a shining city on a hill.

"This is not only the national anniversary," proclaimed Parker. "It is the birthday of whole families of republics we know not of as yet, for it must have a future more glorious than the past or present."

Herndon listened to Parker, spellbound, and then promptly purchased a copy of the speech to bring back home. He shared the pamphlet with his law partner, who had been looking for some useful phrases for an upcoming political campaign.

Imagine that young candidate, sitting alone in his library with the borrowed pamphlet before him. Eyes straining by candlelight, he reads the tiny text of a speech delivered hundreds of miles away. There's plenty of inspiring language in the sermon. Parker makes a powerful case for abolition, condemns "the oligarchy of slave-holders," and extols the virtues of freedom for all.

Yet to the lawyer reading those thirteen pages, one line in particular stands out. It's not about any policy issue. It doesn't champion a moral cause. It's merely a definition. Yet the candidate knows that some definitions are worth fighting for, that this is a passage to be relied on, or perhaps paraphrased, when faith in our republic is at its ebbing and hope is needed most. He reaches for a pencil. He grasps it with long and narrow fingers. And then Abraham Lincoln underlines the following sixteen words: "Democracy is direct self-government over all the people, for all the people, by all the people."

Of the people, by the people, and for the people? I'd sure like to live in a country like that.

ACKNOWLEDGMENTS

I owe this book, like so much else in my life, to people who believed in me before it really made sense to. And now I'm about to leave some of them out by mistake. For that I apologize, but consider this a partial list of people I'm very grateful for.

My agent, Dan Greenberg, for helping me get started on this project more than two and a half years ago.

My editor, Denise Oswald, for pushing, prodding, questioning, challenging, gently rushing, insisting on my best work, and demanding structural reform when it was needed.

The entire Ecco team: Miriam Parker, Meghan Deans, Caitlin Mulrooney-Lyski, Norma Barksdale, and the person in the art department whom I've never met but whom I drove crazy with thoughts about the cover. Their passion for what they do is inspiring, and I'm so lucky I got to work with them again.

My publicist, Whitney Peeling of Broadside PR. Everyone I know who's ever worked with her can't stop talking about how amazing she is, and it turns out everyone is right.

Trey Young, Paul Gross, and Anna Lowenthal, for serving as researchers, proofreaders, sounding boards, and general lifesavers over the past several years. If the three of you represent the next generation of American leaders, I like our odds.

Ben Orlin, for providing bad drawings and excellent insights, math-related and otherwise. You can find more of his work at mathwithbad drawings.com

Kristen Bartoloni and Alex Platkin at Silver Street Strategies, who examined key sections of this book with the same thoroughness and dedication to the truth they brought to team research in the Obama White House.

Daniel Ajootian, who fact-checked the majority of this book and saved me from any number of embarrassments.

All the researchers, scholars, and advocates who were studying our government, and offering ways we might improve it, long before Trump came along. I hope I haven't too badly mangled your work.

The amazing independent booksellers whom I've gotten to know since *Thanks, Obama* was published, including but by no means limited to Politics and Prose, the Elliott Bay Book Company, Books and Books, Kramerbooks, and the organizers of the San Antonio Book Festival, Una Montagna di Libri, Pordenonelegge, the Jewish Book Council, the Miami Book Fair, and the Harrisburg Book Festival.

Jason Richman and Amanda Hymson at UTA, who supported my long-shot aspirations from the beginning.

Abbi Jacobson and Ilana Glazer, for helping me balance decline-of-democracy writing with comedy writing, teaching me a huge amount in a short time, and just generally being great to work with.

Leila Strachan, whose endless patience might just make a TV writer out of me.

My management team, Eric Ortner and Mabry Williams, and my lawyer, Bob Myman, for being there when I needed.

Billy Eichner, Mike Farah, and Brad Jenkins, for glamming up the midterms.

Richard Arenberg, Ian Bassin, Omar Bashir, Ari Berman, Sarah Binder, Tiffany Bond, Meg Bowles, Catherine Burns, Jon Carson, Sam Cornale, E. J. Dionne, Beck Dorey-Stein, Lee Drutman, Marc Elias, Anne Fadiman, Brian Fallon, Joanne Freeman, David Frum, Peter Godwin, Jacob Hacker, Sarah Hurwitz, Debra Jones, Chris Kang, Brent Katz, Elizabeth Kennedy, Brian Klaas, Juliet Lapidos, Amanda Litman, Jane Mayer, Cynthia McFadden, Rob O'Donnell, Norm Ornstein, Marty Paone, Gabe Roth, Robert Rubin, Lillian Schechter, Jeff Shesol, David Simas, Shelly Simonds, Rachel Sklar, Sam Stein, Mike Strautmanis, Zach Wahls, Michael Waldman, Jacob Weisberg, DJ Ybarra, the Taco Cabana Gang, and everyone else who has offered advice, encouragement, a patient explanation of Senate procedure, or some combination of the three.

My friends. Not to brag, but I have excellent taste in friends. I look forward to seeing you all, now that my year-long book hibernation is over.

My parents, Andy and Sara Litt; my sister, Rebecca Litt; and my entire family for always being in my corner.

Jacqui, at the end of my last book I thanked you for everything. Thank you for even more everything.

One final acknowledgment. If you're putting down this book and picking up the fight, thank you. We need you.

SUGGESTED READING

The complete notes on sources can be found at davidlittbooks.com.

Arenberg, Richard A. *Congressional Procedure: A Practical Guide to the Legislative Process in the U.S. Congress—The House of Representatives and Senate Explained*. Alexandria, VA: TheCapitol.Net, 2018.

Benson, Jocelyn F. *State Secretaries of State: Guardians of the Democratic Process*. London: Routledge/Taylor and Francis Group, 2016.

Berman, Ari. *Give Us the Ballot: The Modern Struggle for Voting Rights in America*. New York: Picador/Farrar, Strauss and Giroux, 2016.

Bishop, Bill. *The Big Sort: Why the Clustering of Like-Minded America Is Tearing Us Apart*. Boston, MA: Mariner Books, 2009.

Boorstin, Daniel J. *The Genius of American Politics*. Chicago, IL: University of Chicago Press, 1986.

Buel, Richard. *America on the Brink: How the Political Struggle Over the War of 1812 Almost Destroyed the Young Republic*. New York: Palgrave Macmillan, 2007.

Doherty, Brian. *Radicals for Capitalism: A Freewheeling History of the Modern American Libertarian Movement.* New York: PublicAffairs, 2008.

Drutman, Lee. *The Business of America Is Lobbying: How Corporations Became Politicized and Politics Became More Corporate.* New York: Oxford University Press, 2017.

Eagles, Charles W. *Democracy Delayed: Congressional Reapportionment and Urban-Rural Conflict in the 1920s.* Athens: University of Georgia Press, 2010.

Franklin, Benjamin, and Ralph Ketcham. *The Political Thought of Benjamin Franklin.* Indianapolis, IN: Hackett Publishing Company, 2003.

Freeman, Joanne B. *The Field of Blood: Violence in Congress and the Road to Civil War.* New York: Picador/Farrar, Straus and Giroux, 2019.

Gerson, Noel Bertram. *The Great Rogue: A Biography of Captain John Smith.* New York: David McKay Company, Inc., 1966.

Gienapp, William E. *The Origins of the Republican Party, 1852–1856.* New York: Oxford University Press, 2012.

Grant, James. *Mr. Speaker! The Life and Times of Thomas B. Reed, the Man Who Broke the Filibuster.* New York: Simon and Schuster Paperbacks, 2012.

Grinspan, Jon. *The Virgin Vote: How Young Americans Made Democracy Social, Politics Personal, and Voting Popular in the Nineteenth Century.* Chapel Hill, NC: University of North Carolina Press, 2019.

Hacker, Jacob S., and Paul Pierson. *Winner-Take-All Politics: How Washington Made the Rich Richer—and Turned Its Back on the Middle Class.* New York: Simon and Schuster Paperbacks, 2011.

Hasen, Richard L. *Plutocrats United: Campaign Money, the Supreme Court, and the Distortion of American Elections.* New Haven, CT: Yale University Press, 2016.

Hayduk, Ronald. *Democracy for All: Restoring Immigrant Voting Rights in the United States.* New York: Routledge, 2006.

Judis, John B. *The Paradox of American Democracy: Elites, Special Interests, and the Betrayal of Public Trust.* New York: Pantheon Books, 2000.

Keyssar, Alexander. *The Right to Vote: The Contested History of Democracy in the United States.* New York: Basic Books, 2009.

Kondik, Kyle. *The Bellwether: Why Ohio Picks the President.* Athens: Ohio University Press, 2016.

Kornacki, Steve. *The Red and the Blue: The 1990s and the Birth of Political Tribalism.* New York: Ecco, 2019.

Kropf, Martha E. *Institutions and the Right to Vote in America.* New York: Palgrave Macmillan, 2016.

MacGillis, Alec. *The Cynic: The Political Education of Mitch McConnell.* New York: Simon and Schuster Paperbacks, 2014.

McAuliffe, Terry, and John Lewis. *Beyond Charlottesville: Taking a Stand Against White Nationalism.* New York: Thomas Dunne Books/ St. Martin's Press, 2019.

Millard, Candice. *Destiny of the Republic: A Tale of Madness, Medicine, and the Murder of a President.* Thorndike, ME: Thorndike Press, 2012.

Pogue, Dennis J. *Founding Spirits: George Washington and the Beginnings of the American Whiskey Industry.* Buena Vista, VA: Harbour Books/Mariner Media, 2011.

Rodden, Jonathan A. *Why Cities Lose: The Deep Roots of the Urban-Rural Political Divide.* New York: Basic Books, 2019.

Rauch, Jonathan. *Government's End: Why Washington Stopped Working.* New York: PublicAffairs, 2012.

Shesol, Jeff. *Supreme Power: Franklin Roosevelt vs. the Supreme Court.* New York: W. W. Norton, 2011.

Stein, Mark. *How the States Got Their Shapes.* New York: Smithsonian Books/Collins, 2009.

Stern, Seth, and Stephen Wermiel. *Justice Brennan: Liberal Champion.* Lawrence: University Press of Kansas, 2013.

Toobin, Jeffrey. *The Nine: Inside the Secret World of the Supreme Court.* New York: Anchor Books, 2008.

Tuchman, Barbara W. *The Proud Tower: A Portrait of the World Before the War, 1890–1914.* New York: Random House Trade, 2014.

Waldman, Michael. *The Fight to Vote.* New York: Simon and Schuster Paperbacks, 2017.

INDEX

Page numbers followed by *n* indicate notes.